Search and Destroy

SEARCH AND DESTROY

Inside the Campaign Against Brett Kavanaugh

RYAN LOVELACE

REGNERY
PUBLISHING
A Division of Salem Media Group

Regnery® is a registered trademark of Salem Communications Holding Corporation

Cataloging-in-Publication data on file with the Library of Congress

ISBN 978-1-62157-975-5
ebook ISBN 978-1-62157-976-2

Published in the United States by
Regnery Publishing
A Division of Salem Media Group
300 New Jersey Ave NW
Washington, DC 20001
www.Regnery.com

Manufactured in the United States of America

10 9 8 7 6 5 4 3 2 1

Books are available in quantity for promotional or premium use. For information on discounts and terms, please visit our website: www.Regnery.com.

To my family

CONTENTS

CHAPTER 1
Kavanaugh Wins the 2018 Supreme Court Primary   1

CHAPTER 2
Battle Plans   17

CHAPTER 3
Disrupt, Delay, Deny, and the Silliness of Spartacus   31

CHAPTER 4
Sabotage   53

CHAPTER 5
A #MeToo Gambit   65

CHAPTER 6
Kavanaugh Critics Cry Havoc!   87

CHAPTER 7
Time to Fill or Kill   109

CHAPTER 8
Survival of the Fittest   125

CHAPTER 9
Collateral Damage   139

Acknowledgments   167
A Note on Sources   169
Appendix   225
Index   237

CHAPTER 1

Kavanaugh Wins the 2018 Supreme Court Primary

They hadn't decided how it should happen, but they knew they wanted Justice Neil Gorsuch dead.

The ill-wishers were not theocratic terrorists or ideological extremists plotting in private. They were journalists from major outlets airing their dark fantasies on social media. And they were verified on Twitter, to boot.

The U.S. Supreme Court usually delivers the decisions in its most heated and high-profile cases at the end of the term, and they are often met with flaring tempers by advocates, activists, and agitators. On June 26, 2018, the justices handed down their five-to-four decision upholding President Donald Trump's travel ban on foreign nationals from six predominantly Muslim countries, and Gorsuch, who was concluding his maiden term on the high court, was in the majority.

"Gorsuch's eventual death should be celebrated as a national holiday," tweeted Eric Thurm, a writer for *Wired* and *Rolling Stone*, after the opinion came down.

"Don't wait that long," replied David Klion, a freelancer for publications such as the *New York Times* and the *Nation*. "We need to start impeaching judges and packing courts, or there is no escaping the current

1

nightmare. And we need to elect Democrats ruthless enough to do that, and to primary the ones who prefer to uphold norms."

"Yep, it's literally a matter of life and death, of the future of humanity," chimed in Eric Renner Brown, a writer for *Entertainment Weekly* and *People*. "We don't have 30 years to wait for Gorsuch to kick the bucket or whatever."

Gorsuch replaced Justice Antonin Scalia, who had died in the middle of the 2016 presidential campaign after nearly thirty years on the high court. Republicans, who held a majority in the U.S. Senate, chose not to consider President Obama's nomination of Chief Judge Merrick Garland from the U.S. Court of Appeals for the District of Columbia Circuit, gambling that the outcome of the general election might yield a nominee more to their liking. When the winner of that election, Donald Trump, nominated Judge Neil Gorsuch from the U.S. Court of Appeals for the Tenth Circuit for Scalia's seat, Senate Democrats staged the first successful partisan filibuster of a Supreme Court nominee.

Led by Mitch McConnell, the Republicans responded by exercising the "nuclear option"—changing the Senate rules to eliminate the filibuster for Supreme Court confirmations. (The Democrats had already eliminated it during the Obama years for lower court confirmations.) Gorsuch was promptly confirmed, and the left lost its collective mind. Senator Jeff Merkley of Oregon complained that Gorsuch occupied a "stolen" seat, while former vice president Joe Biden declared the appointment the "single most damaging thing" Trump had done as president.

Perhaps the journalistic pining for Gorsuch's demise was simply posturing for the Twitter trolls who haunt the social media sewers, but neither Congress nor the Supreme Court saw it that way. The political fault lines that fractured the country had already increased concern about the justices' safety. Earlier in 2018, Congress had allocated seven hundred thousand dollars more for the Supreme Court than it had requested. The extra funds went toward security.

The bloodlust grew worse the following day—the close of the term—when Justice Anthony Kennedy announced his retirement. The vacancy on the high court promised to dominate the 2018 midterm elections as the previous vacancy had dominated the 2016 presidential election. One Nation, a hybrid political action committee aligned with McConnell, began running ads the next day in Indiana, Florida, Michigan, Missouri, Montana, North Dakota, Ohio, Pennsylvania, West Virginia, and Wisconsin—states that Trump had carried and where Democratic senators were up for reelection.

McConnell's ads mentioned no prospective replacement for Kennedy, but Don McGahn, the White House counsel, already had a man in mind. He called Brett Kavanaugh, a judge on the U.S. Court of Appeals for the D.C. Circuit, hours after Kennedy announced his retirement. Although Kavanaugh was not yet a household name, he was well-known in Washington and seemed to have first appeared on Trump's radar in 2016. John Malcolm, a senior legal fellow and the director of the Meese Center for Legal and Judicial Studies at the Heritage Foundation, worked to develop a list of potential Supreme Court nominees that Trump's presidential campaign used to woo skeptical conservatives loyal to the GOP competitors whom Trump defeated in 2016. Trump's campaign also relied on the Federalist Society, a national organization of conservative lawyers and judges, for assistance in compiling the public list. In March, Malcolm had included Kavanaugh in his first draft, which informed Trump's decision-making. But neither Kavanaugh nor Gorsuch was on the list that Trump published during the campaign.

"I think that there were some conservatives who were a little skeptical about a couple of decisions that Judge Kavanaugh wrote, probably but most prominently an opinion that he wrote—it's called the *Seven-Sky* case—that involved the challenge to the constitutionality of the individual mandate and Obamacare," Malcolm recalled in July 2018. Kavanaugh dissented from the majority opinion upholding the mandate, arguing that the court did not have jurisdiction to decide the matter. But there were signs in his dissent that he might have upheld the mandate for the same reasons that Chief Justice John Roberts eventually did. The

Seven-Sky dissent was a red flag for many conservatives, but it did not bother Malcolm.

McGahn was likewise unbothered. Kavanaugh was eventually added to President Trump's shortlist of Supreme Court candidates on November 17, 2017. Addressing the Federalist Society's National Lawyers Convention in Washington that day, McGahn announced that the president had "refreshed" the list with five new names. He first cited Judge Amy Coney Barrett, who was confirmed to the U.S. Court of Appeals for the Seventh Circuit one month earlier, alluding to the bitter hearings in which the ranking Democrat on the Senate Judiciary Committee, Dianne Feinstein of California, questioned the compatibility of the nominee's Catholic faith with the duties of a judge. "The dogma lives loudly within you," Feinstein scolded. "Judge Dogma is on the list," McGahn informed the audience, which responded with applause. But when he announced the addition of Kavanaugh to the list, the crowd cheered.

"He's winning on the applause meter," McGahn said of Kavanaugh before proceeding down the list. It was no surprise that Kavanaugh was the fan favorite. A lifelong resident of the Washington area, he had held important White House positions and had been a federal judge for more than a decade. This was his home turf.

Barrett had clerked for the D.C. Circuit and the Supreme Court and had practiced law in Washington, but she had since returned to her native Indiana and joined the faculty of Notre Dame Law School. When the Trump administration began searching for a nominee to the Seventh Circuit, she was not the first choice. Vice President Mike Pence's office, looking for an Indiana judge for the seat, approached Nicole Garnett of Notre Dame Law School. She was not interested, however, and directed Pence's office to her colleague Amy Coney Barrett. The women had become friends during their 1998–1999 Supreme Court clerkships (Barrett with Scalia, Garnett with Clarence Thomas), and Barrett was the godmother to one of Garnett's daughters.

"What do the judges on the list have in common?" McGahn asked the Federalist Society lawyers. "Well, they have a demonstrated commitment to originalism and textualism. They all have paper trails and they all are sitting judges. There's nothing unknown about them. What you see is what you get."

The White House had begun considering Kavanaugh for the Supreme Court long before his name was added to the list. It was important to ensure that there were no skeletons in his closet. Days after Neil Gorsuch's nomination in January 2017, Kavanaugh's name was floated to the *New York Times* as a potential replacement for Kennedy, should he leave the Court next. The White House began looking more intently at Kavanaugh after Gorsuch joined the Court in the spring, according to a former official. America Rising, an opposition research group that had worked with Republican officials and external conservative groups to secure Gorsuch's confirmation, was quietly directed to begin vetting Kavanaugh in the summer of 2017. He had already been vetted for his White House appointments and his seat on the U.S. Court of Appeals for the D.C. Circuit, and the new investigation produced nothing of concern. Nothing was found, said those who knew him best, because nothing was hidden.

"We were in law school together. I actually—when he graduated, I took over his apartment, so I know what's under Brett's bed, I know what's in his closets," John Yoo, a law professor at the University of California, Berkeley, told the Hoover Institution's Peter Robinson in 2018. "And I can tell you: nothing! He's been running for the Supreme Court since he's been twenty-five years old. Spotless!"

Yoo's association with Kavanaugh would later be used as a bludgeon by Kavanaugh's opponents. As deputy assistant attorney general at the U.S. Department of Justice, Yoo drafted memoranda providing legal justification for enhanced interrogation techniques for enemy combatants. When Kavanaugh worked in the White House counsel's office, he advocated for the nomination of Yoo to the Court of Appeals for the Ninth Circuit. Attacked for his so-called "torture memos," Yoo ultimately withdrew from consideration, causing a headache for Kavanaugh and the rest of the White House counsel's office.

Two days after his telephone conversation with McGahn and fifteen years after pondering what to do about John Yoo, Kavanaugh met with the White House counsel in person. Glimpses inside the Trump White House's judicial selection process are rare, but McGahn explained his approach to interviewing appellate court judges in his November 2017 speech to the Federalist Society:

> The interview process is something like the famed Scalia clerkship interview, except with folks from the White House counsel's office. We never ask candidates [for] commitments about substantive issues, but they're pushed and prodded from every angle to give a sense of what method they would employ as a judge, how intellectually capable they are, and whether they possess the fortitude to enforce the rule of law without fear of public pressure.

Scalia clerkship interviews were not for the faint of heart. Few survivors have chosen to tell the tale publicly. But Ian Samuel, a self-described liberal who clerked for Scalia in 2012, wrote about his interview for the *New York University Journal of Law & Liberty*. Scalia reportedly enjoyed sparring with prospective clerks and challenged Samuel, saying, "Why don't you tell me an opinion I've written in the last couple of years that you disagree with, so we can argue about it?" After a half-hour with the candidate, the justice sent him to meet with his quartet of clerks for another interrogation.

Prior administrations had interviewed potential judicial nominees by telephone or not at all, but the Trump administration took a more hands-on approach. Robert Luther, McGahn's former deputy, writes in the *University of Pittsburgh Law Review*:

> In this Administration, the hundreds of judicial candidates that we have considered were personally interviewed at the

White House by White House Counsel's Office and Department of Justice Office of Legal Policy staff. Every candidate who walks through the White House gates for an interview is taken seriously and has a real chance to be nominated if the politics permit it and the background check comes back clean. Why do we do this? While it may be old-fashioned, we think it is important to be able to look a candidate in the eye to be sure that he or she has the fire, poise, temperament, and knowledge required to do this job as well as the President and the members of our office demand.

After his Friday interview with McGahn, Kavanaugh's next stop on Monday, July 2, was a meeting with Trump. Three other candidates met with Trump that day, according to White House press secretary Sarah Huckabee Sanders, and word began to leak out about the candidates moving up Trump's shortlist.

As Kavanaugh got closer to the nomination, conservative skepticism intensified. Exit polls from the 2016 election showed that Trump's voters—especially ideological conservatives and others who supported him reluctantly—had been strongly influenced by his promise, backed up by the list, to appoint a conservative to the Supreme Court. Conservative leaders, elected officials, grassroots organizers, and others who marshaled the conservative coalition made private appeals to the president, the vice president, the president's children, and other advisers, including Leonard Leo, the executive vice president of the Federalist Society.

Kavanaugh's conservative opponents had a plan of attack: brand him as things Trump could not stand—namely, "Swampy," "Bushie," and "Chiefy." They would emphasize Kavanaugh's ties to the Washington legal establishment, the Bush administration, and Chief Justice John Roberts, whom Kavanaugh worked to confirm in the Bush White House.

"Kavanaugh brings with him all the baggage of the George W. Bush administration, including millions of pages of records," a source with knowledge of the judicial selection process said before Kavanaugh met

Trump. "I'd be very surprised if President Trump, in effect, hands over the task of picking the next Supreme Court justice to President George W. Bush."

Kavanaugh's connection to Roberts looked like a point of vulnerability. The chief justice's decisions on Obamacare and its individual mandate so rankled conservatives that Trump used Senator Ted Cruz's support for Roberts as a wedge issue in the campaign for the Republican presidential nomination. Now Cruz was among those privately expressing reservations about Kavanaugh in the days leading up to the Fourth of July holiday, but he never went public.

Instead, conservative talk radio hosts amplified the Kavanaugh skepticism. Rush Limbaugh walked his millions of daily listeners through a piece from The Daily Caller arguing that "Kavanaugh wrote a roadmap for saving Obamacare." Limbaugh said that conservatives' criticism of Kavanaugh "could be legit" before noting that the "long knives" were coming at Kavanaugh from every political direction. "The whisper campaign is that Kavanaugh provided the 'roadmap' for Chief Justice Roberts to uphold the constitutionality of Obamacare," Limbaugh said. "Clearly, there is an effort to keep Kavanaugh off the bench, to keep him away from being nominated. Whether this is accurate or not, time will tell." Limbaugh added that a "lot of people" liked Judge Amy Coney Barrett, but he avoided endorsing a candidate.

The conservative television and radio figure Glenn Beck turned to Twitter to pile on Kavanaugh, hitting him on all the key points. "Brett Kavanaugh 4 #SCOTUS unless something shifts significantly in the next 24 hours," Beck tweeted on July 3. "I cannot get excited about someone who recommended Roberts to Bush, wrote an opinion upholding Obamacare, has hired throngs of liberal law clerks and fed them to liberal justices."

As the pressure mounted on the anti-Kavanaugh conservatives to speak out, Jim Bopp, a veteran Supreme Court litigator, sent a letter to the president and vice president criticizing Kavanaugh and boosting Barrett. A prominent social conservative, Bopp was known for his successful representation of Citizens United in its litigation against restrictions on corporate advocacy for political candidates. At the top of Bopp's long list of concerns about Kavanaugh, according to sources inside and outside of government, was the judge's views on campaign finance law. Those sources said Bopp also noted that liberals were not nearly as concerned about Kavanaugh as they were about Barrett, whose unquestioned conservative credentials would energize the president's base.

Many conservatives, however, did not view the nomination sweepstakes as a two-person race between Kavanaugh and Barrett, which weakened the chance that a single alternative to Kavanaugh would emerge. While the conservative saboteurs were united in their opposition to Kavanaugh, their support was dispersed and many leading D.C. power brokers privately backed their own horses.

Judge Amul Thapar of the U.S. Court of Appeals for the Sixth Circuit was known to be a favorite of Senate Majority Leader Mitch McConnell, who admitted as much to the Associated Press. Following Gorsuch's confirmation in 2017, the first appellate court appointment confirmed by McConnell's GOP Senate majority—by a vote of fifty-two to forty-four—was Thapar, a former federal district court judge from McConnell's home state of Kentucky.

Thapar had just turned forty-eight, and his inexperience on the court of appeals was seen as a disadvantage, but his conservative bona fides were hardly in doubt. When Trump first included Thapar on his Supreme Court shortlist—before his appellate court nomination—the judge's father reportedly told the *Louisville Courier-Journal* that Amul "nearly wouldn't speak to me after I voted for Barack Obama." The elder Thapar did not mean to suggest that his son would reach any particular outcome because of his politics. His reputation for hard work and clearly expressed legal reasoning made him a top competitor for the first two Supreme Court appointments under President Trump. Thapar is poised to remain a leading contender regardless of whether Trump and McConnell are still calling the shots in Washington.

Judge Thomas Hardiman of the U.S. Court of Appeals for the Third Circuit, widely perceived as the runner-up to Gorsuch, was a close associate of Judge Maryanne Trump Barry, who sat on the same court until February 2019. Hardiman was well-connected in the Senate, having enjoyed a close relationship with the late Arlen Specter of Pennsylvania and benefiting from former senator Rick Santorum's unrelenting support. He had been unanimously confirmed to the appellate court less than six months after President George W. Bush nominated him.

Hardiman had an unmatched rags-to-robes story. He worked as a taxicab driver to help put himself through Notre Dame and was the first in his family to graduate from college. But his educational diversity was not attractive to President Trump, who was reportedly interested in an Ivy League pedigree. And Hardiman's conservative critics had successfully painted "Taxicab Tom" as a limousine liberal.

Judge Raymond Kethledge of the U.S. Court of Appeals for the Sixth Circuit had, like Kavanaugh, clerked for Justice Kennedy. Like Hardiman, he was not an Ivy Leaguer, but he had stronger allies in the conservative press. He earned the moniker "Gorsuch 2.0" from Hugh Hewitt, a conservative radio host and contributor to the *Washington Post* who had worked in the White House counsel's office during the Reagan administration. Quin Hillyer, a conservative journalist from Alabama, lauded Kethledge in the *Washington Examiner* as having "the most clear, concise, persuasive writing" among the reported finalists.

No one, however, had the connections and curriculum vitae to compete with Kavanaugh. He moved from an all-boys Jesuit preparatory school in D.C. to the Ivy League—Yale College and Yale Law School—before returning to Washington for a fellowship in the solicitor general's office under Kenneth Starr. After clerkships on the U.S. Courts of Appeals for the Third and Ninth Circuits, Kavanaugh clerked for Justice Anthony Kennedy, alongside Neil Gorsuch, before reuniting with Starr at the independent counsel's office investigating President Bill Clinton.

Kavanaugh later joined President George W. Bush's legal team as associate White House counsel with responsibility for some judicial nominations. He worked on the confirmation efforts for Chief Justice John Roberts. President Bush nominated Kavanaugh to the federal bench in 2003. Senate Democrats, in a sign of things to come, held up his confirmation for three years.

Brett Kavanaugh, then, was a favorite of Justice Kennedy's and a friend of Chief Justice Roberts, and he was intimately familiar with the processes for judicial nominations and confirmations. Sources with knowledge of the relationship between Justice Kennedy and President Trump say that the business dealings between Kennedy's son Justin and the Trump family helped Kennedy feel comfortable leaving the appointment of his successor to Trump. Justin was employed for more than a decade at Deutsche Bank, where he worked directly with Trump on financing his real estate projects.

Kavanaugh's cause had platoons of lawyers whose credentials mirrored his own with experience at the best law schools and the biggest law firms and knowledge of the Supreme Court and K Street. "There is an army of people who stand ready and prepared to spring to action to support him," Travis Lenkner said before Kavanaugh's July nomination. Lenkner, who clerked for both Kavanaugh and Kennedy before embarking on a successful career as a litigator, had already begun assembling Kavanaugh's law clerks and childhood friends for the effort of supporting his candidacy. Thirty-nine of Kavanaugh's forty-eight clerks had gone on to clerk for the Supreme Court, and his high school classmates were eager to support their old friend.

This infrastructure was an important selling point because Trump and his fellow Republicans were keen on starting the Supreme Court's next term with a full complement of justices. The Senate minority leader, Chuck Schumer of New York, urged Republicans to wait until after the 2018 midterm elections to consider any nominee to the high court, but the Senate Judiciary Committee chairman, Chuck Grassley of Iowa, was eager to receive the nomination. McConnell also made it a priority.

"We will vote to confirm Justice Kennedy's successor this fall," McConnell promised in June—more than a month before Kennedy officially left the court. The seat Gorsuch filled had sat open for more than four hundred days because of McConnell's desire to give voters the chance to pick the president responsible for filling the seat. McConnell's action was exceptional, but not unprecedented. The longest vacancy, 841 days, ended with the confirmation of Robert C. Grier to take Justice Henry Baldwin's seat in 1846. In modern times, vacancies have typically lasted less than two months. A Pew Research Center analysis of the fifteen Supreme Court vacancies immediately preceding Kennedy's retirement, dating back to 1970, found that vacancies were filled within an average of fifty-five days. Trump's nomination would need to stick close to that average to meet the Republicans' goal of seating a justice before the new term began in October 2018.

"If the president nominates someone extraordinary like Neil Gorsuch again, I think it's very hard to stop that kind of a nomination," Leonard Leo, Trump's advisor on the Supreme Court and judicial nominations, told Fox News on Thursday night, June 28. "The American people were widely supportive of Neil Gorsuch, and Justice Gorsuch had bipartisan support in the Senate."

When asked about Kavanaugh's likelihood of overcoming Democrats' opposition, Leo answered, "Ultimately, I think red-state Democrats in the Senate will understand that someone like Brett Kavanaugh or another Neil Gorsuch–type nominee would be quite suitable for our country."

Trump was not waiting to find out. The same evening, the president met with three red-state Democratic senators and two fence-sitting Republican women senators about the vacancy. Democrats Joe Donnelly of Indiana, Heidi Heitkamp of North Dakota, and Joe Manchin of West Virginia met with Trump that night, according to Sarah Huckabee Sanders. Trump had carried their states in 2016, and all three were facing tough reelection bids that fall.

Trump also met with Lisa Murkowski of Alaska and Susan Collins of Maine, both pro-choice Republicans who were expected to be leery of an appointment that might tip the court in a pro-life direction. Trump and the White House staff also met with Senator Grassley that night, and the White House staff talked to more than a dozen other senators throughout the day.

On his flight to Bedminster, New Jersey, the home of a Trump National Golf Club, the president called the looming announcement "exciting" and was uncharacteristically coy about his shortlist, saying only, "I like them all" and "It is a group of highly talented, very brilliant, mostly conservative judges." He added, "Outside of war and peace, of course, the most important decision you make is the selection of a Supreme Court judge, if you get it."

Kavanaugh met with the president on Monday and with the vice president on Wednesday. By Sunday, July 8, Trump had made his decision. He and Kavanaugh spoke over the phone that morning, and the judge met the president and first lady that night when Trump formally extended the offer and Kavanaugh accepted it.

The news of Kavanaugh's selection remained a secret until Trump made it public in a Monday night announcement from the East Room of the White House. Kavanaugh stayed up past midnight working on a speech, but he was scrupulous not to inform the clerks and advisers who had labored on the vetting process. As the notoriously leaky Trump White House prepared the list of guests for the announcement ceremony, the likelihood that the name of the president's choice would get out increased. But the best-kept secrets of the Trump administration have been the identities of his nominees for the Supreme Court.

The press realized that no leak was forthcoming, so cable news cameras staked out Judge Barrett's home in Indiana. Nearly ninety minutes before the scheduled announcement, CNN's Erin Burnett interrupted her program to announce "breaking news": "Amy Coney Barrett was seen moments ago at her home in South Bend, Indiana." The camera cut to images of the judge retrieving laundry from a clothes line, and Burnett explained, "Now, okay, I mean private jets can do a lot, but that was less than two hours—she's [going to] have to change and everything else, so that's how that looks."

Kavanaugh, meanwhile, was reportedly on the move from the federal courthouse in Washington. "Brett Kavanaugh spotted leaving in a black sedan accompanied by four black SUVs with security agents presumed to be Secret Service, per source," tweeted Peter Baker, the chief White House correspondent for the *New York Times*. Reporting the identities of men in black SUVs departing a federal courthouse based on a single anonymous source's guesswork might ordinarily not meet the reporting standards for the *Times*, but it did on the day Kavanaugh was selected.

Even those headed to the White House for the announcement were uncertain whom Trump had selected. The Heritage Foundation's John Malcolm explained, "I received the invitation about three hours beforehand, and I was delighted to get it. I wasn't even sure at that point who the nominee was going to be. But when I was standing in line outside the White House and I saw who was [in] the line with me, I had a pretty good idea at that point that it was going to be Brett Kavanaugh, and of course I was very pleased."

Malcolm walked inside and was shown to a front-row seat, squeezed in alongside Maureen Scalia, Justice Scalia's widow, former attorney general Ed Meese, and White House counsel Don McGahn. The president then strode down the red carpet into the East Room and announced that he was nominating Brett Kavanaugh.

"Judge Kavanaugh has impeccable credentials, unsurpassed qualifications, and a proven commitment to equal justice under the law," Trump said. "Throughout legal circles, he is considered a judge's judge, a true thought-leader among his peers. He is a brilliant jurist, with a clear and effective writing style, universally regarded as one of the finest and sharpest legal minds of our time."

After the room burst into applause at the mention of Kavanaugh's name, Trump paused and said, "I know the people in this room very well, they do not stand and give applause like that very often, so they have some respect."

There were no Democratic senators in the room, but the president had a message for them too. He thanked Republicans and Democrats and then issued a challenge: "This incredibly qualified nominee deserves a swift confirmation and robust bipartisan support. The rule of law is our nation's proud heritage. It is the cornerstone of our freedom. It is what guarantees equal justice, and the Senate now has the chance to protect this glorious heritage by sending Judge Brett Kavanaugh to the United States Supreme Court."

Everyone knew that Trump had selected a formidable champion to do battle with those who were intent on denying him a second appointment to the high court.

CHAPTER 2

Battle Plans

B efore Brett Kavanaugh said a single word at the White House announcement of his nomination, a crowd of protesters began gathering at One First Street, steps away from the Supreme Court. It wasn't precisely an anti-*Kavanaugh* protest; they were there to oppose anyone President Trump nominated.

This pre-planned opposition was not a new tactic. One year earlier, liberal groups such as Alliance for Justice, the Center for American Progress, People for the American Way, and the Leadership Conference on Civil and Human Rights did something similar ahead of Trump's selection of Neil Gorsuch. They notified reporters that activists would descend on the Supreme Court one hour after Trump announced a nominee to replace the late Justice Antonin Scalia.

But something was different the second time around. In 2018, the leftist protest had a professional sheen. Hand-lettered signs were vastly outnumbered by professionally printed signs. Blue signs emblazoned with "Stop Kavanaugh" in bold yellow letters spread throughout the crowd. The *Weekly Standard*'s Haley Byrd spotted them within thirty minutes of Trump's uttering Kavanaugh's name. Signs had been prepared with the names of all the leading candidates—Amy Coney Barrett, Raymond

Kethledge, and Thomas Hardiman. Protesters told reporters they did not know who made them.

The rally and signs were the work of a new liberal group, Demand Justice, which was formed in May 2018 to "prod Democrats to show more guts when it comes to opposing Trump's extreme nominees," according to Brian Fallon, the organization's executive director. As Hillary Clinton's lead mouthpiece in her failed 2016 presidential campaign, Fallon had previously served as the spokesman for Attorney General Eric Holder and as an aide to the Senate's Democratic leader, Chuck Schumer of New York. Demand Justice, Fallon wrote in a column for *USA Today*, was a direct response to the Left's failure to stop Gorsuch and a sign of its determination to block future conservative judicial nominees.

For Fallon, the fight over Kennedy's seat was not about stopping a particular nominee, but was about teaching leftists—in the press, in the Senate, and on the street—how to take one down. The day before Trump made his selection, Fallon chided a progressive *New York Times* columnist, saying, "I think you underestimate the chances we could pull off an upset." "If we don't contest [the nomination] at this inflection-point moment," Fallon said, "we will never build the muscle memory to organize around the courts."

Fallon intended to slime anyone Trump picked for Kennedy's seat. One day after Kennedy announced his retirement, Demand Justice led a #SaveSCOTUS rally of progressive activists and Democratic senators demanding that President Trump "ditch the list," which referred to his well-known Supreme Court shortlist. "We will not accept a single nominee from Trump's previous list of presidential nominees, which does not have a single fair-minded judge on that list," declared Anisha Singh, then the senior organizing director for the Center for American Progress, at the rally.

The message resonated, and Fallon had little trouble finding funding. In May 2018, Demand Justice began its efforts to "change minds and sensitize rank-and-file progressives to think of the courts as a venue for their progressive activism and a way to advance the progressive agenda," hoping to raise ten million dollars in its first year. By July 2—a full week before Kavanaugh's nomination—the organization announced its plan to spend five million dollars opposing Trump's nominee. A line on its website said the millions of dollars would be routed to television, radio, and digital ads, as well as voter mobilization. The effort would target "moderate Senate Republicans" like Susan Collins of Maine and Lisa Murkowski of Alaska and "vulnerable Senate Democrats" like Joe Donnelly of Indiana, Heidi Heitkamp of North Dakota, and Joe Manchin of West Virginia, all of whom were up for reelection in 2018.

Despite liberals' complaints about the political influence of "dark-money," Demand Justice is itself a "dark-money" group—that is, a project of a 501(c)(4) organization, Sixteen Thirty Fund, according to documents filed with the Federal Election Commission. Nearly all of Demand Justice's board members were tied to the Clintons or the leftist billionaire financier George Soros:

- Board member Cristóbal Alex, national deputy director of voter outreach and mobilization for Hillary Clinton's 2016 campaign, was the program officer for George Soros's Open Society Foundations and was in charge of the civic engagement portfolio with an annual budget of seven million dollars.
- Board member Eric Kessler, an official in the Clinton administration and a member of the Clinton Global Initiative, is also the founder of Arabella Advisors, which manages the New Venture Fund, the beneficiary of at least $150,000 from George Soros's Open Society Foundations.
- Board member Doug Hattaway was a senior communications advisor to Hillary Clinton's 2008 campaign.
- Board member Monica Dixon is a consultant with ties to the Clintons.
- Board member Dara Freed was a fundraiser for Hillary Clinton since her Senate campaign of 2000.

- Nat Chioke Williams, the only board member without an ostensible tie to the Clintons or George Soros, is the executive director of the Hill-Snowdon Foundation, which supports "youth organizing" and "economic justice organizing," including its "Making Black Lives Matter Initiative."

Despite the connections to Soros and the Clintons, Fallon boasted in *USA Today* of "thousands of grassroots donors," seeking to give the impression that his dark-money group was a popular initiative. Prominent Democrats with designs on the White House were soon drawn to Demand Justice like moths to a flame. Rallies in June and July 2018 attracted senators Cory Booker of New Jersey, Kirsten Gillibrand of New York, Kamala Harris of California, and Elizabeth Warren of Massachusetts—Democrats who would launch their presidential campaigns within the year. Asked at the June rally how far she would go to stop Trump's next nominee to the Supreme Court, Harris replied, "As far as possible— I don't know how you define that."

The reason Democrats with their eyes on the White House would care more about grassroots donors than ever before became apparent in 2019. For the first time, the party would consider fundraising as well as poll numbers in determining a candidate's eligibility for its televised debates during the primary season. Any candidate who received donations from sixty-five thousand unique donors and at least two hundred unique donors in twenty states would not have to worry about polls or name identification. The early primary states of Iowa, New Hampshire, South Carolina, and Nevada saw their influence diminished, while the special-interest groups conducting PR campaigns against Trump's Supreme Court nominee—groups largely run by the Clinton alumni network—gained more power than they ever had before.

The Supreme Court vacancy was something a Democratic presidential hopeful could build a campaign on, but the liberal politicking did not seem to be at the top of Kavanaugh's mind when he accepted the nomination. The significance of replacing Kennedy—the justice for whom he had clerked—came first. Just after thanking President Trump—before he thanked his parents or introduced himself—Kavanaugh paid tribute to the man he would succeed: "Thirty years ago, President Reagan nominated Anthony Kennedy to the Supreme Court. The framers established that the Constitution is designed to secure the blessings of liberty. Justice Kennedy devoted his career to securing liberty. I am deeply honored to be nominated to fill his seat on the Supreme Court."

Anthony Kennedy had replaced Justice Lewis Powell, who had been appointed by President Richard Nixon and was part of the seven-justice majority that legalized abortion in *Roe v. Wade* (1973). And like Powell, Kennedy was a swing-vote who usually voted with the conservatives, but joined the liberals on issues like abortion and marriage. But Kennedy took Powell's seat only after the Senate rejected President Reagan's nomination of Judge Robert Bork in 1987. Like Kavanaugh, Bork sat on the U.S. Court of Appeals for the D.C. Circuit and had worked in a Republican administration (Nixon's) that Democrats regarded as toxic. Senator Edward Kennedy of Massachusetts opened the attack with his infamous "Robert Bork's America" speech, evoking a dystopia of back-alley abortions, segregated lunch counters, and rogue police. What doomed Bork, however, were his statements about the legal reasoning by which the court had recognized a constitutional right to privacy in *Griswold v. Connecticut* (1965), a decision which struck down state restrictions on contraceptives.

Bork found the opinion in *Griswold*, which was written by Justice William O. Douglas for a seven-to-two majority, flawed—even if he did not disagree with the outcome. "[T]he right of privacy, as defined or undefined by Justice Douglas, was a free-floating right that was not derived in a principled fashion from constitutional materials," Bork said at his Senate Judiciary Committee hearings in response to a question from the committee chairman, Joe Biden. "One of the problems with the right of privacy, as Justice Douglas defined it, or did not define it, is not simply that it comes out of nowhere, that it does not have any rooting in the Constitution, it is also that he does not give it any contours, so you do not know what it is going to mean from case to case."

Bork went on to link the flawed reasoning of *Griswold* to the rationale for legalizing abortion. "If *Griswold v. Connecticut* established or adopted a privacy right on reasoning which was utterly inadequate, and failed to define that right so we know what it applies to, *Roe v. Wade* contains almost no legal reasoning," Bork said in response to a question from Senator Orrin Hatch, a Republican from Utah. Although Bork responded "no" when Hatch asked if he would necessarily vote to reverse *Roe*, he had given his liberal opponents the ammunition to sink his nomination.

The liberal activist organization People for the American Way took it from there, attacking Bork in television ads featuring the actor Gregory Peck, who won an Academy Award for his performance as Atticus Finch in *To Kill a Mockingbird*: "Robert Bork wants to be a Supreme Court Justice, but the record shows that he has a strange idea of what justice is," Peck intoned. "Robert Bork could have the last word on your rights as citizens, but the Senate has the last word on him. Please urge your senators to vote against the Bork nomination because if Robert Bork wins a seat on the Supreme Court it will be for life. His life and yours."

Bork's nomination failed in the Senate by a vote of fifty-eight to forty-two, and the verb "to bork"—to attempt to defeat a nomination with an organized campaign of vilification—entered the lexicon. A. B. Culvahouse, President Reagan's White House counsel, called the failed Bork nomination "the one thing I regret most in the White House." Caught flat-footed by the tactics of the left, Culvahouse admitted that he was "surprised" by Senator Kennedy's attack on Bork and the ferocity of Bork's enemies. He told an audience at the University of Virginia:

> [W]here I really think we made a mistake was in not seizing
> control of the confirmation process preparation and saying,
> "This ain't a legal thing. This is not preparing for a Supreme
> Court argument. This is hand-to-hand political combat,

and this is the way you're going to do it." Whether Bork would have agreed, I don't know, but that's the way Kennedy was prepared. I helped prepare Souter, I helped prepare Clarence Thomas. It was a political process, not a legal debate over the meaning of justiciability or the antitrust paradox or whatever.

Next on the firing line came Douglas Ginsburg, another judge from the D.C. Circuit, who was nominated less than one week after Bork's defeat. Ginsburg withdrew a month later after admitting to using marijuana decades before becoming a federal judge. Reagan's team, said Culvahouse, decided the Supreme Court seat ought to go to Anthony Kennedy "for lots of reasons, including his own persona and political skill."

Don McGahn was a high school student when Bork became a verb, and the hearings motivated him to become a lawyer. "My father taped [the hearings] on a VHS player and made me watch them, and it was fascinating because I was inspired and it made me go to law school," McGahn recalled in remarks at the Ronald Reagan Presidential Library. "And then I was in law school with the Thomas hearings."

Kavanaugh, McGahn noted, was a first-year law student when Bork was nominated for the Supreme Court and a recent graduate when Clarence Thomas faced an even uglier confirmation ordeal. "So we studied [the hearings] intently, and we really paid attention to what happened, and I think we took a lot of lessons learned, and we were very prepared from sort of how we launched it to how we did it," McGahn said at the Reagan Library.

Culvahouse seemed sickened by the state of judicial nomination battles when we talked in July 2018. The nation was "lucky" to have wound up with Kennedy, he said, adding that the "infrastructure on the left and the right that make[s] a lot of money and [has] a lot of staff pursuing the business of supporting or opposing Supreme Court and other judicial nominees" is "harming the institution."

Many conservatives view the external infrastructure that supports Trump's judicial nominees as necessary after the failures of the administrations of Reagan and both Bushes. Reflecting on his own experiences, Don McGahn bemoaned the Supreme Court skirmishes but made no apologies for the Trump administration's efforts to confirm its nominees. Unlike Culvahouse, McGahn was not "surprised," and unlike Bork, Kavanaugh became a Supreme Court justice. Speaking at the Reagan Library in January 2019, McGahn reflected:

> It's unfortunate that modern Supreme Court nominations are essentially run like political campaigns, but that's what it's become.... It was inevitable that they were going to come after whoever was up [for Kennedy's seat] on something. It was just going to be tough to predict. But we weathered the storm and survived. Previous generations may not have survived because they may not have seen it coming.

Previous generations also did not have the team that Kavanaugh had. The White House tapped Jon Kyl to be Kavanaugh's "sherpa," the point man to lead him through the Senate. The former senator from Arizona had spent eighteen years on the Senate Judiciary Committee—a tenure that overlapped with Kavanaugh's service in the Office of the White House Counsel and included the confirmation of four Supreme Court justices. Sources with knowledge of the judicial selection process say the Trump administration had wanted Kyl to be Gorsuch's sherpa as well, but the job ultimately went to Kelly Ayotte, a former senator from New Hampshire fresh off a narrow reelection loss to Democrat Maggie Hassan. Kyl had successfully led Jeff Sessions's confirmation as attorney general and had a reputation for making barriers to confirmation look like speed bumps.

Kyl is famous not only for his expertise with confirmations and his sterling reputation with senators on both sides of the aisle, but also for his discretion. Reached by phone on the morning of Kavanaugh's appointment, Kyl refused to say that he was indeed going to be the sherpa for Kavanaugh. The consummate team player, he said not a word until White House spokesman Raj Shah confirmed the news.

McGahn and Kyl had known Kavanaugh for decades, and most of the team members preparing for the confirmation battle had longstanding connections to the judge. The one person on the small platoon accompanying Kavanaugh around the Senate who had no prior connection was Kerri Kupec, a spokeswoman for the Justice Department's Office of the Solicitor General whose familiarity with the media's coverage of the Supreme Court was valuable. A former legal counsel and communications director for Alliance Defending Freedom, a right-leaning civil liberties law firm, Kupec was used to being targeted as a member of a "hate group." ADF's opposition to certain progressive priorities earned the ire of the Southern Poverty Law Center (SPLC), which is notorious for its promiscuous use of the "hate group" label.

After months of working in the trenches with Kavanaugh, Kupec said she was struck by a quality she had not found in many other lawyers eager to get ahead in the nation's capital: "He's a very good listener, a very empathetic listener, that was I think one of the things that struck me—even his body language, his facial expressions. He knows how to listen well, which I think is unusual in Washington, D.C."

In addition to McGahn, Kyl, and Kupec, who knew the lay of the land at the White House, the Senate, and the Supreme Court, the confirmation team was assisted by several of Kavanaugh's former law clerks. Claire McCusker Murray, who had gone on to clerk for Justice Samuel Alito and became a partner at Kirkland & Ellis, was helping to run the confirmation effort out of the White House counsel's office. She was joined there by Zina Gelman Bash, who had worked on the Trump transition team and later entered the White House as a special assistant to the president for regulatory reform on the Domestic Policy Council.

Bash had left the White House and moved to Texas when her husband, John Bash, became the U.S. attorney for the U.S. District Court for the Western District of Texas (sworn in by then-Judge Kavanaugh) in 2018. Like several other of Kavanaugh's clerks, colleagues, and friends, she dropped everything and returned to D.C. to help him when the nomination became a reality.

The personal toll of working on Kavanaugh's confirmation effort was not limited to uprooting her life and the private pressure of critical work in support of a high-stakes appointment. Bash, who had been included in *The Hill*'s "Fifty Most Beautiful" people list in 2017, attracted attention in her visible role shadowing Kavanaugh throughout the confirmation process—but not the kind she was used to. During the hearings, she was visible on television sitting behind the judge, and her habit of holding her thumb and forefinger in a way that resembles an "OK" gesture while folding her arms was interpreted as a bat signal for white supremacists by the anti-Trump #Resistance. Eugene Gu, a Twitter-verified medical doctor, tweeted to his two hundred thousand followers: "Kavanaugh's former law clerk Zina Bash is flashing a white power hand sign behind him during his Senate confirmation hearing. They literally want to bring white supremacy to the Supreme Court. What a national outrage and a disgrace to the rule of law." Amy Siskind, an investment banker turned anti-Trump #Resistance writer, piled on, declaring that Bash's gesture should "disqualify" Kavanaugh from the Court. The British-based *Daily Mail* followed up with a story headlined "Who is Zina Bash? John's wife revealed after being accused of white supremacy at Kavanaugh's hearing."

As the white-supremacist accusation and Bash's picture bounced around the Internet, her husband tweeted back in her defense, calling the attacks on his wife "repulsive" and noting that neither he nor his wife was familiar with the hateful symbol. He also explained why the accusation of white supremacy was particularly offensive:

> She was born in Mexico. Her grandparents were Holocaust survivors.... We of course have nothing to do with hate groups, which aim to terrorize and demean other people—never have and never would. Some of the Twitter comments have even referred to our baby daughter. I know that there are good folks on both sides of the political divide. I hope that people will clearly condemn this idiotic and sickening accusation.

Women working in support of Kavanaugh faced a backlash that their male counterparts did not for a simple reason: women viewed as favoring a nominee who would not explicitly prostrate himself before the abortion lobby were viewed as traitors to "women's rights." Kavanaugh understood this. In his remarks at the White House during the evening his nomination was announced, he emphasized his coaching of his daughters' basketball teams and his mother's work as a "trailblazer" in the legal profession. He also pointed out that a "majority of my law clerks have been women" and that Justice Elena Kagan had hired him to teach at Harvard Law School when she was dean.

In those same remarks, Kavanaugh also emphasized that he was not a judicial activist intent on implementing a conservative agenda: "My judicial philosophy is straightforward. A judge must be independent and must interpret the law, not make the law. A judge must interpret statutes as written. And a judge must interpret the Constitution as written, informed by history and tradition and precedent."

As he was speaking, the Judicial Crisis Network disseminated photos of Kavanaugh coaching his daughters to soften the ground, but their counterparts at Demand Justice had already begun working to weaponize the #MeToo movement. Brian Fallon, attempting to tap into the #MeToo anger, charged that Kavanaugh, who clerked for Judge Alex Kozinski on the Ninth Circuit in 1990, must have known about the sexual harassment of which Kozinski was accused in 2017.

When Heather Gerken, the dean of Yale Law School and a self-described "progressive," praised Kavanaugh's nomination in a statement on Yale's website, calling him a "longtime friend" of his alma mater and expressing admiration for his teaching and mentoring, 250 Yale Law students, faculty, and alumni responded with a letter criticizing her judgment and warning that "people will die if he is confirmed." The mob continued:

> Without a doubt, Judge Kavanaugh is a threat to the most vulnerable. He is a threat to many of us, despite the privilege

bestowed by our education, simply because of who we are.... Overturning [*Roe v. Wade*] would endanger the lives of countless people who need or may need abortions—including many who sign this letter. Trump's nomination of Judge Kavanaugh is a reliable way to fulfill his oath [to appoint judges who will vote to overturn *Roe*].

Gerken went silent. The message was clear: women ought not to support Kavanaugh, and those who do are accomplices to murder. But the left was just getting started. Demand Justice's warnings about the hell on earth that Kavanaugh's confirmation would usher in made "Robert Bork's America" look like Reagan's shining city on a hill in comparison.

Demand Justice partnered with Planned Parenthood and NARAL Pro-Choice America on a "Rise Up for Roe Tour" that visited a mixture of liberal hotbeds, home states of vulnerable Republicans, and key battlegrounds for the 2020 election. The first stop on the tour in August—a month before Kavanaugh's hearing in the Senate—was New York City, where the freelance feminist scribbler Lauren Duca shared that she would not shave her legs for the duration of the tour. Chelsea Clinton then addressed the faithful. Seated in front of a wall with the words "Rise Up for Roe" splattered in a purple and green design similar to the Nickelodeon logo ubiquitous in her youth, she recalled, "I did a lot of campaigning in 2016 for my mom, whom I'm deeply biased towards and very proud of, and I talked about the Supreme Court I think at every event I did." The insight she gained from this experience was that allowing Brett Kavanaugh onto the Supreme Court would necessarily maim countless women:

It's not only about the hundreds of women who died every year, it's about the tens of thousands of women who were left terribly scarred and disabled from back-alley abortions or self-induced abortions.... We cannot go back, but we will go back if we do not stop Kavanaugh.

For Chelsea Clinton, Judge Kavanaugh was not the federal appellate court judge with a decade of experience on the top-feeder circuit for the nation's highest court. He was a Republican boogeyman who helped Ken Starr attack her family in the 1990s. Her remarks suggested that not only had she failed to accept the results of the 2016 election, but that she also had not yet moved beyond 1999. She expressed her pain over Rush Limbaugh's remarks about her family in the 1990s, showing what had been gnawing on the Clinton psyche for more than twenty years.

Before Brett Kavanaugh ever appeared before the Senate for a hearing on his nomination, he was charged with murder by Ivy League law professors. The Senate Judiciary Committee's Democrats had vowed to oppose whomever Trump picked, and one of the Democrats' 2020 frontrunners had vowed to stop at nothing to ruin the nomination. The failed 2016 Democratic presidential nominee's family made clear that the Kavanaugh battle was evidence that the 2016 election was not yet over and that the judge was a personal enemy of the Clinton family.

CHAPTER 3

Disrupt, Delay, Deny, and the Silliness of Spartacus

"**G**ood morning, I welcome everyone to the confirmation hearing of—"

"Mr. Chairman!"

The chairman of the Senate Judiciary Committee, Chuck Grassley, had not uttered a dozen words before Senator Kamala Harris, one of the committee's newest members, sought to prevent him from naming Brett Kavanaugh. Harris would be the first of three Judiciary Committee Democrats to announce a run for president in 2020, and she was the first to try to turn Kavanaugh into he-who-must-not-be-named.

Throughout the Labor Day weekend, Democrats plotted in private to turn the confirmation hearings into a circus. Senate Minority Leader Chuck Schumer led a phone call with Democrats to coordinate the strategy, and he tried to manipulate the Senate rules to postpone the hearings.

The strategy was simple: disrupt, delay, and deny Kavanaugh's confirmation by any means necessary. The first wave of disruptors, organized by Demand Justice, were women dressed up in red robes and white bonnets who lined the balconies overlooking the hearing room entrance used by spectators, staff, and, most importantly, the press. Their costumes evoked *The Handmaid's Tale*, a Hulu television series based on

Margaret Atwood's dystopian novel about a society that consigns women to submission and servitude.

The Handmaid's Tale had inspired anti-Trump fashionistas across the country to ditch their pink knitted "pussy hats" from the 2017 Women's March on Washington in favor of the robes and bonnets. Shortly after the show debuted in the spring of 2017, "handmaids" were spotted in Texas carrying a Planned Parenthood banner, shadowing GOP legislators on Capitol Hill, and following Vice President Mike Pence around the country. Lori Lodes of Demand Justice told ABC that the women in red trained their sights on Kavanaugh because "he represents the greatest threat to legal abortion since *Roe* was decided."

The handmaids were far from alone at Kavanaugh's hearings. A group of Texas doctors waiting in line for the hearings made a video saying they saw people accept cash to enter the hearing room and protest by yelling and screaming. Dr. Chris Dundas of Corpus Christi said some of the women who made it through the hearing room were disappointed they were not arrested.

"When they were arrested, they were keeping a record and celebrating who got arrested without any regard for open discussion or even the possibility of being convinced of anything," added Dr. Burton Purvis of Arlington, Texas. "It was just for the purpose of disruption."

The coordination of the protests was obvious enough to those present, but it was inconspicuous on television. Megaphone Strategies, a self-described "social justice media strategy firm" co-founded by the progressive activist Van Jones, sent reporters periodic tallies of arrests from the organizations it represented, including the Women's March, Center for Popular Democracy (CPD) Action, and People for the American Way. Two hours into the first day's hearings, Megaphone Strategies sent reporters an update. The early tabulation had "over 30 women" arrested, and some "were dragged out of the hearing without warning from police officers."

"Women are disrupting this hearing today because our lives are at risk. Women will die if Kavanaugh is confirmed," said Rachel O'Leary

Carmona, the chief operating officer of the Women's March. She explained that "hundreds of women" were still waiting in line to get into the hearing room. "The gloves are off, the rings are on, and we're ready to resist the fight that chose us."

On day one of the hearings, which were expected to last four days in September, seventy people were arrested for disrupting the committee's questioning of what Megaphone Strategies called a "well-documented anti-woman judge." A few of them were well known, such as Linda Sarsour, an anti-Israel activist and member of the Women's March board, and actress Piper Perabo. As the protesters were hauled out of the room, the organizers shepherded them to reporters.

Megaphone Strategies arranged for more than a dozen other "experts and activists" to speak to the press on designated topics such as "Women's Rights and Roe," "Donald Trump, Russia Investigation, and Impartial Courts," and "Presidential Accountability, Impeachment, Civil Liberties." Other were deployed to disparage female Republican senators who had the temerity to listen to Kavanaugh before making a decision. Megaphone Strategies enlisted Jeff King, a "four-time Iditarod sled dog race champion," to take aim at Lisa Murkowski of Alaska, while it pushed a student organizer from "Maine Student Action" in front of reporters to criticize Susan Collins of Maine.

Not content with seventy arrests on the first day, Megaphone Strategies looked for more ways for people to get arrested and intimidate public officials on the Hill. On the afternoon of the second day, when another thirty protesters had been arrested at the hearing, a handful of women staged a sit-in at Senator Rob Portman's office and were arrested. Through Megaphone Strategies, Carmona said the protesters went to Portman to explain "how they could die if Kavanaugh is confirmed."

Some of Megaphone Strategies' protesters wanted not simply to get arrested, but also to get elected. Deb Haaland's campaign for the House of Representatives from New Mexico's first congressional district worked with Megaphone Strategies to garner national attention so she could explain why "a vote for Brett Kavanaugh is a vote against Native

Americans." Specifically, she warned, Kavanaugh's "positions on climate change and women's reproductive rights will hit Native Americans especially hard." Precisely what Kavanaugh's "positions" on such issues were and why climate change and reproductive issues affect Native Americans more than others did not matter. Haaland saw an opening, and it worked. A couple of months later, she was one of two Native American women elected to Congress.

All along, the Democrats hoped to delay a vote on Kavanaugh's nomination until after the November elections. If they could campaign against Kavanaugh, perhaps they could flip the Senate and hold Kennedy's seat open until 2020. The Republicans' push to get Kavanaugh on the bench by October was motivated as much by their desire to remove the nomination as a campaign issue as by the desire to have a full complement of nine justices when the Supreme Court's new October term began.

The first delaying tactic was to drown the Senate in documents. Conservatives who had opposed Trump's selection of Kavanaugh had warned that the Judiciary Committee would be overwhelmed by paperwork, a warning that had become a reality. Deputy Attorney General Rod Rosenstein reportedly directed all ninety-three U.S. Attorney offices around the country to deploy as many as three prosecutors, as warranted, to assist the Justice Department with its document review. Candice Wong, a former Kavanaugh clerk and an assistant U.S. attorney in the District of Columbia, was moved to the Justice Department's Office of Legal Policy to help with the confirmation effort, a source with knowledge of the move said at the time. While former law enforcement officials sought the cover of anonymity to express their concerns about the reassignments, Main Justice put a brave face on the moves. Sarah Isgur Flores, a Justice Department spokeswoman, said that moves like Wong's were not "unusual in the slightest" and that plenty of other persons had been reassigned within the Justice Department to work on the Kavanaugh detail.

The volume of papers submitted to the Senate was unprecedented. By far the largest document dump associated with a Supreme Court nomination, it amounted to more than was submitted for the preceding five confirmed Supreme Court justices combined. The Senate received more than 440,000 pages of presidential records connected with Kavanaugh's work as a lawyer in the White House. The Senate Judiciary Committee also had to comb through Kavanaugh's 120-page answer to the committee's questionnaire, which included an attachment of 17,000 pages. After getting through the presidential records and questionnaire, the committee still faced Kavanaugh's judicial records, which amounted to more than 10,000 pages, including 307 opinions authored by Kavanaugh and hundreds of more opinions that he joined.

To tackle the paperwork, the Senate permitted the majority and minority staffs of the Judiciary Committee to add lawyers as special counsels to help process the nomination. Mike Davis served as chief counsel on judicial nominations for the committee chairman. He had begun as an intern opening mail for Grassley some seventeen years earlier. In the ensuing years, he served as a law clerk to Justice Neil Gorsuch at both the court of appeals and the Supreme Court, served as associate political director in President George W. Bush's office of political affairs, and worked as an assistant attorney general for the criminal division of the Justice Department and as a special assistant U.S. attorney for the Eastern District of Virginia. He also opened and operated his own law practice in Denver. With experience in all three branches of government, Davis knew how judicial nominations are processed and the nature of political warfare in D.C.

Davis's Democratic counterpart was Marc Hearron, the chief counsel on nominations for the ranking Democrat, Senator Dianne Feinstein, and a former partner at Morrison & Foerster. Hearron told the *National Law Journal* that one noticeable difference between his work as a litigator and his work on judicial nominations was the absence of a judge who "is going to decide who's right and is going to issue a ruling. On the Hill, there is no judge. The judge is the court of public opinion, and so you have to really work to try to get the public to care about issues that are going on."

Hearron revealed the Democrats' strategy when he continued, say-ing, "[T]he closest you get to having a judge [is] talking to a reporter and trying to explain to them what's going on and then hoping that their story will reflect what is actually happening. You know that the report-er's also talking to the Republicans, and they're going to give them a spin, and you're hoping that your view of the facts actually is what's reflected in the story." The Democrats intended to try Kavanaugh in the court of public opinion—not in a hearing room or an actual courtroom—because pliant reporters were "the closest you get to having a judge."

Perhaps no lawyer had a heavier lift ahead of the Senate Judiciary Committee hearings on Kavanaugh's nomination than Bill Burck, a former law clerk to Justice Kennedy and deputy counsel to President George W. Bush. Burck had been Bush's Presidential Records Act repre-sentative since 2009, which meant that he assisted the former president in the review of documents requested by the Senate for Kavanaugh's confirmation. A leading white-collar criminal defense lawyer in Wash-ington since leaving government, Burck was simultaneously representing White House counsel Don McGahn, former White House chief of staff Reince Priebus, and former White House strategist Steve Bannon in Special Counsel Robert Mueller's probe.

Burck met with Feinstein's and Grassley's staff members for the first time on July 18, the week after Kavanaugh's nomination. He answered their questions, offered to have records from Kavanaugh's White House counsel's office stint ready in a matter of weeks, and suggested that he would help the committee staffers find software that would make the document review process easier. Burck found the Senate Democrats to be rather unresponsive. "The best way to put it was that it was not friendly, it wasn't quite hostile," he recalled. "Republicans took the posi-tion that [the records request] was going to be a certain set of documents, and the Democrats did not commit. They just said, 'Well, we'll have to talk to our bosses about it.' But they just kind of listened and didn't react."

One day after the meeting, Grassley sent Feinstein a draft letter for Bush's team that proposed the committee request all emails sent and received by Kavanaugh in the counsel's office, all paper documents from his office files, all files on his confirmation to the Court of Appeals in 2006, and all emails and paper documents from Kavanaugh's time as staff secretary that fell under defined categories and arose from specific search terms. Feinstein's staff was noncommittal, declined to meet in person, and told Grassley that they would have an answer soon.

Instead of responding to Grassley's proposed request, Feinstein's staff waited until the end of the week—Friday at five o'clock in the evening—to share a draft of a letter Feinstein intended to send to David Ferriero, the archivist of the United States. The National Archives has jurisdiction over the George W. Bush Presidential Library, so Feinstein's staff members were attempting to go over the heads of Bush's staff. Ferriero was appointed by President Obama, so the Democrats expected him to be sympathetic. Feinstein told Grassley that she would send her letter to the archivist the following day regardless of whether Grassley agreed to co-sign it. Grassley declined, citing insufficient time to review the proposal, and Feinstein sent the letter on Saturday.

Grassley sent his own letter to the archivist disputing Feinstein's assertions, and the next week began with a ninety-minute meeting between their staffs. Feinstein was demanding the records of *anyone* who handled documents in the Bush White House in case any of them mentioned Kavanaugh's name, and her staff would not budge from their no-compromise approach. The two senators spoke the following day. According to Grassley, Feinstein said she wanted to review Kavanaugh's staff secretary records to determine whether they mentioned anything relating to "torture" in connection with the Bush administration's approval of enhanced interrogation techniques for terrorists. Grassley replied that they were voting on the nomination of Judge Kavanaugh to the Supreme Court, not on a third term for President Bush. The two were at an impasse, and according to Grassley's account, he suggested a search of the staff secretary records on the issue Feinstein cared about, but Feinstein's staff refused to comply.

As the two staffs continued to lock horns, Ferriero responded to Feinstein, and his answer was not what the Democrats were expecting:

> We are aware of discussions that have taken place between the former President's representatives and the Senate Judiciary Committee, and we have had discussions with both parties, as well as with your staff, which is our normal practice.... Any decisions or agreements that may be reached between former President Bush and the Committee would be independent of [our] role and responsibilities under the [Presidential Records Act].

The Democrats were infuriated that someone they considered one of their own would stick to the letter of the law. Feinstein's response was blistering:

> Your unduly restrictive reading of the law results in one political party having complete control over what records the Senate will be able to see before deciding whether a nominee should receive a lifetime appointment to the Supreme Court of the United States. [Y]our letter indicates that the National Archives is retreating from its role as the neutral nonpartisan decision-maker over what records will be produced to Congress. Instead, under an agreement reached between former President George W. Bush's lawyers and the Chairman, private, partisan lawyers are being granted decision-making authority as to which records will be provided to Congress.

While Feinstein raged in public, the Senate's top-ranking Democrat, Chuck Schumer, leaned on Ferriero in private, imploring him over the telephone "to do the right thing." He also made a private, written appeal to former President Bush, but the Democrats were too late. Grassley had already set the document-production wheels in motion with a letter to retired Brigadier General Patrick X. Mordente, the director of the Bush Library, formally requesting Kavanaugh's presidential records.

On August 2, Bush's representative, Bill Burck, responded to Grassley's request with 45,083 documents totaling 125,035 pages. "As you know," Burck reminded the Judiciary Committee, "President Bush is under no obligation to produce records of his Administration but has authorized this production to assist the United States Senate Committee on the Judiciary in its assessment of Judge Kavanaugh's nomination to the United States Supreme Court and to advance education and research about his Administration."

Ferriero, meanwhile, was still under pressure from Democrats. On the same day that Burck turned over the 125,000 pages of documents, Ferriero informed Grassley that he expected to complete the document production "by the end of October 2018"—just days before the November midterm elections that might flip control of the Senate to the Democrats. They seemed to have finally found a government official who would help them delay Kavanaugh's confirmation.

Bush's staff, however, paid little attention to Ferriero's estimate. Burck talked to the archives and learned of the "constraints" on the agency's resources, so Bush's team decided to service the Judiciary Committee's request "on a rolling basis." Since Ferriero had slowed the document review process, on August 9, Burck handed over 16,641 documents—49,344 pages in all—on the condition that they be labeled "committee confidential." The Bush team was still reviewing whether the documents could be made public and would send copies of those that could be made public as they became available.

In a show of efficiency unprecedented in the ranks of government, Bush's team continued to hand over hundreds of thousands of presidential records in the ensuing weeks. Despite the efforts of the National Archives to slow the process down, the Bush team continued to provide documents, including some forty-two thousand pages the day before Kavanaugh's September hearings began.

When Senator Kamala Harris interrupted the opening of the first day of Kavanaugh's hearings, she was referring to this newest batch of documents, which the committee members had received the night before. This senator, who told reporters three months earlier that she would go "as far as possible" to stop Kavanaugh, argued that she had not had enough time to review the documentation and make a decision she said she already made. Little more than an hour into the hearings, Harris blasted out an email solicitation that read, "I am prepared to do everything in my power to stop this nomination," and asked recipients to sign a petition during the hearings.

Following Harris's interruption, Senator Amy Klobuchar of Minnesota, another early entrant in the 2020 Democratic presidential field, added to the cacophony by repeating Harris's concerns about the newest batch of documents. Neither presidential candidate was able to sidetrack Senator Grassley, so Senator Cory Booker—the third Judiciary Committee Democrat who launched a presidential campaign within six months of the hearing—decided to make it personal.

Interrupting the hearing, Booker declared that he was appealing to Grassley's "sense of decency and integrity." The Democrats had sought a meeting about the documents, he contended, but were denied one, and he made no mention of the rest of the back-and-forth between Republicans and Democrats. "I appeal to your sense of fairness and decency, your commitments that you've made to transparency," Booker shouted. "Based upon your own principles, your own values, I call for at least to have a debate or a vote on these issues and not to rush through this process."

This was not the first time Booker called into question the decency of Kavanaugh's supporters. Standing alongside Senator Elizabeth Warren of Massachusetts—yet another 2020 presidential candidate—in July, Booker called the nomination of Kavanaugh a "moral moment" in which "there are no bystanders." Those who supported Kavanaugh, he said, were "complicit to that evil." Booker's inflammatory rhetoric did not gain widespread attention then, but in front of millions of people at the hearing he had found an audience.

Booker's barb provoked a response from Grassley. Maintaining his Iowa-nice demeanor, the chairman explained that while he had respect for Booker, "I think you are taking advantage of my decency and integrity." Sensing an opportunity, Booker continued to push. On the second day of the hearings, he raised the issue of racial profiling, which Kavanaugh had discussed after the September 11, 2001, attacks in private email correspondences with his colleagues in the White House. Booker said that Kavanaugh had not demonstrated sufficient outrage that a colleague had suggested looking for guidance to *Korematsu v. United States*, the Supreme Court decision that approved the internment of Japanese Americans during World War II.

Kavanaugh asked to see the correspondence, but Booker did not provide it before questioning him. Senator Thom Tillis of North Carolina sought to get the document for Kavanaugh, but Booker objected and continued grilling Kavanaugh about the seventeen-year-old email. Eventually Senator Mike Lee of Utah interjected that Booker was reading from an email labeled "committee confidential":

> The rules of fairness and the rules of the committee require us to treat our witnesses with respect, with certain minimum standards of respect, such that you can't cross-examine somebody about a document that they can't see.... Now in this circumstance, the document that was referred to by my distinguished friend and colleague from New Jersey, Senator Booker, was designated as "committee confidential." Now, there are ways we can deal with this, we can deal with this either in a closed session so that he can see the document to which you are referring, or we can also go about different procedures to make it public.

Lee noted that they had already made similar confidential documents public for Senator Klobuchar—the only Democrat to request before the hearings that specific confidential documents become public—and Senator Patrick Leahy of Vermont, the longtime Democratic leader of the Judiciary Committee before Feinstein. Booker refused to follow the rules and had no interest in showing Kavanaugh due respect. "That's why this system is rigged," Booker said in reply to Lee. "That process is unfair, it's unnecessary, it's unjust, and it's unprecedented on this committee."

Lee offered to work with Booker "hand-in-hand, literally," to expedite the publication of confidential documents, but Booker was not as interested in the public's seeing the emails as he was in the public's seeing him. Senator Grassley started the next day's hearings by noting that Booker had made no request for the confidential document to be made public until after the hearing in which he read it aloud. The Justice Department worked with the committee in the early-morning hours to comply with Booker's requests that the documents be made public. Booker complained that he would have to "reveal to you what questions [I] wanted to ask" by making such a formal request. Booker wanted to spring his questions on Kavanaugh.

Angered by Booker's flaunting of the committee's rules, Senator John Cornyn, the majority whip, interjected that there could be "consequences" for the violation of Senate rules. Booker excitedly replied that he knew he was violating the rules, which he viewed as a form of "civil disobedience."

"I am right now, before your process is finished, I am going to release the email about racial profiling, and I understand that the penalty comes with potential ousting from the Senate," Booker said. "And if Senator Cornyn believes that I violated Senate rules, I openly invite and accept the consequences of my team releasing that email right now." Booker repeated several times that he was deliberately violating the rules, until Grassley interjected, "Okay, how many times are you going to tell us that?"

Booker then began posting what he described as the "committee confidential" documents to his Twitter feed, prompting Cornyn to reply, "Running for president is no excuse for violating the rules of the Senate or the confidentiality of the documents that we are privy to." For all his posturing as an outlaw, Booker had actually failed to break the rules. The documents in question had been made public before the hearings resumed. As Senator Lee noted, "The process worked."

Booker, determined to find a way to slow the committee and break the rules, further delayed the hearings to "clarify" that he did not violate a *Senate* rule but only a rule of the Judiciary Committee. "I did willingly violate the chair's rule on the committee confidential process. I take full responsibility for violating that sir, and I violated it because I sincerely believed that the public deserves to know this nominee's record," Booker said. "Now, I appreciate the comments of my colleagues. This is probably the closest I'll ever have in my life to an 'I am Spartacus' moment. My colleagues, numerous of them, said that they too accept the responsibility."

Precisely who had joined in Booker's "Spartacus" escapade was unclear. In the Stanley Kubrick film *Spartacus*, a group of Roman slaves all claim to be Spartacus to save their friend. Klobuchar and Harris did not appear eager to raise their 2020 competitor's profile. If his fellow presidential candidates would not help him, perhaps Booker could rile up the senior senator from Texas. He challenged Senator Cornyn to take action against him if he was "sincere" and not full of "political bluster." "If he is not a tempest in a teapot…then bring the charges," Booker said. "Go through the Senate process to take on somebody that you said is unbecoming to be a senator."

These furious assaults on the English language failed to move anyone to take action against him, but Booker persevered. As the Judiciary Committee prepared to meet in private with Kavanaugh—a forum that Feinstein skipped—the junior senator from New Jersey continued throughout the afternoon to post more supposedly confidential documents to Twitter. That effort failed too, as Bush's staff had approved the confidential documents for public view. Bill Burck wrote in an email, "We were surprised to learn about Senator Booker's histrionics this morning because we had already told him he could use the documents publicly. In fact, we have said yes to every request made by the Senate Democrats to make documents public."

Finding no adversary among the Republicans to act as a foil for his heroism, Booker turned instead to cable news for approbation and applause. He first regaled Chris Hayes of MSNBC with an account of how his fearless rule-breaking had sent Republicans "scrambling." "Were the documents already clear or were you violating the rules?" asked a confused Hayes, pointing to Burck's statements that they were cleared for public release.

"I violated the rules, and I am violating the rules. The reality is it's all moot at this point because I'm continuing to release documents that they haven't approved yet," insisted the senator.

Booker next pleaded his case on CNN, where he was again unable to kindle a flame. "This morning you said you were going to break Senate rules so you could release documents pertaining to Kavanaugh. You said you were willing to risk expulsion from the Senate to do that, [and] now Republicans on the committee have said that the documents had already been approved for release before four a.m. this morning," Anderson Cooper said. "Senator Cornyn basically accused you of a stunt to bolster a possible run for the presidency. Was that just a stunt?"

"Well, I mean the amusing thing about that is what Cornyn first said is he threatened me, he threatened me with expulsion," Booker replied. Then he repeated his account of renegade rule-breaking and insisted he was still breaking all kinds of rules even as he was speaking: "I am violating those laws, I have been doing [it] all day. And it was an unjust law, you see there was no consequence. They will not move to expel me from the Senate for violating the committee confidential rules."

Cooper remained unimpressed. "I guess the question is, was it really a violation because at this point, to be clear, Bill Burck, President Bush's Presidential Records [Act] representative, said he cleared the documents before four a.m. per your staff's request and that they had told you you could use them publicly," Cooper said, repeating himself. "Grassley's office also confirmed you were told that the restrictions on the documents had been waived before you spoke today, so how do you square that with the idea that, with what you've said?"

"Well, I square that very easily," Booker said. "Number one, last night I broke the rules. Then they scrambled to release the document, but I continue to release documents.... I am breaking the rules, I am breaking the sham rules. Twenty documents—if you check my Twitter feed anybody in the public now can have access to the ones they wanted to hide. They haven't cleared those yet, maybe they're rushing to catch up to me and clear those as well."

And so the interview continued painfully with Senator Spartacus insisting that he was a no-good rule-breaker. The Democrats' efforts to delay the confirmation hearings with an extended fight over documents fizzled with his cable news performance.

Reflecting on the Democrats' histrionics, Grassley said he thought his decision to continue the hearings amid the disruptions truthfully irked the right more than the left.

"Instead of getting done at 2:30, we got done at 5:30, and probably the only people I made mad was the Republicans because I didn't gavel [Democrats] down beforehand," Grassley said. "And a lot of people said to me, 'Why don't you shut 'em up, you know?'... And I said I've learned a long time ago that you spend more time trying to shut people up than letting them talk, see."

The Democrats next sought to disqualify Kavanaugh before his confirmation came up for a vote in the full Senate. In thirty-minute rounds beginning on day two of the hearings, they took turns trying to tie the nominee to conservative policies and to any scandal—perceived or real—of the Trump administration. Senator Feinstein, the ranking member, got the first crack at Kavanaugh. She announced that she would question him about his views on guns and *Roe v. Wade*, but her first question about *Roe* was actually about a different case—*Planned Parenthood v. Casey*.

"Do you agree with Justice O'Connor that a woman's right to control her reproductive life impacts her ability to 'participate equally in the economic and social life of the nation'?" Feinstein asked. Kavanaugh replied:

Well as a general proposition, I understand the importance of the precedent set forth in *Roe v. Wade*. So *Roe v. Wade* held, of course, and it was reaffirmed in *Planned Parenthood v. Casey*, that a woman has a constitutional right to obtain an abortion before viability subject to reasonable regulation by the state up to the point where that regulation constitutes an undue burden on the woman's right to obtain an abortion. And one of the reasons for that holding, as explained by the court in *Roe*, and also in *Planned Parenthood v. Casey* more fully, is along the lines of what you said, Senator Feinstein, about the quote from Justice O'Connor, so that's one of the rationales that undergirds *Roe v. Wade*. It's one of the rationales that undergirds *Planned Parenthood v. Casey*.

As Kavanaugh noted, Feinstein quoted from *Planned Parenthood v. Casey*, not *Roe*. By asking him whether he agreed with O'Connor's opinion in a different case, Feinstein was tempting him to disagree with the first woman justice of the Supreme Court, an appointee of President Ronald Reagan. When he demurred, the senator revealed that she was interested not in whether he agreed with the reasoning of *Roe* but in what he thought of the Court's subsequent application and justification of *Roe*. She then peppered him with questions about whether *Roe* was "settled law," what "settled law" means to him, and whether a settled law is, in fact, correct law. The volleys produced no "viral moment" for California's senior senator, and Kavanaugh survived.

Most of the other Democratic senators probed Kavanaugh's views on abortion, health care, and related issues in an effort to make him appear hostile to women, but the Kavanaugh confirmation team had a plan to push back. The Supreme Court advocate Lisa Blatt, then a partner of Arnold & Porter Kaye Scholer, introduced Kavanaugh to the committee with a ringing endorsement:

I am also a liberal Democrat and an unapologetic defender of a woman's right to choose.... My hero is Justice Ruth Bader Ginsburg, for whom I had the great fortune of serving as a law clerk. I proudly voted for Hillary Clinton, I voted for President Obama twice, and with my apologies Mr.

Chairman for this one, I wish Senator Feinstein were chairing this committee. And yet, I am here today to introduce Judge Kavanaugh and urge the Senate to confirm him as the next associate justice of the Supreme Court.

Blatt told the senators that she had received angry phone calls and emails from friends and strangers alike for her support of Kavanaugh, but "I was raised to call it like I see it, and I don't see the choice before you as difficult." She described Kavanaugh's opinions as "instant classics" that are "invariably thoughtful and fair" and pronounced him qualified for the nation's highest court "by any objective measure." Blatt's endorsement was a gut punch for Kavanaugh's pro-choice opponents, and they swung back hard. The animosity directed at Blatt before her appearance at the hearing was mild compared with what came afterward. Before the hearings, Demand Justice's Brian Fallon called her a traitor and a puppet of "corporate interests," and when she switched law firms the year after Kavanaugh's confirmation, he put "liberal feminist" in scare quotes when referring to her on social media. In private, she faced much worse.

After Feinstein failed to land a punch, Senator Dick Durbin stepped into the ring. The minority whip had viewed Kavanaugh as an archenemy since his nomination in 2003 to the federal appellate court in the District of Columbia—a nomination that the Democrats held up in the Senate for three years. In a confirmation hearing in 2004, Durbin, irked by Kavanaugh's work on Kenneth Starr's Whitewater investigation of the Clintons, called him the "Forrest Gump of Republican politics": "You show up at every scene of the crime." After Kavanaugh was confirmed, Durbin accused him of lying to the committee. Now Durbin had another shot at Kavanaugh, and he was ready to pick up where he had left off a decade and a half ago.

"I'm going to throw you a pitch which you've seen comin' for twelve years," Durbin began. "I want to talk to you about the 2006 testimony, which you gave before this committee." In the twilight of the Bush administration, Durbin had asked Kavanaugh about the federal appellate court nomination of William "Jim" Haynes IV, a former Pentagon general counsel who helped formulate interrogation policies for detainees at Guantanamo Bay. Kavanaugh answered that he knew Haynes but did not handle his nomination, adding, "I was not involved and am not involved in the questions about the rules governing the detention of combatants." Durbin never bought it.

Reading Kavanaugh's testimony from a poster held by a staffer, Durbin chastised him for having given a complete answer: "When I was back in the day a trial attorney preparing a witness for interrogation testimony deposition, giving testimony at trial, I said two things: Tell the truth and don't answer more than you're asked, don't volunteer information. Judge Kavanaugh, you failed on the second count."

"I adhered to the first part. I told the truth," Kavanaugh replied.

The senator insisted: "Well you volunteered more information than I asked, and you went further than you should have."

The Democrats' progressive base was overwhelmingly interested in one subject—abortion. The perceived threat to *Roe v. Wade* was why Kavanaugh—and indeed, *any* Trump nominee—must be kept off the Supreme Court. Senator Kamala Harris understood this as well as anyone, of course, and had vowed to defeat the nomination by any means necessary. She used her questions on this second day of the hearings to raise suspicion that Kavanaugh might be implicated in the Trump administration's supposed efforts to obstruct the Mueller investigation of Russian "collusion" in the 2016 presidential election.

She asked the nominee if he had ever had a conversation about the Mueller investigation with anyone from the law firm Kasowitz Benson Torres, which had represented President Trump. The firm had more than 260 attorneys in nine offices around the world, and Kavanaugh fumbled as he searched to think of whom he knew there. Without a roster of all attorneys, staff, and other employees, he said, he could not answer with any confidence. Noting that the investigation had produced cases in his courthouse, he asked whether Harris had someone particular in mind.

Harris declined to be more specific and would not concede that her question was at all unclear. Lacking the information necessary for a complete answer, Kavanaugh did not give the senator a categorical *yes* or *no* and so appeared to the untrained eye as though he had something to hide. The fact that the special counsel's investigation eventually found no evidence of Russian collusion with the Trump campaign did not matter. The important thing was to make Kavanaugh the man at "every scene of the crime," as Durbin said.

The Democrats' attacks on Kavanaugh proved less effective than the attacks on earlier Republican nominees because in the age of the Internet, rebuttals could be disseminated immediately and widely. Judge Bork was taken out by Ted Kennedy's speech and a television ad. When Clarence Thomas faced the Anita Hill hearings in 1991, he had the benefit of conservative talk radio—mainly Rush Limbaugh—and not much else. When the Democrats hit Kavanaugh, their attacks were answered in real time. A legion of right-leaning allies on social media functioned as a rapid-response team to Democratic attacks, and an unofficial leader of the operation was seated in the front row in the first days of Kavanaugh's hearings. Shoshana Weissmann, a purple-haired social media maven at the libertarian R Street Institute, was live-tweeting the hearings about a dozen seats away from the judge. Invited by the Justice Department, she said she was offered a seat behind the judge but opted for a slightly less visible perch.

The stream-of-consciousness tweets from @senatorshoshana, similar to those a campaign puts out during a presidential debate, demystified the confirmation process. When Democrats complained about the "committee confidential" designation on allegedly secret documents, Weissmann shared the news of Senator Feinstein's private letters urging that certain documents related to Kavanaugh be kept secret. When Democrats decried the influence of the nefarious Federalist Society, she tweeted, "I've been a member of the evil secret Federalist Society since I was 16. Join them!!! #FF @FedSoc." An untraditional player, she proved invaluable. "People were watching it live like it's a pop culture event, which is bad," she said. "They should be watching it and trying to learn. And they took everything out of context, where I had to go back and then explain, 'No, you f—ing idiots, this is how this stuff works.'"

Independent of the Kavanaugh confirmation team, Weissmann was free to mock the opposition as she pleased. "It's so weird how on TV it looks so legit, but sitting there, it's a room full of people," she tweeted after leaving the hearings. She said she regrets that since she did not sit through all four days of the hearings, she missed the opportunity to "flash my @fedsoc gang sign," a tongue-in-cheek reference to Zina Bash's supposed white supremacist hand signals.

Weissmann thought the hearings, with their irresistible opportunity for showboating, constituted a hazard for senators with electoral aspirations. Abandoning substance for show, they were tempted to pander to the small-dollar donors with an ostentatiously hostile grilling of Trump's nominee. The hearings were "all politics and no courts," complained Weissmann, who was struck by how many questions had nothing to do with the law—a remarkable change from past hearings. She and her R Street Institute colleague Anthony Marcum compiled a searchable and sortable database of the text of the confirmation hearings for every Supreme Court nominee since Lewis Powell and William Rehnquist, who were both nominated on the same day in 1971 by President Nixon.

"If you look at any Judiciary Committee hearing and compare it to past ones, the substance is just dead," Weissmann said. "What stood out to me [at Kavanaugh's] was no one knew anything, or if they knew they were pretending not to, which is really depressing. For the left and right, it was just crap. Crap everywhere."

Kavanaugh emerged from the first days of his Senate Judiciary Committee hearings largely unscathed, in some measure because of his supporters' preparation and his opponents' misbegotten strategy. Kavanaugh's female defenders and Lisa Blatt's testimony made a first impression that undermined the arguments that he was hell-bent on criminalizing abortion. Senator Booker's misfire on cable news killed the notion that documents were being wantonly withheld. Weissmann and the other social media rapid-responders had adroitly executed their whack-a-mole defense.

Their attempts to bloody Kavanaugh in his hearings having failed, the progressive left now turned to their last resort to stop the appointment. They had begun laying the groundwork months earlier, but their strategy was just now becoming apparent. Judicial confirmations in the Trump era have been an occasion for Senator Sheldon Whitehouse, a Rhode Island Democrat, to roast conservative legal groups. He did not deviate from his script in the Kavanaugh hearings and again decried the influence of the Federalist Society and the Pacific Legal Foundation. But Whitehouse also revealed something about how the left planned to stop Kavanaugh if all else failed: "You know perfectly well," he said to the nominee, "that the Court depends on, as much as anything, on its reputation. You don't have a purse and you don't have an army. You stand on your reputation in the judiciary. And you must not only act justly, but be seen to act justly."

The power and legitimacy of the Supreme Court depend not only on the decisions the justices render, Whitehouse was telling Kavanaugh, but on the court of public opinion, as well. That was the court to which the Democrats would now resort.

The originalists and textualists that Whitehouse despised took a much different view of the source of the Court's authority. Soon after Kavanaugh's first hearings, Justice Clarence Thomas was asked at a Federalist Society event about what preserves the legitimacy of the Supreme Court. It is built "brick by brick," he said, on an ethical and moral foundation bolstered by jurists' honesty, integrity, and adherence to the law and their oaths of office. He continued:

> If we could use that word ["honorable"] about more people who are in public life, people who actually ask the questions at confirmation hearings instead of Spartacus [here he was interrupted by laughter from his Federalist Society audience]—if we could use the word honorable more often, think

about the difference it'll make. Then you'll have a legacy. We will have left the country in better shape, morally, structurally, than we found it. But as long as we're looking at our interests, or scoring points, or looking cute, or being on TV... or what editorials we're getting, especially the legal system, how do we maintain it? If you can't debate hard issues honestly, with honor, with integrity, how do we keep a civil society?

If at the outset some Senate Democrats had reservations about resorting to the court of public opinion, they had since abandoned them. Senator Feinstein's staff would soon demonstrate the extent of their reliance on public opinion when they sent Christine Blasey Ford to high-powered D.C. lawyers rather than to law enforcement officials or the full Judiciary Committee.

CHAPTER 4

Sabotage

"**P**otential Supreme Court nominee with assistance from his friend assaulted me in mid 1980s in Maryland. Have therapy records talking about it. Feel like I shouldn't be quiet but not willing to put family in DC and CA through a lot of stress."

That's the anonymous message Christine Blasey Ford sent through an encrypted application to the *Washington Post* on the morning of Friday, July 6, 2018. Her opening salvo against Brett Kavanaugh did not identify him by name and did not include her name either.

At the time she sent her message, Trump was three days away from making his selection of Kavanaugh, whose momentum was well documented in the press. Kavanaugh's allies began organizing in support of him as soon as Justice Anthony Kennedy announced his retirement, and by the morning of Ford's anonymous message, cable news was talking hour after hour about the respective strengths of the finalists. The *Washington Post*'s Ruth Marcus, a vehement opponent of the president and a critic of Kavanaugh, had appeared on MSNBC that morning to assess which Supreme Court candidate was, in her view, "the biggest danger to abortion rights."

An hour went by, and no one at the *Post* responded to Ford. She sent the *Post* another message eighty-one minutes after her first one, according to the time-stamps on her encrypted messaging app. She appeared to name her attackers.

"Brett Kavanaugh with Mark Judge and a bystander named PJ," she wrote.

Ford again received no reply. Determined to see her allegation published, she called the office of her congresswoman, Anna Eshoo, a liberal Democrat from the San Francisco Bay area. Ford told the receptionist that "someone on the president's shortlist attacked me."

By the time she testified before the Senate Judiciary Committee little more than two months later, her story had changed several times over. The timing of the assault changed by a matter of years. First her encrypted message to the *Washington Post* said "mid 1980s," but later she wrote to Senator Feinstein that it occurred in the "early 1980's." She then told the *Washington Post* that it happened precisely in the "summer of 1982" before ultimately testifying, "I can't give the exact date."

Ford testified that on the day she first submitted the allegations to the *Washington Post*, she "had a sense of urgency to relay the information to the Senate and the president as soon as possible." "I felt like the best option was to try to do the civic route," she testified. "I wasn't interested in pursuing the media route, particularly." Yet she also testified that before July 6 she never made any attempt to reach any senator, the White House, or any staffer at any level working for a senator or the president. She did, however, continue to pursue the *Washington Post*.

Kavanaugh's nomination was announced on the evening of July 9. Later that night, Ford testified, she received a return call from Congresswoman Eshoo's office. Early the next morning, Ford again submitted an anonymous message to the *Washington Post* through the encrypted app. "Been advised to contact senators or NYT," she wrote, before pointedly adding that the *Post* had not responded. She testified that Eshoo later directed her to Senator Feinstein, the ranking Democrat on the Judiciary Committee, but that her unnamed "beach friends" told her to go to the *New York Times*.

Within ninety minutes of threatening to go to the *Washington Post*'s competition, Ford received a reply: "I will get you in touch with a reporter." That reporter was Emma Brown, a graduate of Stanford University and former seventh-grade teacher. She began at the *Post* in 2009 writing obituaries before moving to the education beat, where her work on the accomplishments of Arne Duncan, President Obama's secretary of education, won plaudits from fellow journalists. She also was a finalist for an award from fellow education journalists for her reporting on sexual assaults at colleges. (She would take a leave from the *Post* in 2019 to write a book about raising boys after the #MeToo reckoning.) In response to the tip from a California academic with purported connections to Stanford accusing the president's nominee for the Supreme Court of trying to rape her, the *Post* turned to its Stanford-educated reporter with experience covering sexual assault.

As much as she wanted to make her story known, Ford wanted her conversation with Brown to remain off the record. "She really wanted to tell somebody her story," the reporter later told CNN, "but she also didn't want to have her life upended, and she was terrified of what would happen if she came forward. She struggled with that all summer long."

To assure the *Post* that her allegation against Kavanaugh pre-dated his emergence as a candidate for Kennedy's seat on the Supreme Court, Ford provided the newspaper with details that she never gave the Senate Judiciary Committee—the "therapy records" from 2012, which she cited in her first encrypted message.

In March 2012, Jeffrey Toobin wrote in the *New Yorker*, "If a Republican, any Republican, wins in November, his most likely first nominee to the Supreme Court will be Brett Kavanaugh," predicting that he would be a departure from the Republican-appointed justices who had voted with the majority in *Roe v. Wade* and later had reaffirmed that decision in *Planned Parenthood v. Casey*. "[M]oderate Republicans held sway for years at the Supreme Court," Toobin observed, "but that species vanished on both sides of First Street," the road that runs between the Capitol and the high court.

Two months after Toobin's article was published, Ford and her husband went to couples' therapy, where she first shared details of her allegation. She said her husband remembered her uttering Kavanaugh's name, but as for her own recollection of the discussion, she testified, "I recall saying that the boy who assaulted me could someday be on the U.S. Supreme Court and spoke a bit about his background at an elitist all-boys school in Bethesda, Maryland."

Toobin's article was not the first time that Brett Kavanaugh had been in the public eye, of course. Yet Ford did not air her allegations when Kavanaugh was part of the Whitewater special prosecutor's team or when he was a key aide to President George W. Bush. And she did not accuse Kavanaugh of sexually assaulting her when he was nominated to the U.S. Court of Appeals for the D.C. Circuit, even though his confirmation was hotly contested and dragged on for three years. It was only after he was mentioned in the press as a possible Supreme Court nominee that her account of being attacked by young Brett Kavanaugh found expression.

Ford attributed her 2012 allegation in therapy to a disagreement over a "very extensive, very long remodel" of her home in her testimony to the Senate Judiciary Committee. But there was another major event in Ford's life in 2012—a job change. She left work as director at Corcept Therapeutics, a pharmaceutical company that has been dogged by congressional investigators and a class-action lawsuit by investors accusing the company's management of conflicts of interest, pay-to-play schemes, and an ends-justify-the-means corporate ethos.

Corcept Therapeutics' only drug is Korlym, which may be dispensed in the United States only to treat patients with Cushing Syndrome, an illness in which the body produces too much cortisol. The active ingredient in Korlym is mifepristone, better known as the abortion drug. Mifepristone was approved by the U.S. Food and Drug Administration for use in abortions in 2000. At that time, Stanford University Medical School's psychiatry department began studying the use of mifepristone as a cortisol-blocker to treat depression and psychosis. The Stanford researchers formed Corcept Therapeutics in 1998, shortly before Ford became a research psychologist at that university in 1999.

Dr. Alan Schatzberg, a co-founder of Corcept Therapeutics and the former chairman of the psychiatry department at Stanford, said in 2002 that the drug he was developing "may be the equivalent of shock treatments in a pill" for patients with major depression. Ford formally joined Corcept Therapeutics in 2005, first as associate director and later as director. Her responsibilities as a biostatistician included leading "statistical activities of Phase 3 program for development of new medicines," according to paperwork she submitted to the U.S. Senate. A drug usually goes through several phases of clinical trials before the manufacturer applies to the FDA for permission to market it. Following the completion of a Phase 3 trial in 2006, Corcept Therapeutics did not publish the results at the U.S. National Library of Medicine online.

This failure to publish results led critics to label the work of Corcept Therapeutics and Stanford as "experimercials"—that is, medical research undertaken to produce publicity for a specific drug. Schatzberg was particularly susceptible to such criticism because he owned millions of shares of Corcept Therapeutics stock while researching the only drug Corcept Therapeutics produced with funding from the federal government. In 2008, the curious arrangement piqued the interest of Senator Chuck Grassley, then the ranking member of the Finance Committee. Grassley's staff began investigating Christine Blasey Ford's employer ten years before Grassley presided over Ford's hearing before the Judiciary Committee. According to a 2008 letter from Stanford's general counsel, Schatzburg forfeited his responsibility for Stanford's research into mifepristone because of Grassley's investigation. The Project on Government Oversight, a nonprofit watchdog, later uncovered internal emails from the U.S. National Institutes of Health revealing that the federal government wanted the clinical trial component of its grant to Stanford to be "terminated immediately and permanently."

The unraveling of Corcept Therapeutics' scheming nearly undid Ford's employer. But Corcept Therapeutics secured FDA approval under the Obama administration in 2012—the year Ford left the company—for the specific use of treating Cushing Syndrome in a select set of patients.

The full extent of Corcept Therapeutics' alleged shady business practices has emerged since then. The Southern Investigative Reporting Foundation discovered in 2019 that the pharmaceutical company undertook a pay-to-play plot to induce physicians to prescribe the drug. Blue Orca Capital, a self-described "activist investment firm," then revealed that Corcept Therapeutics used an undisclosed specialty pharmacy and distributor of its drug that appeared to be a component of Corcept Therapeutics designed "to boost sales, hide losses or engage in other financial shenanigans." Corcept Therapeutics responded that its critics were motivated by short-sellers looking to enrich themselves at the expense of the company, an answer that did not satisfy all of its investors.

The fraud allegedly perpetrated by Corcept Therapeutics spawned a class action lawsuit by the company's investors, filed on March 14, 2019, which threatened to dismantle the entire operation. The investors alleged that the company "aggressively promoted Korlym for off-label uses," paid doctors "improperly" to promote the drug, and artificially inflated its revenue and sales figures through "illicit sales practices," all while keeping the company's investors in the dark. The lawsuit does not describe the full scope of the alleged off-label uses of Korlym, including whether it was prescribed to patients with depression or to patients seeking an abortion.

In sum, while Kavanaugh's chief accuser presented herself to the Senate and to the public as Dr. Christine Blasey Ford, leader of "statistical activities" in the "development of new medicines," it appears that she worked for a company that benefited from federal research grants while routinely failing to deliver the results it predicted. The company also stands accused of allegedly defrauding its investors, "aggressively" pushing the abortion drug for unknown off-label uses, and falsifying its financial data to line the wallets of those working for Corcept Therapeutics. To be clear, Ford is not named in the class action lawsuit, nor was she directly implicated in the congressional investigation of the company. But her work to make the abortion drug accessible to a wider group of patients through Corcept Therapeutics may shed some light on her motivation to halt the nomination of a justice perceived as ready to over-rule *Roe v. Wade.*

Ford is not a medical doctor. She obtained a Ph.D. in psychology from the University of Southern California in 1996, where she specialized in marriage and family therapy. She trained as a clinical psychologist at Pepperdine University, graduating with a master's degree in 1991. While working at Corcept Therapeutics, which was heavily reliant upon Stanford, Ford received a master's degree in epidemiology from the Stanford University School of Medicine, which employed Corcept Therapeutics' co-founder.

Despite holding several advanced degrees and working as a teacher herself, Ford testified that she "did not know how" to contact the U.S. Senate with her allegations about Kavanaugh. According to Ford's testimony, Congresswoman Eshoo and her staff, who met with Ford multiple times in July, directed her to write to Senator Feinstein. She complied with a letter dated July 30, 2018, and marked "CONFIDENTIAL," which Eshoo's staff delivered to Feinstein's office. Ford's letter contained an account of the alleged assault that differed from the one she initially gave to the *Washington Post.* On July 6, Ford had told the *Post* that the assault occurred in the "mid 1980s," but in her letter to Feinstein, she said it was "in the early 1980s." The number of people present had changed too. Ford had told the *Post* on July 6 that the assault involved "Brett Kavanaugh with Mark Judge and a bystander named PJ." P. J. was omitted from Ford's letter to Feinstein, which reads, "The assault occurred in a suburban Maryland area home at a gathering that included me and 4 others." It continues:

> Kavanaugh physically pushed me into a bedroom as I was headed for a bathroom up a short stairwell from the living room. They locked the door and played loud music, preclud-ing any successful attempts to yell for help. Kavanaugh was on top of me while laughing with Judge, who periodically jumped onto Kavanaugh. They both laughed as Kavanaugh

tried to disrobe me in their highly inebriated state. With Kavanaugh's hand over my mouth, I feared he may inadvertently kill me. From across the room, a very drunken Judge said mixed words to Kavanaugh ranging from "go for it" to "stop." At one point when Judge jumped onto the bed, the weight on me was substantial. The pile toppled, and the two scrapped with each other. After a few attempts to get away, I was able to take this opportune moment to get up and run across to a hallway bathroom. I locked the bathroom door behind me. Both loudly stumbled down the stairwell, at which point other persons at the house were talking with them. I exited the bathroom, ran outside of the house and went home.

Ford wrote that she had "not knowingly seen Kavanaugh since the assault." She said she had spotted Judge once at a Safeway, however, and knew that "he was extremely uncomfortable seeing me." Ford did not mention her repeated attempts to contact the press, but she wrote to Feinstein that she notified her "local government representative" because she "felt guilty as a citizen about the idea of not saying anything." She concluded by sharing her schedule, noting that she was "currently vacationing in the mid-Atlantic until August 7th" and would be back in California after August 10.

Ford testified that after a "fairly brief phone call" with Feinstein before August 7 she began "interviewing" lawyers to represent her. Feinstein's staff, she said, directed her to the law firm of Debra Katz, a well-known #Resistance instigator and #MeToo litigator. Katz was part of the anti-Trump resistance before it even had a name, taking to the streets of Washington in the Women's March the day after Trump's inauguration. She had a talent for attracting media coverage. When Jeff Sessions was confirmed as attorney general one month later, ABC's *Good Morning America* featured Katz, identified only as a "protester," pledging to "fight back." But Katz cut her teeth in television defending

President Bill Clinton against Paula Jones, an Arkansas state employee who accused him of sexual harassment when he was governor.

"Paula Jones' suit is very, very, very weak," Katz told CNN in 1998. "She's alleged one incident that took place in a hotel room that, by her own testimony, lasted ten to twelve minutes. She suffered no repercussions in the workplace." In those pre-#MeToo days, she told the CBS Evening News that Jones's allegation was "not enough to create a sexually hostile work environment claim," and the New York Times reported that Katz would have told Jones, "[Y]ou don't have a case." Jones ultimately collected an $850,000 settlement from Clinton, while the Clintons collected thousands of dollars in campaign contributions from Katz in the ensuing decades. Katz raised money for the Clintons too, raking in twenty-nine thousand dollars for Hillary Clinton's 2016 campaign a full year before the election, according to an internal campaign memo revealed by WikiLeaks.

Katz simultaneously built a successful law firm—Katz, Marshall & Banks—specializing in sexual harassment, sexual discrimination, and whistleblower cases. Her clients have included victims of such high-profile defendants as Harvey Weinstein and former New York attorney general Eric Schneiderman. Katz's practice benefitted from the attention of Ronan Farrow in the New Yorker. The former State Department official and adviser to Secretary of State Hillary Clinton wrote about Weinstein and Schneiderman and other sexual misconduct cases involving Katz's clients, sometimes naming Katz as a source. If her clients were muzzled in public by nondisclosure agreements, Farrow could see to it that the plaintiff's side of the story was prominently expressed.

As effective as Farrow has been, Katz has not relied on him exclusively. Jodi Kantor and Megan Twohey of the New York Times wrote articles about Weinstein that, in Katz's view, "should have won [them] the Nobel Prize" for activism instead of the Pulitzer Prize they won for journalism.

Katz's skill at winning her cases entirely in the court of public opinion is well-documented, and she has not let friendly journalists take all the credit. She was dubbed "DC's Leading #MeToo Lawyer" in the summer of 2018 by *Washingtonian* magazine and one of the "Top 10 Plaintiff's Attorneys to Fear Most" by *Human Resource Executive* magazine. In an admiring profile in the alumni magazine of the University of Wisconsin in August 2018, she explained that the #MeToo movement had forced cases to end "more quickly and for higher dollar amounts than before," acknowledging that she turns to the press to win cases that would never reach a courtroom. "Sometimes people come to us and because of the time that has passed, there isn't a legal claim, but they have an important story to share," Katz said. "In those cases, we may help them to be empowered to share their story."

Preferring to win by "taking a public stand," her litigation tactics include "attending a protest," "penning an op-ed," and getting the mainstream media to write about her. Her assiduously cultivated relations with the press would prove invaluable in Ford's cause. Two days before the Wisconsin alumni magazine profile was published, Katz's newest client—Christine Blasey Ford—sat for a polygraph test. Katz did not direct Ford to law enforcement, to the White House, or to the Senate Judiciary Committee. The committee did not receive any component of Ford's polygraph results until one day before the hearing in which she testified.

Vacationing in Delaware, Ford had already spoken with the Judiciary Committee's ranking Democrat when she decided to sit for the polygraph. She testified that she traveled directly from her grandmother's funeral to a hotel near the Baltimore airport to take the polygraph in August 2018. She was on a "tight schedule" to get to New Hampshire. She later revised her testimony, saying that the funeral may have occurred after the polygraph. Though she could not remember with any precision what happened on the day she took the polygraph, she did "remember being hooked up to a machine, like, being placed onto my body, and being asked a lot of questions, and crying a lot."

Ford did not recall where she took the test or where she was beforehand or afterward. The name of the hotel, however, is the Hilton BWI

Baltimore Airport Hotel on 1739 West Nursery Road in Linthicum Heights, Maryland. Jeremiah P. Hanafin, a polygraph examiner from a Virginia suburb of Washington, administered the test on August 7, 2018, identifying the subject as "Christine Blasey." An attorney from the Katz firm, Lisa Banks, accompanied Ford into the room for the test and asked Hanafin to leave the room while they composed a handwritten statement, signed "Christine Blasey," that would serve as Ford's account for the polygraph test.

Ford's story had changed again; indeed, it appeared to change as she was writing it. She first wrote that the assault took place in the "early 80's" before scratching out the word "early." She wrote that "4 people" had been present and then crossed out the word "people" and wrote that "4 boys and a couple of girls" were present. Previously she described the assault as involving "Brett Kavanaugh with Mark Judge and a bystander named PJ." In the polygraph version, she did not name the four boys or two girls.

"Brett lay, laid on top of me and tried to remove my clothes while groping me," Ford wrote. "He held me down and at [sic] put his hand on my mouth so to stop me from ye [sic] screaming for help. His friend Mark was in the room and both were laughing. Mark jumped on top of us 2 or 3 times. I tried to get out from under unsuccessfully. Then Mark jumped once again and he toppled over. I managed to run out of the room across, to the bathroom and lock the door. Once they [sic] I heard them go downstairs, I ran out of the house and went home."

When Hanafin returned and administered the polygraph, he had Ford retell the story. This time she reintroduced the character of P. J., now a "very nice person," not a "bystander" to the assault as she had previously told the *Washington Post*. In a private report submitted to Ford's attorneys on August 10, Hanafin told them what they wanted to hear: her performance was "not indicative of deception."

Ford testified that her lawyers advised her to take the polygraph, but she would not say why she decided to do so or what purpose she thought it would serve. It could serve to bolster her credibility and make her more attractive to the *Washington Post*. Debra Katz certainly seemed to think so.

CHAPTER 5

A #MeToo Gambit

A frustrated Debra Katz told a meeting of the bipartisan Congressional Caucus for Women's Issues on Wednesday, September 12, 2018, that she was worried about the "Weinstein effect—if you haven't assaulted eighty people, it doesn't count.... If you haven't raped people and done the most egregious things, it's more of a 'huh.' It's not even worthy of the *Washington Post* anymore."

That's because in the Internet Age, the legacy press's business depends more on defending its reputation than on breaking sensational news that gains attention. This insight was first spotlighted by Ryan Holiday, a marketing industry turncoat who wrote *Trust Me, I'm Lying: Confessions of a Media Manipulator*. One of the Internet's first expert purveyors of fake news in the service of bestselling authors and billion-dollar businesses, Holiday explained how he concocted falsehoods which he got major news organizations to report as fact. His method, which he called "trading up the chain," turns nonsense into the nightly news by exploiting the corrupt journalistic standards of online publications—their perverse prioritization of page views, their hunger for any and all content, and their appetite for aggregated news, which borders on plagiarism.

"Online publications compete to get stories first, newspapers compete to 'confirm' it, and then pundits compete for airtime to opine on it," Holiday noted. "The smaller sites legitimize the newsworthiness of the story for the sites with bigger audiences. Consecutively and concurrently, this pattern inherently distorts and exaggerates whatever they cover."

Holiday succeeded by seducing smaller sites with fewer barriers to publication into writing about his falsehoods, which would then gain too much attention from larger websites and online audiences for the larger and more established news outlets—online, print, and television— to ignore. His work became the stuff of legend, and by the time President Trump took office, Holiday wrote in the *New York Times* that he had fielded a job offer as a "communications director for a cabinet member," which he turned down.

"The Clintons famously alleged a 'vast right-wing conspiracy,' and as self-serving and unreliable as the couple is, they weren't totally wrong," Holiday wrote in *Trust Me, I'm Lying*. "They just didn't mention the left wing can and does use the same strategy." In fact, his analysis helps explain how Christine Blasey Ford's anonymous allegation went from being ignored by the *Washington Post* to nearly destroying a Supreme Court nomination.

Media manipulation, Holiday wrote, involves three levels: the entry point, the legacy media, and the national press. The entry point must be an outlet that is "traffic-hungry, always on the lookout for a big story that might draw a big spike of new viewers." Enter the Intercept, an "online magazine" founded in 2013 with support from eBay founder Pierre Omidyar on the promise of blogger Glenn Greenwald turning his exclusive reports of Edward Snowden's leaks into a hub of investigative journalism for an anarcho-leftist audience.

On September 12, hours after Debra Katz's complaint about the "Weinstein effect" and the day before the Judiciary Committee's first scheduled "markup" of the Kavanaugh vote, Ryan Grim reported in the Intercept that Senator Dianne Feinstein was refusing to share a "Brett Kavanaugh–related document" with her fellow Democrats on the

Judiciary Committee. The content of the document was "unclear," Grim wrote, but it was a "letter" that "purportedly describes an incident that was relayed to someone affiliated with Stanford University, who authored the letter and sent it to Rep. Anna Eshoo, a Democrat who represents the area." Grim reported that Eshoo had passed the letter to Feinstein and that the author of the letter was represented by Debra Katz. Feinstein's, Eshoo's, and Katz's offices all declined to comment, and Grim offered no other names in an article that simply cited "multiple sources."

Grim, a left-wing author, had arrived at the Intercept one year earlier from the Huffington Post, a left-leaning website that for years was one of Ryan Holiday's favorite entry points for fake news. The Intercept's struggle keeping prickly investigative journalists united and on task has been well documented. One former staffer turned to a rival, *Politico*, to dismiss the Intercept as "where journalism goes to die." By 2018, the Intercept was not able to count solely on the star power of its boldface names to sustain its position in the market.

An outlet in need of clicks and a blogger with an agenda were not going to stall a story like "Feinstein Withholding Brett Kavanaugh Letter." In addition to writing for the Intercept, Grim ran Strong Arm Press, an anti-Trump publishing house that relies on crowdfunding and solicits cash in return for mentions in its books. His willingness to bypass journalistic standards for the sake of a damaging story was in line with the mission of his tiny publishing house.

Grim's initial report was riddled with inaccuracies (the letter was not "relayed to someone affiliated with Stanford University," for example) and ambiguities (such as Feinstein's harboring a "document" that "purportedly describes an incident"). His account was refuted by its very subjects as Democrats flocked to CNN to say that the allegations "caught [Judiciary] committee Democrats by surprise." But Grim had achieved his goal.

The next day, in a short statement, Feinstein gave his story a boost: "I have received information from an individual concerning the nomination of Brett Kavanaugh to the Supreme Court. That individual strongly requested confidentiality, declined to come forward or press the matter further, and I have honored that decision. I have, however, referred the matter to federal investigative authorities."

Feinstein had not previously shared the letter with her Judiciary Committee colleagues, and sources with knowledge of the closed-door portion of the hearings said she did not bring it up there either. But her amplification of Grim's report breathed new life into the effort to #CancelKavanaugh. By amplifying the Intercept's report, she elevated Ford's allegation to the previously unattainable second level of Holiday's trading-up-the-chain scheme: the legacy media.

However enticing the traffic that would follow stories about the Intercept's posting, the legacy media did not dare risk damaging their reputations by repeating the allegations without verifying them independently. As soon as Feinstein had confirmed the allegations' existence, however, the legacy media jumped in. News aggregators such as the Drudge Report and RealClearPolitics and social media users made it clear that everyone was talking about the confidential document that no one could describe. Although the legacy media were usually far behind the aggregators and Twitter, reporters were treating aggregators and the social media hordes as their assignment editors in this case. The authority of the few editors still adhering to basic journalistic standards was usurped by the gatekeepers of viral online gossip.

The instrument for accomplishing the next step—advancing the allegation from a poorly-constructed blog post and a senator's hastily-worded statement—was Ronan Farrow. As he had done before, Farrow published Katz's client's anonymous allegations on the *New Yorker* website. His article was co-authored by Jane Mayer. Her effort to sink Justice Clarence Thomas's nomination thirty years earlier had failed, but now she had a second chance to take a Republican judicial scalp. Many publications would not run defamatory or criminal allegations without naming their source—the *Washington Post* had followed this formula when Ford made her first approach—but Farrow and Mayer were less squeamish. Feinstein's actions over the previous days helped to justify their publication of anonymous and scurrilous allegations.

"The complaint came from a woman who accused Kavanaugh of sexual misconduct when they were both in high school, more than thirty years ago," Farrow and Mayer wrote. "The woman, who has asked not to be identified, first approached Democratic lawmakers in July, shortly after Trump nominated Kavanaugh. The allegation dates back to the early nineteen-eighties, when Kavanaugh was a high-school student at Georgetown Preparatory School, in Bethesda, Maryland, and the woman attended a nearby high school. In the letter, the woman alleged that, during an encounter at a party, Kavanaugh held her down, and that he attempted to force himself on her."

Farrow and Mayer missed or ignored important pieces of the story. Yes, the accuser "first approached Democratic lawmakers in July shortly after Trump nominated Kavanaugh," but before the nomination she repeatedly contacted the *Washington Post*. Katz's client declined to be interviewed on the record, leaving Farrow and Mayer with partial context for a partial report.

With no way of verifying the veracity of the allegation against Kavanaugh, Farrow and Mayer tied it to the allegation against Clarence Thomas when his nomination to the Supreme Court was up for confirmation, offering it as a warning to Feinstein. A failure to believe the anonymous woman would be dangerous. The writers noted that Feinstein had a primary challenger "from her left" and that the "political risks of mishandling the allegation were acute."

"During Clarence Thomas's Supreme Court confirmation hearing, in 1991, the Senate was accused by some of failing to take seriously enough Anita Hill's allegations that Thomas had sexually harassed her while acting as her boss at the Equal Employment Opportunity Commission," Farrow and Mayer wrote, pointing out that Joe Biden, who had presided over those hearings, felt it necessary for his survival as a presidential candidate to offer a public apology for failing to believe the woman with sufficient fervor. Farrow and Mayer's #MeToo message was clear: Democrats who did not believe the anonymous woman's last-minute allegations against Kavanaugh would find themselves accused of failing to take the allegations seriously. Litigating the case in the court of public opinion as self-appointed special counsel for the Resistance, Farrow and Mayer were intent on ensuring that the seriousness of the charge trumped the reliability of the evidence.

The *New Yorker* article had the desired effect on the jurors on social media and cable news. But most importantly for Christine Blasey Ford and her lawyers, Farrow and Mayer accomplished what Ford and Katz on their own could not: capturing the attention of the *Washington Post*. Ford's allegation had reached the national press, Ryan Holiday's third level.

On Thursday, September 13, after the Intercept revealed the existence of a document "purportedly describ[ing] an incident" and Senator Feinstein acknowledged its existence, Katz publicly refused to say she was representing the accuser, as the Intercept had reported, telling BuzzFeed, "There's nothing to say." By Friday, Farrow and Mayer had published her client's anonymous allegations against Kavanaugh, and the *Washington Post* was preparing to run its story revealing Ford's identity. Katz was elated. I know this because she wrote to me on Saturday about my coverage of her representation of the still unknown Kavanaugh accuser, telling me that she laughed at reading about how she flouted time constraints on her congressional testimony. "This really is quite a moment in history," she wrote of the importance of her work.

Katz made no apparent effort to reach the Senate Judiciary Committee majority or law enforcement before repeatedly messaging me about her work. No lawyer working on Ford's behalf contacted or responded to the Judiciary Committee for several more days, until Tuesday, September 18. By that point, Ford had outed herself in the *Washington Post* on Sunday and Katz had gone on CNN and *CBS This Morning* on Monday. And yet no one had talked to the people responsible for vetting Kavanaugh or the people preparing to vote on his nomination the following week. Katz was showing that no one knew more than she about winning cases in the court of public opinion.

"I think what's really important, when I have these cases, is to try to figure out where the pressure points are," Katz told an "Applied Feminism and #MeToo" conference at the University of Baltimore in 2019. "If you just bring these cases and [say] 'This is what the law says, and this is how we're going to approach it,' it's not going to get you your best result for the client, and it's not going to bring the change that you want. I'm a big believer in working with nonprofits, who are subject-matter experts, and thinking about a press strategy, a legislative strategy, because we do this work because we are committed to social justice."

Emma Brown's Sunday *Washington Post* story focused not on Ford's allegations against Kavanaugh, but on her decision to speak out. The *Post*'s headline took it for granted that the public was already familiar with Ford's letter: "California Professor, Writer of Confidential Brett Kavanaugh Letter, Speaks Out About Her Allegation of Sexual Assault." "Since Wednesday," Brown wrote, Ford "has watched as that bare-bones version of her story became public without her name or her consent, drawing a blanket denial from Kavanaugh and roiling a nomination that just days ago seemed all but certain to succeed. Now, Ford has decided if her story is going to be told, she wants to be the one to tell it."

The first sentence of the story noted Ford's confidential letter to Feinstein. But it was not until the fourteenth paragraph, buried in the online version beneath videos and commentary from Ford's husband, that the *Post* acknowledged that she had first made contact with the newspaper through a "tip line." The story did not mention that Ford had contacted the newspaper before writing the letter to Feinstein, or that the *Post*, unlike Ronan Farrow and Jane Mayer, had not run her anonymous allegations. She had submitted to a polygraph examination, Brown wrote, on the counsel of Katz, who "said she believed Ford would be attacked as a liar if she came forward."

By late August, Brown wrote, "Ford had decided not to come forward, calculating that doing so would upend her life and probably would not affect Kavanaugh's confirmation." At that point, she had repeatedly tried to get the *Washington Post*'s attention, hired a lawyer, talked to a senator, and talked to a congresswoman. Yet she was not making the effort to "come forward," according to Brown, and was watching as others told her story "without her name or her consent." The only reason anyone had her story to share was because Ford had provided it, yet "she expected her story to be kept confidential."

The success of Ford's story in trading "up the chain" was so thorough that Katz was not asked to explain her client's purported desire for confidentiality. CNN's Alisyn Camerota, for example, said to Katz, "[A]s we know the story, she really did not want to come forward, she wrote a confidential letter, so tell me the trajectory of her willingness now to go to such a public forum."

"Well, you're right," Katz replied, "there was a great deal of ambivalence about whether she wanted to be publicly associated with these allegations, and essentially that choice was made by her to remain confidential…. She asked Senator Feinstein to keep her letter and her allegations confidential, and Feinstein agreed to do that, and that decision was essentially taken away from her as those allegations were leaked."

The first news outlet to receive word of Ford's allegation, the *Washington Post*, got it from Ford. Avoiding the fact that her client had repeatedly contacted the press during the summer, Katz portrayed her as coming under a "great deal of pressure" from reporters. Katz did let it slip that Ford was aware that her allegations were going to become public, and she may have made an effort to catch herself mid-sentence: "She knew that she was going to be, um, uh, her allegations were going to be outed, and that in fact is what occurred, and as a result she decided to take control of this and tell this in her own voice." A lawyer who must distinguish what her clients "know" from what they think or believe, Katz made it clear that her client was not caught by surprise when her allegations began trading up the chain.

In that CNN interview, Katz carefully painted a picture of Ford as a professor "at Stanford, where she teaches," without explaining that Ford was actually a professor at Palo Alto University, which participates in a consortium with Stanford. Katz completed her opening argument on CNN by depicting her client as a whistleblower: "She's told the truth, she's done it at great personal risk.... She's telling the truth, she took a polygraph, she mentioned this to her—in her therapy sessions in 2012, she came forward before this nominee was nominated. This is someone who told the truth at great personal cost, and we all know what she's going to have to withstand as a result of having come forward."

Katz said on television that Ford was willing to testify before the Senate Judiciary Committee, although she had not been in touch with the committee. "She is willing to, hopefully, tell her story in a manner that is a fair proceeding. Unfortunately, what we're already hearing this morning is that the Republicans intend to play hardball, they intend to grill her. This is not an exercise that is designed to get at the truth." Neither Katz nor Ford made an effort to reach the committee before talking to reporters and appearing on television. Katz charged the Republicans with playing "hardball," though she had not talked to them directly, and Ford's legal team would not do so until the following day on Tuesday, September 18.

Just before eight o'clock on Tuesday night, Katz's law firm sent an email to the Senate Judiciary Committee. Katharine Willey, counsel for Chairman Grassley, responded the next morning with a letter from Grassley saying the committee intended to hold a hearing on Ford's allegations on Monday, September 24, at ten o'clock in the morning. Katz's firm responded that they would wait a day to reply in full because it was Yom Kippur. The next day, Thursday, September 20, Katz sent an email to Jennifer Duck, a lawyer for Feinstein's staff:

Dear Ms. Duck:

We authorize Senator Feinstein to provide Sen. Grassley's staff with the unredacted letter to Senator Feinstein dated July 30, 2018 provided that Senator Grassley's staff agrees not to publish or disseminate the letter.

Please do not transmit the letter electronically, Ms. Duck.

Sincerely,

Debra S. Katz

Several days after the *Washington Post* had published Ford's account detailing the letter and Katz had appeared on CNN and CBS, Katz finally agreed to let the Republicans see it.

Willey emailed Katz to set up a phone conference, but Katz responded that she was unavailable at the requested time and asked that Democratic staffers be included on the call. The committee staff members and Ford's attorneys spoke on September 20. When the various parties could not find an agreeable time to talk by phone on September 21, Grassley's staff wrote back that the committee had offered Ford the opportunity to testify at an open hearing, a closed hearing, a public interview by staff, a private interview by staff, and by flying female committee staff investigators to meet with Ford in California. Grassley's team wanted the hearing on September 24, but was willing to accommodate Ford. Willey sent a lengthy email to Katz and her law partner Lisa Banks before three o'clock in the afternoon:

> Yesterday, you issued ten demands to us regarding the conditions under which Dr. Ford is willing to testify. Consistent with our sincere desire to hear Dr. Ford's testimony in her preferred setting—while, at the same time, respecting fundamental notions of due process and Committee practice—we are willing to meet you halfway. You demanded that we not hold the hearing on Monday because Dr. Ford needs time to prepare her testimony. Because Dr. Ford's testimony will concern only her personal knowledge of events, events which she already described to the *Washington Post*, holding a hearing more than one week after she aired these allegations is more than reasonable. We will nevertheless reschedule the hearing for later in the week, as you requested. The Committee will take Dr. Ford's and Judge Kavanaugh's testimony on Wednesday, September 26.
>
> We deplore that Dr. Ford has faced serious threats and harassment over the past week, and we will make every

effort to guarantee her safety. At the same time, Judge Kavanaugh and his family, including his two young daughters,
have also faced serious death threats and vicious assaults as
a result of these allegations. And they're getting worse each
day. Judge Kavanaugh unequivocally and categorically
denied these allegations. He was willing to testify last week
after the allegations were made publicly, and he already
accepted our invitation to testify on Monday. It is not fair
to him or to his family to allow this situation to continue
without a resolution and without an opportunity for him to
clear his name. Holding the hearing on Wednesday honors
your request for a later hearing date while recognizing that
Judge Kavanaugh is entitled to due process. It is the fairest
option for both parties.

We also accept some of your other demands. You
demanded that Judge Kavanaugh not be in the hearing room
during Dr. Ford's testimony. We have no objection to that.

You demanded that only one camera be permitted in the
hearing room and that there be limited press access. We have
no objection to that.

You demanded that the number of rounds and minutes
per round of questions be equal for all senators. We have no
objection to that.

You demanded that Dr. Ford be given adequate breaks
during her testimony. We of course have no objection to that.

You also expressed concerns about Dr. Ford's safety and
that the Senate provide adequate security. This, of course, we
will do. The Capitol Police offers more than adequate security.
The Senate hosts the President, Vice President, Cabinet secretaries, heads of state, and other prominent public figures all
the time with the necessary precautions.

Some of your other demands, however, are unreasonable
and we are unable to accommodate them. You demanded that

Judge Kavanaugh be the first person to testify. Accommodating this demand would be an affront to fundamental notions of due process. In the United States, an individual accused of a crime is entitled to a presumption of innocence. And, further, the accused has the right to respond to allegations that are made about him. Judge Kavanaugh cannot be expected to respond to allegations that have been made to the press. He is entitled to hear the full, detailed testimony of Dr. Ford before he testifies. You have indicated that Dr. Ford has allegations that she would like to make in public and under oath. She will have the opportunity to do so before we give Judge Kavanaugh the opportunity to respond.

You also demanded that only senators be permitted to ask questions of the witnesses. We are also unable to accommodate this demand. There is no rule of the Senate or the Committee that precludes staff attorneys from asking witnesses questions. We reserve the option to have female staff attorneys, who are sensitive to the particulars of Dr. Ford's allegations and are experienced investigators, question both witnesses. We believe this will allow for informed questioning, will generate the most insightful testimony, and will help de-politicize the hearing.

You demanded that the Committee issue subpoenas for the testimony of Mark Judge and other unidentified witnesses. The Committee is unable to accommodate this demand. The Committee does not take subpoena requests from witnesses as a condition of their testimony.

You went on television earlier this week and said Dr. Ford wants the chance to tell her story in public and under oath. This is the opportunity we have given her. We don't need to subpoena additional witnesses to do that.

You demanded that the Committee call additional witnesses that Dr. Ford requests. We are unable to accommodate this demand. The Committee does not take witness requests from other witnesses. Mark Judge and one other alleged witness to the events Dr. Ford has described have already denied the allegations under penalty of felony to the Committee. We can obtain additional testimony through staff interviews, obtaining statements, or other means that are subject to penalties of felony, if necessary.

This Committee has been extremely accommodating to your client. We want to hear Dr. Ford's testimony and are prepared to accommodate many of your demands, including further delaying a hearing that is currently scheduled for Monday. We are unwilling to accommodate your unreasonable demands. Outside counsel may not dictate the terms under which Committee business will be conducted.

Please respond by 5:00 pm to accept the invitation for Dr. Ford to testify on Wednesday according to the terms outlined above. We will have to issue various Committee notices soon after, so timeliness is extremely important.

Within five minutes of the letter's delivery to Katz, another attorney for Grassley, Kolan Davis, asked that Katz keep their discussions confidential. Both sides were concerned about the press's learning of their private negotiations and the effect of leaks on the nomination process. Katz did not heed Grassley staff's requests and did not accept the invitation before the deadline of Friday at five o'clock in the evening. The committee moved the deadline to ten o'clock in the evening, and Katz finally sent a reply to Willey and Davis at about a quarter past nine:

The imposition of aggressive and artificial deadlines regarding the date and conditions of any hearing has created tremendous and unwarranted anxiety and stress on Dr. Ford. Your cavalier treatment of a sexual assault survivor who has been doing her best to cooperate with the Committee is completely inappropriate.

Yesterday, we had what I thought was a productive dialogue about the conditions Dr. Ford would find acceptable to be able to testify before the Senate Judiciary Committee about her allegations of sexual assault involving Judge Brett Kavanaugh. Rather than continuing that dialogue, Senator Grassley today conveyed a counterproposal through the media, insisting that she appear for a hearing on a date I had expressly told you was not feasible for her. Hours after those media accounts first appeared, you sent me a response to the proposals that we had conveyed in good faith yesterday. You rejected a number of the proposals that are important to Dr. Ford to ensure that the process would be a fair one, including subpoenaing Mark Judge to testify.

Instead, you spent much of your email making points that distorted the requests we had made and the sequence of events. It would be fruitless to review each of those misstatements as it is now abundantly clear that regardless of the assurances Senator Grassley has made, you have been tasked with pressuring Dr. Ford to agree to conditions you find advantageous to the nominee and also with denying Democratic members of the Senate Judiciary Committee any input about how this hearing would proceed. When I urged you to include them in our discussions today, you rejected my request outright, accusing them of being the source of leaks. Even more disturbing, while you took almost a full day to consider our proposal, you demanded a 5:00 p.m. response to your proposal this evening.

By email sent today at 4:01 p.m., I advised you that Dr. Ford had traveled to meet with the FBI for several hours about the death threats she had been receiving, and we would need until tomorrow to confer with her and to be able to provide you with a well-considered response. Rather than allowing her the time she needs to respond to the take-it-or-leave-it demand you conveyed, you sent us an email at 5:47 p.m.— which you again gave to the media first—insisting that we accept your "invitation" for a Wednesday hearing by 10:00 p.m. tonight. I now have learned that Senator Grassley has scheduled the Committee's vote for this Monday.

The 10:00 p.m. deadline is arbitrary. Its sole purpose is to bully Dr. Ford and deprive her of the ability to make a considered decision that has life-altering implications for her and her family. She has already been forced out of her home and continues to be subjected to harassment, hate mail, and death threats. Our modest request is that she be given an additional day to make her decision.

Sincerely,

Debra S. Katz

Willey replied within fifteen minutes to say that the 10:00 p.m. deadline coming at the bottom of the hour had not changed. The next day at 2:17 p.m. Katz wrote to Willey, "Dr. Ford accepts the Committee's request to provide her first-hand knowledge of Brett Kavanaugh's sexual misconduct next week." Ford was coming to D.C.

Following repeated requests from Chairman Chuck Grassley's staff to interview Ford—including on the West Coast—she ultimately made her way to Washington for the televised hearings. She later testified that she wanted "to avoid having to get on an airplane, but I eventually was able to get up the gumption with the help of some friends, and get on the plane." Fear of flying had not prevented her from traveling to Hawaii, Costa Rica, and the South Pacific islands in the past. Air travel was "easier for me…when it's a vacation," she testified, than when it involved Kavanaugh.

Once Ford overcame her fear of flying and agreed to appear in Washington, D.C., the newest addition to her legal team, Michael Bromwich, sought to stage-manage the hearing. A lawyer with extensive political and prosecutorial experience, he had testified before Congress forty times, himself. A member of the independent counsel team investigating the Iran-Contra affair, he had prosecuted Lieutenant Colonel Oliver North and served as inspector general of the Justice Department in the Clinton administration. More recently he had represented Andrew McCabe, the former deputy director of the FBI who was fired by President Trump.

A late addition to the legal team, joining just one week before the hearings, Bromwich had not helped formulate the legal strategy that Ford had followed throughout the summer, such as the decision to take the polygraph. By the time he joined Katz's team, the number of persons advising Ford was growing. Ricki Seidman, an investigator for Senator Edward Kennedy during the Clarence Thomas confirmation hearings and an aide in the Clinton White House, had helped guide Sonia Sotomayor to the nation's highest court. Now she was preparing Ford for the hearings. Ford's advisers also included Kendra Barkoff, a consultant at the PR firm SKDKnickerbocker and a former press secretary to Vice President Biden.

There had been an internal conflict at Bromwich's firm over his representing Kavanaugh's accuser. His partners made no secret of their desire to have nothing to do with Christine Blasey Ford. When Bromwich resigned on the Saturday before the hearings, the firm released a statement saying he had been planning to leave and that Ford's allegations did not cause his departure, but did "accelerate" his exit.

Bromwich made the most of the week before the hearings, demanding that photographers from certain news organizations be allowed in the hearing room, seeking to determine the number of television cameras, and requesting that only a handful of wire services be present.

The Republicans bowed to most of these demands. While 156 seats had been available for print reporters at the first set of hearings, only forty-eight would be available when Ford testified. Approximately fifty photographers were admitted to the first hearings, but no more than eight could enter the hearing room for Ford's testimony. More than twenty-eight video cameras captured Kavanaugh's testimony in early September, but for Ford's testimony, only C-SPAN was allowed to bring video cameras into the hearing room.

The Republican capitulation extended beyond limiting press access. The hearing was scheduled with regard for Ford's convenience rather than with what was necessary to ensure that the Court opened its new term with a full complement of nine justices. The Republicans also hired a female sex-crimes prosecutor from Arizona, Rachel Mitchell, to question Ford on their behalf, although they did not share the news immediately. Katz and Bromwich were livid. Katz wrote to Grassley's nominations counsel, Mike Davis:

> Are there reasons—other than strategic advantage and unfair surprise—that you will not tell us the name of the experienced sex crimes prosecutor Senator Grassley hired to question our client? Please send us her name and cv [curriculum vitae] immediately. It is impossible to square the Chairman's promise of a fair hearing with his staff's refusal to provide us with this most basic of information or to speak with us about the outstanding issues.

When the hearing began, televisions flickered with images of eleven Republican men peering down from a dais over Mitchell at Ford. The impression of one woman squaring off against a dozen men was exactly what Bromwich and Katz wanted.

"When we entered the Capitol that day," Katz said afterward, "we had powerful tailwinds—activists and everyday people, of unions and other organized groups, and of those who were so moved by [Ford's] courage, they just wound up at the Capitol. And a lot of people have congratulated the lawyers for prepping Dr. Ford so well, but what you see is Dr. Ford. What we did was we made it safe for her to talk."

Bromwich and Katz treated the hearing like a trial, from lodging objections to counseling their witness to slow down and remain composed. Mitchell, on the other hand, treated the hearing like a deposition.

The problem was that her questioning was interrupted every five minutes for a five-minute round of friendly questions from a Democrat. It was difficult, therefore, for many observers to follow what Mitchell was doing.

For example, Senator Sheldon Whitehouse, a Democrat from Rhode Island, began by showering Ford with praise and then asked her to agree that she had requested an FBI investigation of her claims but that "there has been no sincere or thorough investigation of your claims."

"You have met all of the standards of what I might call preliminary credibility with your initial statement," Whitehouse said, referring to the prepared remarks Ford read at the start of the hearing, which reporters received in advance. "You have vivid, specific and detailed recollections, something prosecutors look for. Your recollections are consistent with known facts." Ford responded simply with a modest "yes."

Mitchell, by comparison, picked up after Whitehouse with questions that followed not the senator's line of thought, but her own inquiry. "Dr. Ford, the *Washington Post* reported in their September 16th article that you did show them therapist notes, is that incorrect?" Mitchell asked. "I don't remember physically showing her a note," Ford answered.

A casual viewer of the hearings was unlikely to recall which article appeared in the *Washington Post* on September 16, what the therapist's notes had to do with anything, and whether the "her" Ford was referring to was her therapist or the reporter who had been in her attorney's offices and may have reviewed the therapy records there. But the report in the *Post* on September 16 was the first to identify Ford by name, and the therapist records were the materials Ford first presented as corroborating evidence for her allegations in her initial messages to the *Washington Post* in July.

It was likewise easy to overlook Ford's acknowledgment that every person she identified as having attended the party where Kavanaugh allegedly assaulted her had told the committee under penalty of felony that he or she had no memory or knowledge of any such party. This included Ford's high school friend Leland Keyser, whom Ford suggested might be less than reliable: "Leland has significant health challenges, and I'm happy that she's focusing on herself and getting the health treatment that she needs," Ford told the committee. "And she let me know that she needed her lawyer to take care of this for her, and she texted me right afterward with an apology and good wishes, and et cetera, so I'm glad she's taking care of herself."

Responding to Senate Judiciary Committee investigators, Keyser's attorney, Howard Walsh, wrote, "Simply put, Ms. Keyser does not know Mr. Kavanaugh and she has no recollection of ever being at a party or gathering where he was present, with, or without, Dr. Ford." Kavanaugh would read that part of Walsh's letter in his opening statement, imploring the senators, "Listen to Ms. Keyser. She does not know me."

Coming under enormous pressure after the hearing, Keyser revised her previous statement through her attorney: "Notably, Ms. Keyser does not refute Dr. Ford's account, and she has already told the press that she believes Dr. Ford's account. However, the simple and unchangeable truth is that she is unable to corroborate it because she has no recollection of the incident in question."

Keyser then told FBI investigators that she felt pressured by Ford's allies to revise her statement. Former FBI agent Monica McLean, a friend of Ford's, was leaning on Keyser to alter her statement. So were many others, both in public and in private. Speaking more than six months after Kavanaugh's confirmation, Keyser explained in an email the deliberative steps she took to try to help Ford:

> When my longtime friend Christine Blasey Ford brought allegations against Judge Kavanaugh, I found myself in a difficult situation. I wanted to support my friend and have great empathy for the predicament she described in her statement to the Judiciary Committee. However, after a week of dutifully studying pictures of the Judge, I could not recollect him currently or back in High School. I could also not recollect the evening in question per Christine Ford's allegations.

Keyser said she tried to look into Kavanaugh's past on her own when she learned she was going to be involved in the vetting of his nomination. She discovered that her "personal politics do not fall in line with Judge Kavanaugh being promoted to the Supreme Court," but she found his record to be "very impressive." Keyser could not in good conscience assert that she had any reason to believe Ford was telling the truth.

The boy Ford identified as "PJ," who was allegedly at the party, was Patrick J. Smyth. His attorney, former federal prosecutor Eric Bruce, delivered Smyth's sworn statement to the Judiciary Committee:

> I understand that I have been identified by Dr. Christine Blasey Ford as the person she remembers as "PJ" who supposedly was present at the party she described in her statements to the Washington Post. I am issuing this statement today to make it clear to all involved that I have no knowledge of the party in question; nor do I have any knowledge of the allegations of improper conduct she has leveled against Brett Kavanaugh. Personally speaking, I have known Brett Kavanaugh since high school and I know him to be a person of great integrity, a great friend, and I have never witnessed any improper conduct by Brett Kavanaugh towards women. To safeguard my own privacy and anonymity, I respectfully request that the Committee accept this statement in response to any inquiry the Committee may have.

Like "PJ," Mark Judge had to retain a high-powered Washington lawyer to respond to questions about Christine Blasey Ford's allegations. Judge, who Ford said witnessed the assault, turned to a top criminal defense lawyer, Barbara "Biz" Van Gelder, at the firm Cozen O'Connor. Judge issued a letter making clear that he had no desire to enter the circus around Kavanaugh's nomination:

> I did not ask to be involved in this matter nor did anyone ask me to be involved. The only reason I am involved is because

Dr. Christine Blasey Ford remembers me as the other person in the room during the alleged assault.

In fact, I have no memory of this alleged incident. Brett Kavanaugh and I were friends in high school but I do not recall the party described in Dr. Ford's letter. More to the point, I never saw Brett act in the manner Dr. Ford describes.

I have no more information to offer the Committee and I do not wish to speak publicly regarding the incidents described in Dr. Ford's letter.

Those watching Ford's testimony did not hear the detailed and lengthy responses from her named witnesses or from the approximately fifteen classmates of Kavanaugh and Ford whom the committee contacted. Viewers were confused by the proceedings but sympathetic to the middle-aged woman shuffling papers to keep the dates, articles, and therapy records straight, whose youthful "uptalking," characteristic of her adoptive Southern California home, produced an aura of innocence. The line that especially resonated with the audience, perhaps triggering memories of their own traumas, was "I thought that Brett was accidentally going to kill me." Despite her acknowledgment that her "group of friends intersected with Brett and his friends for a short period of time" more than thirty years earlier, she referred to him alternately as "Brett" and as "Mr. Kavanaugh" but never as "Judge Kavanaugh," avoiding the title that conferred his authority or credibility.

Mitchell did not push back. She was simply gathering facts. Republicans were deathly silent, Ford's team was aggressively defensive, and the Democrats on the Judiciary Committee focused their questions on her emotions and alleged trauma. Conservatives were livid. Broadcast networks and many radio stations carried the hearings gavel to gavel, but the conservative talk-radio host Rush Limbaugh provided instant insight into the mind of the pro-Kavanaugh crowd, digesting Ford's testimony and Mitchell's questions. He did not let the hearings preempt his three-hour show but gave director's-cut-DVD-style commentary, talking over the Senate proceedings:

> It's frustrating folks, it's maddening to watch this.... [Mitchell] asks five minutes of questions, but nobody knows what she's driving at, unless you arrive at this with some information and knowledge beforehand. Well we can't rely—I don't know how many people across the country are watching this. I'll assume it's a lot, and it's a big stretch to assume that most everybody in the public watching already has a baseline of information so that her questioning would be understood in context. You can't do that this way! Despite how repulsive it might be or seem, this is theater! This is performance! All trials are, all hearings are.

The Ford drama was compelling. More than twenty million people watched the entirety of the Ford-Kavanaugh hearings on cable and broadcast television, according to the *Hollywood Reporter*, with viewership ebbing and flowing throughout. But 7.2 million viewers stuck with Fox News alone. After Act I, those Fox viewers were presented with a crew of analysts ready to bury Kavanaugh. Chris Wallace declared Ford's testimony a "disaster for Republicans...and meanwhile the Democrats are landing haymakers."

"This was extremely emotional, extremely raw, and extremely credible, and nobody could listen to her deliver those words and talk about the assault and the impact it had had on her life and not have your heart go out to her," Wallace said, without qualifying the assault as "alleged." Swayed by Ford's emotion, he found her testimony "extremely credible." Other journalists had made up their minds long before Ford or Kavanaugh ever testified in public.

CHAPTER 6

Kavanaugh Critics Cry Havoc!

Christine Blasey Ford's decision to testify against Brett Kavanaugh before the Senate Judiciary Committee set off a flurry of new allegations and rumors of additional accusers. Hours after Ford agreed to testify, Ronan Farrow and Jane Mayer published in the *New Yorker* more accusations of sexual misconduct against Brett Kavanaugh—again without any direct corroborating evidence. This time, the accuser was willing to identify herself, but she acknowledged that she was not immediately certain that Kavanaugh had actually done anything. Nevertheless, she knew that she wanted any vote on Kavanaugh's nomination delayed.

Deborah Ramirez, who was an undergraduate at Yale at the same time as Kavanaugh, told Farrow and Mayer about a college party at which, she said, she became extremely drunk and was sexually assaulted.

In her initial conversations with the *New Yorker*, she was reluctant to characterize Kavanaugh's role in the alleged incident with certainty. After six days of carefully assessing her memories and consulting with her attorney, Ramirez said that she felt confident enough of her recollections to say that she remembered Kavanaugh had exposed himself at a drunken dormitory party, thrust his penis in her face, and caused her to touch it without her consent as she pushed him away. Ramirez was calling for the FBI to investigate Kavanaugh's role in the incident.

The reliability of Ramirez's newly recovered memory was initially called into doubt by the *New York Times*, which reported:

> The Times had interviewed several dozen people over the past week in an attempt to corroborate [Ramirez's] story, and could find no one with firsthand knowledge. Ms. Ramirez herself contacted former Yale classmates asking if they recalled the incident and told some of them that she could not be certain Mr. Kavanaugh was the one who exposed himself.

No one who knew Ramirez's story—including Ramirez herself—would say it was true. The *New York Times* and the *New Yorker* found no eyewitnesses who could confirm Ramirez's "memories," which were recovered only after six days of consulting with an attorney. Farrow and Mayer ran with the allegations anyway, citing as corroboration one anonymous source who said he had heard about the incident from someone else. To limit the damage to their reputations, Farrow and Mayer appeared on CNN and CBS the morning after the *Times* report.

Ramirez's recovered memory was "a fairly high level of evidence for this kind of a case," Farrow assured CNN, although he was not a lawyer and had neither cases nor evidence. "When you look at the other reporting I've done, for instance, on sexual assault and harassment, the last story Jane Mayer and I did was about a Democratic politician, Eric Schneiderman, your New York attorney general, and we used the same caution and standards there."

Mayer, meanwhile, went on CBS and tried to explain how someone who lived in the same building as Kavanaugh thirty years ago but did not witness the incident could corroborate Ramirez's accusation. "Did he see it?" John Dickerson asked.

"No," acknowledged Mayer, "as I've said, he heard it from someone who was there and, as I've said, um, we interviewed him, and I said to him, 'Are you sure that it was Brett Kavanaugh?' He said, 'I am 100 percent sure.'"

Given Ramirez's own uncertainty and the lack of evidence or first-hand corroboration, the way this allegation made its way into the pages of the *New Yorker* reveals much about Farrow's "caution and standards." First, according to Farrow and Mayer, Ramirez's allegation was "conveyed to Democratic senators by a civil-rights lawyer." When the Democrats on the Judiciary Committee received the allegation from Ramirez—a registered Democrat who opposed Kavanaugh's appointment to the Court—they did not turn it over to the committee chairman or to anyone responsible for vetting Kavanaugh. They went to Senator Michael Bennet of Ramirez's home state of Colorado, a Democrat who would soon announce his candidacy for the presidency. As first reported by the *Colorado Sun*, Bennet helped put Ramirez in touch with a lawyer named Stan Garnett of the Denver-based firm Brownstein Hyatt Farber Schreck, who considered running for the Senate seat held by Republican Cory Gardner. Garnett's firm was not enthusiastic about his representing Kavanaugh's latest accuser, however, so he handed Ramirez off to John Clune at another firm.

Why Bennet directed Ramirez to a prospective Democratic Senate candidate over a less politically ambitious lawyer is not clear, but Bennet's loyalties have shifted from his state's wealthy donors toward the Democratic Party's far-left base. In 2017, Bennet introduced the Supreme Court nominee Neil Gorsuch to the Senate Judiciary Committee, expressing the hope that doing so would "help restore the Senate's strong history of comity and cooperation." He then voted against Gorsuch's confirmation, rankling Coloradans of all stripes from the *Denver Post*'s editorial board to the wealthy special interests that helped Bennet gain his footing when he first arrived in Colorado in the late 1990s. Bennet knew that he would have no shot at the Democratic presidential nomination in 2020 if he bucked the progressive interests opposing Trump's Supreme Court nominees. After opposing Gorsuch, he had to commit to tanking Kavanaugh, too.

The *New York Times* likewise did not want to harm the progressive interests attacking Trump's Supreme Court nominees. As Farrow and Mayer squirmed on television trying to explain why they wrote the Ramirez story with no corroborating evidence, the *Times* altered a published story that was seen as damaging to the Resistance's #CancelKavanaugh agenda. The *Times* excised a paragraph stating that Ramirez had told former classmates she was unsure whether Kavanaugh exposed himself and that the *Times* "interviewed several dozen people over the past week in an attempt to corroborate Ms. Ramirez's story, and could find no one with firsthand knowledge." The objectionable paragraph was replaced with an attack on Republicans:

> In the #MeToo era, Republicans cannot afford to attack Judge Kavanaugh's accusers. So they have instead trained their fire on Senate Democrats, accusing them of waging a campaign of character assassination, and the news media—in particular the New Yorker. Many cited a Times article that said The Times had conducted numerous interviews but was unable to corroborate Ms. Ramirez's story. But the Times did not rebut her account.

The *New York Times*' taking sides appears less surprising when viewed in the context of the alleged duplicitous and deceitful means by which its reporters solicited dirt on Kavanaugh. Robin Pogrebin allegedly did not identify herself as a reporter when she approached Karen Yarasavage, a friend from college of both Deborah Ramirez and Brett Kavanaugh. A reporter for the "Culture Desk," where she covers art, architecture, and theater, Pogrebin was an undergraduate at Yale at the same time as Kavanaugh, Ramirez, and Yarasavage. Taking advantage of the old college tie, she tried to get Yarasavage to share dirt on Kavanaugh. Pogrebin also allegedly sought to put words in Yarasavage's mouth, but Yarasavage blocked her from doing so and said she wanted nothing to do with Pogrebin. Undaunted, Pogrebin co-authored an article in the *Times* about Ramirez's accusation—"In a Culture of Privilege and Alcohol at Yale, Her World Converged with Kavanaugh's"—attributing to "several friends" details identical to what she had wanted to attribute to Yarasavage and not mentioning that she was a classmate of Kavanaugh.

Pogrebin's methods were not necessarily illegal, but her alleged conduct was certainly unethical. The Society of Professional Journalists' Code of Ethics admonishes reporters, "Avoid undercover or other surreptitious methods of gathering information unless traditional, open methods will not yield information vital to the public." Through the *New York Times* vice president of communications, Danielle Rhoades Ha, Pogrebin disputed that she did not identify herself as a reporter with the *Times*. Pogrebin made use of her personal connections with Kavanaugh's classmates to land a book deal with a co-author, Kate Kelly, who has employed similar methods of reporting and leveraged her school connections in her work.

Kelly too was not a legal or political reporter, but she had graduated from the National Cathedral School, an all-girls prep school in Washington, in 1993—ten years after Kavanaugh graduated from Georgetown Preparatory School. For the *Times*, Kelly followed Kavanaugh at his thirty-fifth-anniversary high school reunion festivities, reporting on what he was wearing—"a red cap, khaki slacks, and a black coat"—and published the names of his classmates who also attended the private celebration. She did not disclose her own connection to the event as an alumna of a sister school, but reported on where Kavanaugh's classmates, their spouses, and their friends went for an after-party without Kavanaugh. She also reported what she overheard in the bar's parking lot—one man shouting, "That was a great party."

In her pursuit of Kavanaugh, Pogrebin picked up the unfinished business of her mother, Letty Pogrebin, a co-founder with Gloria Steinem of the feminist *Ms.* magazine, to which Debra Katz is a regular contributor. In the #MeToo moment, a failure to #BelieveTheWoman did not simply draw attacks from an agenda-driven press and partisan politicians, but also drew them from friends. Anyone who did not blindly believe Deborah Ramirez or who shared Ramirez's own doubts about her memories was vulnerable to attacks from leftists of all walks of life in all corners of Washington. Karen Yarasavage divulged her unsettling experience with Robin Pogrebin's allegedly unethical reporting techniques in an exchange of texts with her friend Kerry Berchem, a lawyer at Akin Gump Strauss Hauer & Feld and a vocal critic of Kavanaugh and President Trump on social media.

"She caught me off guard the other day," Yarasavage texted to Berchem. "Never identified herself as NYT, but just Robin Pogrebin as [though] we knew each other."

"She did the same to me," Berchem replied. "Tho u had forewarned me."

Berchem told Yarasavage she thought "Dems" in search of any unflattering details of Kavanaugh's teenage past might reach out to her "so as to sabotage" him. When reporters spurred by Ramirez's allegation began poking around, Yarasavage wrote that she was skeptical of the charge. "I never heard a word of this ever happening," Yarasavage texted Berchem, alluding to Kavanaugh's brief courtship of her in college. But Berchem would have none of it. "Breathe," Berchem texted. "I understand your emotions. I really do."

Yarasavage was losing patience with the public portrayal of Kavanaugh but did not want to insert herself into the controversy. "When I say Brett was vanilla with me, I mean it," Yarasavage texted. "He turned his back when I changed in his room."

Berchem tried to keep a lid on Yarasavage's recollections of Kavanaugh's college days, which contradicted the Left's narrative. Berchem texted Yarasavage that it was "maybe better to not" go on the record; doing so might hurt Ramirez more than Kavanaugh. The high-powered lawyer then put the screws to her friend, who had information that would not help Democrats win: "If [Ramirez] is making these allegations now, either she has conviction they happened or she might be crazy. But if it's the latter, and your commentary publicly makes it worse, would you really want that? Because I think that you would find it harder to live with that then if you just stayed silent. If there's nothing there then Brett…will be fine right? Bretz [sic] career is on the line. Maybe her life is on the line?"

Berchem was telling Yarasavage that her decision to tell the truth could end Ramirez's life, while staying silent about the truth would merely blunt Kavanaugh's professional ambitions. Yarasavage did not respond, but Berchem continued to text her: "Just be careful. There would be no going back."

Berchem then decided to speak out against Kavanaugh even though she had not been on Yale's campus at the time of the alleged assault. She informed Yarasavage that she was providing reporters with an on-the-record statement: "Debbie [Ramirez] is not innately brave, she is being brave. If she has anything to gain, it's closure, not fame. I believe her."

"I believe Deb," Berchem texted to Yarasavage. "Brett is a selfish prick." And she accused Yarasavage of letting Kavanaugh use her for his own political gain. Berchem then shared a photo belonging to Yarasavage, showing Yarasavage, Ramirez, Kavanaugh, and others together, posting it on a private Facebook group.

Having failed to stymie Kavanaugh's confirmation, Berchem then took screenshots of her texts with Yarasavage and sent a memo to Senator Richard Blumenthal, a Democrat on the Judiciary Committee, and to the FBI. Neither the Senate nor the FBI seemed interested in her gossipy attempts to intimidate a friend into silence, so she turned to NBC News. "I am in receipt of text messages from a mutual friend of both Debbie and mine that raise questions related to the allegations," Berchem told NBC. "I have not drawn any conclusions as to what the texts may mean or may not mean but I do believe they merit investigation by the FBI and the Senate."

Berchem's inability to draw conclusions about the meaning of her own text messages did not dissuade NBC. The network amplified her story, reporting that government officials were ignoring evidence involving Kavanaugh and Deborah Ramirez. "Berchem's efforts also show that some potential witnesses have been unable to get important information to the FBI," the network reported, citing references in Yarasavage's text messages to "Brett's guy" and "Brett's team" as evidence that someone somewhere must have been trying to keep her quiet. Omitted from the story were all of Yarasavage's text messages saying that she "never heard a word of this happening" and that "Brett was vanilla."

Not content with a misleading and incomplete account of an implied cover-up orchestrated by Kavanaugh, NBC also aired allegations of sexual assault by yet another accuser: Julie Swetnick, who also had no evidence. She did, however, have Michael Avenatti, the celebrity lawyer who gained a platform on cable news because of his representation of Stephanie Clifford, the porn star who picked a fight with President Trump and was better known as Stormy Daniels. Avenatti's unparalleled publicity skills earned him more than 250 appearances on cable and broadcast television networks in 2018. The press, thoroughly seduced, proclaimed him a top contender for the Democratic presidential nomination for 2020. In September, *Politico* declared, "Michael Avenatti Is Winning the Democratic Primary," and the largest cable news networks and most heavily trafficked news sites trumpeted his every thought. He was feted as the "man of the hour" at the *Hollywood Reporter*'s Most Powerful People in New York Media gala. *Vanity Fair* spotted Avenatti talking to an MSNBC executive, purportedly about hosting his own cable television show.

"I represent a woman with credible information regarding Mark Judge," Avenatti tweeted. "We will be demanding the opportunity to present testimony to the committee and will likewise be demanding that Judge and others be subpoenaed to testify. The nomination must be withdrawn."

Ten minutes after Avenatti's tweet, Senator Grassley's staff requested that he share his information with Senate investigators. He posted his private correspondence with Grassley's staff on Twitter alongside this message:

> We are aware of significant evidence of multiple house parties in the Washington, D.C., area during the early 1980s during which Brett Kavanaugh, Mark Judge, and others would participate in the targeting of women with alcohol/drugs in order to allow a "train" of men to rape them.

Avenatti went on to tweet allegations about the hidden meanings of passages in Brett Kavanaugh's high school yearbook before "warning" the nominee's defenders, "The GOP and others better be very careful in trying to suggest that she is not credible." Then on the eve of Christine Blasey Ford's public testimony, Avenatti tweeted that his client was Julie Swetnick and submitted a sworn statement that he said Swetnick wrote to the Judiciary Committee. The statement said Swetnick saw Kavanaugh "engage in abusive and physically aggressive behavior toward girls, including pressing girls against him without their consent, 'grinding' against girls, and attempting to remove or shift girls' clothing to expose private body parts." Swetnick knew, she said, that Kavanaugh spiked punch at parties and targeted vulnerable women, orchestrating a massive gang rape by teenage boys at house parties. She stated:

> I also witnessed efforts by Mark Judge, Brett Kavanaugh and others to cause girls to become inebriated and disoriented so they could then be "gang raped" in a side room or bedroom by a "train" of numerous boys. I have a firm recollection of seeing boys lined up outside rooms at many of these parties waiting for their "turn" with a girl inside the room. These boys included Mark Judge and Brett Kavanaugh. In approximately 1982, I became the victim of one of these "gang" or "train" rapes where Mark Judge and Brett Kavanaugh were present.

After receiving Swetnick's sworn declaration, the Senate Judiciary Committee Democrats sent Grassley a letter demanding that the vote on

Kavanaugh's nomination be canceled. Through Avenatti, Swetnick declined to be interviewed by Senate investigators, but she decided to appear on NBC to share her story on television for the first time in an interview with Kate Snow. From the start, Swetnick's account differed from her sworn statement. While she had written that she was aware of Kavanaugh's spiking the punch at parties, she told Snow, "I don't know what he did." She also described seeing Kavanaugh wearing his school uniform at the rapist parties and recalled boys lined up outside a bedroom for their turn to rape the girl inside—a scenario she backed away from in the interview:

> *Swetnick*: I didn't know what was occurring, I would see them laughing, a lot of laughing.
> *Snow*: Standing in line outside a room?
> *Swetnick*: Not a line, but definitely huddled by doors, and I didn't understand what it could possibly be.
> *Snow*: And in your declaration, you describe Brett Kavanaugh and his friend Mark Judge standing outside, seeing them stand outside a door?
> *Swetnick*: Yes, with other boys.
> *Snow*: So you're suggesting that, in hindsight, you think he was involved in this behavior?
> *Swetnick*: I would say, yes. It's just too coincidental.

Swetnick gave NBC the names of four people she said would corroborate her story. One of them told NBC he did not recall knowing a Julie Swetnick, one was dead, and the other two did not respond. The Senate Judiciary Committee's investigators talked to ten people who knew Swetnick from junior high school to the present. None of them could corroborate any of her allegations. Instead, the committee investigators found that Swetnick had "a history of making false legal claims and false accusations of sexual misconduct." Richard Vinneccy, who had a romantic relationship with Swetnick for seven years, provided the committee a sworn statement that after the two broke up, Swetnick threatened to murder him, his girlfriend, and his unborn child. She also threatened to tell police he raped her, she claimed to be pregnant with his twins, she said she would not grant him a divorce although the two never married, and she threatened to have him deported—even though he was a U.S. citizen.

A decade before accusing Kavanaugh of rape, Swetnick engaged Debra Katz's firm to file a sexual harassment complaint against a former employer. Avenatti, however, assured CNN there was "no coordination whatsoever" between Katz and his client's last-minute allegations against Kavanaugh. After their story fell apart, Grassley referred Swetnick and Avenatti to the Justice Department and FBI for a criminal investigation of their false statements. The criminal referral, however, soon became the least of Michael Avenatti's problems. Less than six months later, he was facing up to 333 years in prison for bank fraud, bankruptcy fraud, extortion, and wire fraud. The political press was shocked by the sudden fall of its anointed presidential frontrunner, but Stormy Daniels, the porn star client who made him famous, said she was not surprised by the charges.

Neither was the Senate Judiciary Committee. Grassley had cited Avenatti's tax problems and alleged financial frauds in his criminal referral as evidence of a lack of credibility. There was no shortage of material, but the referral said, "Committee investigators determined that delving into additional [stories of wrongdoing] would be beating a dead horse." There were more than twenty staffers on Grassley's Oversight and Investigations Unit and his Nomination Unit investigating the allegations coming in from Christine Blasey Ford and Debra Katz, Deborah Ramirez and the *New Yorker*, Julie Swetnick and Michael Avenatti, and others. Ford, Ramirez, and Swetnick declined to talk to committee investigators under oath, but Brett Kavanaugh did as soon as each allegation arose. One day after Christine Blasey Ford outed herself in the *Washington Post* as his accuser, he was on the phone with the Judiciary Committee investigators, issuing a categorical denial of the allegations and insisting,

"I want a hearing tomorrow." He was emphatic: "I did not do this. I did not do this to Ms. Ford or anyone.... I want to be categorical and unequivocal that I did not commit sexual assault. That is not me. That was not me."

Kavanaugh referred to the approximately 220 high school–era friends, including sixty-five women, who promptly came to his defense, saying he always "behaved honorably and treated women with respect." Ford's, Ramirez's, and Swetnick's witnesses challenged the three accusers' claims, said they did not know the accusers, said they did not know Kavanaugh, or were dead. As questions about the accusers' allegations multiplied, left-wing activists and their media allies shifted gears, arguing that marshalling sixty-five women to sign the testimonial within twenty-four hours of the first allegations against Kavanaugh was suspicious. Before Ford contacted anyone about her accusations, however, Travis Lenkner had said that Kavanaugh's high school friends were already organizing to support his confirmation in whatever way they could. One of Ford's friends from high school, Virginia Hume, writing in the *Weekly Standard*, explained how that letter was drafted and disseminated among Kavanaugh's friends. "Those surprised at the speed with which it came together should see it as yet another testament to Brett's excellent reputation," she wrote. Hume addressed some of the specific objections to the authenticity of the effort:

> To those who responded to my tweet saying "I knew Brett in high school" by asking if I had gender reassignment surgery: I went to an all-girls school in Bethesda. He went to an all-boys school in Bethesda. We were permitted on occasion to speak to people of the opposite sex.
>
> To those hearing the thwap thwap thwap of black helicopters because my father is a journalist or because I worked in politics: In a group of 65 graduates of D.C. area schools, it would be odd *not* to find someone related to or working as a journalist or politician. It is entirely unremarkable. This is a

company town. (That said, it might explain why people happened to see my tweets on the subject).

Finally, to the one person who said I'm too young to know Brett Kavanaugh: Truly, I thank you from the bottom of my heart.

Because of the growing uncertainty about Ford's willingness to testify, Kavanaugh did not get his desired hearing the day after his first phone call with the Senate investigators about Ford's allegations. He then decided to share his side of the story in a televised interview with Martha MacCallum on Fox News. During his conversations with Senate investigators, Kavanaugh had an attorney at his side from Wilkinson Walsh + Eskovitz, a small, trial-focused firm. On camera with MacCallum, Kavanaugh sat with his wife and was less feisty than with adversarial investigators. His mood was careful and cautious, and he avoided speculation about the motives of those slinging accusations at him. His story was consistent, and he shared intimate details of his private life with the national audience watching cable news.

Kavanaugh: I've never sexually assaulted anyone. I did not have sexual intercourse or anything close to sexual intercourse in high school or for many years thereafter. And the girls from the schools I went to and I were friends—

MacCallum: So you're saying that through all these years that are in question, you were a virgin?

Kavanaugh: That's correct.

MacCallum: Never had sexual intercourse with anyone in high school—

Kavanaugh: Correct.

MacCallum: —and through what years in college, since we're probing into your personal life here?

Kavanaugh: Many years after, I'll leave it at that, many years after.

As the hearings approached and more allegations were flung at him, Kavanaugh grew testier with Senate investigators. In an interview under oath on September 25, after the *New Yorker* ran its second round of uncorroborated allegations and Avenatti tweeted that more allegations were on the way, Kavanaugh noted that he had already undergone six FBI background checks and multiple Judiciary Committee confirmation hearings over the course of two decades, and nothing had come up until days before the Senate was about to vote on his Supreme Court nomination. "I think this is, this is crazy town. It's a smear campaign," Kavanaugh exclaimed. "It's just outrageous, trying to take me down, trying to take down my family. It's bad. It's doing damage to the Supreme Court. It's doing damage to the country. It's doing damage to this process. It's become a total feeding frenzy, you know? Every—just unbelievable."

Senate investigators then pressed him about an allegation that had not yet received widespread attention. Senator Sheldon Whitehouse, a Democrat from Rhode Island, announced that he had received a phone call from a constituent who alleged that Kavanaugh sexually assaulted a woman on a boat in Newport, Rhode Island, early one August morning in 1985. Kavanaugh responded that he was not in Newport in 1985, had not been on a boat in Newport, and had never sexually assaulted a woman in Rhode Island or anywhere else. The man who made the allegation, Jeffrey Catalan, recanted his allegation one day after Kavanaugh's response to Senate investigators, tweeting, "Do [sic] everyone who is going crazy about what I said I have recanted because I have made a mistake and apologize for such mistake."

The day after Catalan recanted—Thursday, September 27—Ford and Kavanaugh appeared before the Senate Judiciary Committee. By the time Kavanaugh finally got his wish of testifying under oath in public, the *New Yorker* had asserted that there were numerous allegations of sexual assault against him with a "high level of evidence," the *New York Times* had dismissed the challenges to the accusations as Republican efforts at character assassination, and the *Washington Post* had aired allegations that it had not been able to corroborate for several months. CNN and CBS gave an uncritical platform to Ford's attorney, Debra Katz, and all of the television news networks shared the sworn statement of Michael Avenatti's client Julie Swetnick accusing Kavanaugh of serial gang rape.

Ford appeared first, and her testimony was all the Democrats hoped it would be. Images of her being sworn in led nightly newscasts around the world and were splashed across the front pages of newspapers the next day. Rachel Mitchell, the sex-crimes prosecutor selected by Republicans to probe her allegations, decided not to cross-examine her, but proceeded as though the hearing were a deposition.

By the time Kavanaugh entered the room, the media had all but declared his appointment dead, and his allies were whispering about who would replace him as the nominee if Senate Majority Leader Mitch McConnell pulled the vote or President Trump withdrew the nomination. But Kavanaugh took his seat ready to fight—as much for his reputation as for a seat on the nation's highest court.

Kavanaugh had prepared with a mock hearing two days earlier. Earlier practice sessions had resulted in leaks, so this time Don McGahn limited the number of people in the room. They met in McGahn's office with Kavanaugh's private attorney, Alex Walsh; a Justice Department lawyer; and Mark Paoletta, the general counsel to the Office of Management and Budget. Paoletta had been on the White House legal team that guided Clarence Thomas through the Anita Hill hearings and later, while chief counsel to Vice President Mike Pence, worked on Justice Gorsuch's confirmation. Paoletta was brought in to spar with Kavanaugh, while the Justice official took a methodical approach with deeply researched questions about Kavanaugh's past and writings. Seated opposite the nominee at the end of a long table, Paoletta started by grilling Kavanaugh over his high school yearbook. The exchange quickly grew heated, Kavanaugh giving as good as he got from Paoletta.

The session concluded after ninety minutes with some final advice for the nominee: "You need to be talking to the American people. You may think that nobody in that room believes you, or she's just walked out and everybody believes her. Don't worry. Tell your story. Go after the committee. They're the ones who did this. Not her." Kavanaugh knew that Thomas had taken a similar approach, treating the Judiciary Committee as his adversary at the Anita Hill hearings. Kavanaugh explained that though he did not have Thomas's "voice of God," he would try to channel some of Thomas's "righteous indignation."

Kavanaugh came out swinging on Thursday, evoking Thomas's famous denunciation of his hearing as a "high-tech lynching for uppity blacks" and a "national disgrace." Kavanaugh boomed:

> This confirmation process has become a national disgrace. The Constitution gives the Senate an important role in the confirmation process, but you have replaced advice and consent with search and destroy.
>
> Since my nomination in July, there's been a frenzy on the left to come up with something, anything to block my confirmation. Shortly after I was nominated, the Democratic Senate leader said he would, quote, "oppose me with everything he's got." A Democratic senator on this committee publicly—publicly referred to me as evil—evil. Think about that word. It's said that those who supported me were, quote, "complicit in evil." Another Democratic senator on this committee said, quote, "Judge Kavanaugh is your worst nightmare." A former head of the Democratic National Committee said, quote, "Judge Kavanaugh will threaten the lives of millions of Americans for decades to come."
>
> I understand the passions of the moment, but I would say to those senators, your words have meaning. Millions of Americans listen carefully to you. Given comments like those, is it any surprise that people have been willing to do anything, to make any physical threat against my family, to send any violent email to my wife, to make any kind of allegation

against me and against my friends. To blow me up and take me down. You sowed the wind for decades to come. I fear that the whole country will reap the whirlwind.

The behavior of several of the Democratic members of this committee at my hearing a few weeks ago was an embarrassment. But at least it was just a good old-fashioned attempt at Borking. Those efforts didn't work. When I did at least okay enough at the hearings that it looked like I might actually get confirmed, a new tactic was needed. Some of you were lying in wait and had it ready. This first allegation was held in secret for weeks by a Democratic member of this committee and by staff. It would be needed only if you couldn't take me out on the merits.

When it was needed, this allegation was unleashed and publicly deployed over Dr. Ford's wishes. And then—and then as no doubt was expected—if not planned—came a long series of false last-minute smears designed to scare me and drive me out of the process before any hearing occurred. Crazy stuff: Gangs, illegitimate children, fights on boats in Rhode Island. All nonsense, reported breathlessly and often uncritically by the media.

This has destroyed my family and my good name. A good name built up through decades of very hard work and public service at the highest levels of the American government. This whole two-week effort has been a calculated and orchestrated political hit, fueled with apparent pent-up anger about President Trump and the 2016 election, fear that has been unfairly stoked about my judicial record, revenge on behalf of the Clintons, and millions of dollars in money from outside left-wing opposition groups.

This is a circus. The consequences will extend long past my nomination. The consequences will be with us for decades. This grotesque and coordinated character assassination will dissuade competent and good people of all political persuasions from serving our country. And as we all know, in the United States political system of the early 2000s, what goes around comes around. I am an optimistic guy. I always try to be on the sunrise side of the mountain, to be optimistic about the day that is coming. But today, I have to say that I fear for the future. Last time I was here, I told this committee that a federal judge must be independent, not swayed by public or political pressure. I said I was such a judge, and I am. I will not be intimidated into withdrawing from this process. You've tried hard. You've given it your all. No one can question your effort, but your coordinated and well-funded effort to destroy my good name and to destroy my family will not drive me out. The vile threats of violence against my family will not drive me out.

You may defeat me in the final vote, but you'll never get me to quit. Never. I'm here today to tell the truth. I've never sexually assaulted anyone. Not in high school, not in college, not ever.

Forcefully denying that he had ever committed sexual assault, Kavanaugh stated that he nevertheless was not questioning that someone had assaulted Christine Blasey Ford and that he wished no ill will to her or her family. "The other night, [my wife] Ashley and my daughter Liza said their prayers," Kavanaugh told the committee. "And little Liza—all of ten years old—said to Ashley, 'We should pray for the woman.' It's a lot of wisdom from a ten-year-old. We mean no ill will." Alyssa Milano, a pro-choice #MeToo activist who campaigned against Kavanaugh and was intentionally seated directly behind him in view of the television cameras, was moved to tears.

In addition to Kavanaugh's sworn denial of the allegations and the witnesses supporting him, the nominee had also provided investigators with his detailed personal calendar from the summer of 1982, which was when Ford said he had assaulted her. (She revised her memory after Kavanaugh provided the calendar.) The calendar indicated with specificity the friends he met and the events he attended, with down-to-the-minute detail.

"Some have noticed that I didn't have church on Sundays on my calendars. I also didn't list brushing my teeth," Kavanaugh testified. "And for me, going to church on Sundays was like brushing my teeth: automatic. It still is."

Kavanaugh's opponents had ridiculed the granular detail of the calendar, suggesting before the hearing that the documents had been doctored. But Kavanaugh explained in his opening statement why he had kept such remarkably careful records:

> My dad started keeping detailed calendars of his life in 1978. He did so as both a calendar and a diary. He was a very organized guy, to put it mildly. Christmastime, we'd sit around and he regales [sic] us with old stories, old milestones, old weddings, old events from his calendars. In ninth grade, in 1980, I started keeping calendars of my own. For me, also, it's both a calendar and a diary. I've kept such calendars as diaries for the last thirty-eight years. Mine are not as good as my dad's in some years. And when I was a kid, the calendars are about what you would expect from a kid; some goofy parts, some embarrassing parts. But I did have the summer of 1982 documented pretty well.

Kavanaugh's opening statement anticipated attacks on his high school yearbook and its inside jokes. He said some students and editors of the Georgetown Prep yearbook had taken their inspiration from *Animal House*, *Caddy Shack*, and *Fast Times at Ridgemont High*, causing everyone involved to cringe at the sight of it more than three decades later.

Ed and Martha Kavanaugh had always been conscientious about their only child's welfare. Now seated with his wife in the Senate hearing room, they had to listen to him talk about his sex life before millions of people watching on television across the country and around the world.

"As to sex, this is not a topic I ever imagined would come up at a judicial confirmation hearing, but I want to give you a full picture of who I was," Kavanaugh said in his opening statement. "I never had sexual intercourse, or anything close to it, during high school, or for many years after that. In some crowds, I was probably a little outwardly shy about my inexperience, tried to hide that. At the same time, I was also inwardly proud of it. For me and the girls who I was friends with, that lack of major rampant sexual activity in high school was a matter of faith and respect and caution."

The question-and-answer portion of Kavanaugh's testimony proceeded much as Christine Blasey Ford's had—Rachel Mitchell plodded through her five-minute rounds of questions on behalf of Republicans, while Democrats spoke for themselves—the key difference being that the Democrats cross-examined Kavanaugh and brought up every embarrassing detail of his youth they could think of—especially his high school yearbook. Senator Sheldon Whitehouse was particularly concerned with the sardonic accolade "Beach Week Ralph Club—Biggest Contributor":

Whitehouse: What does the word "ralph" mean in that?

Kavanaugh: That probably refers to throwing up. I'm known to have a weak stomach and I always have. In fact, the last time I was here, you asked me about having ketchup on spaghetti. I always have had a weak stomach.

Whitehouse: I don't know that I asked about ketchup on spaghetti.

Kavanaugh: You didn't. Someone did. And this is well-known. Anyone who's known me, like a lot of people behind me—known me my whole life—know. I got a weak stomach, whether it's with beer or with spicy food or with anything.

Whitehouse: So the vomiting that you reference in the Ralph Club reference—related to the consumption of alcohol?

Kavanaugh: Senator, I was at the top of my class academically, busted my butt in school. Captain of the varsity basketball team. Got into Yale College. When I got into Yale College, got into Yale Law School. Worked my tail off.

Whitehouse: And did the word "ralph" you used in your yearbook refer to alcohol?

Kavanaugh: I already answered the question. If you're—

Whitehouse: Did it relate to alcohol? You haven't answered that.

Kavanaugh: I like beer. I like beer. I don't know if you do. Do you like beer, Senator, or not?

Whitehouse: Okay, next one is—

Kavanaugh: What do you like to drink? Senator, what do you like to drink?

Whitehouse: Judge, have you—I don't know if it's boofed or boofed, how do you pronounce that?

Kavanaugh: That refers to flatulence. We were sixteen.

Whitehouse was going line by line through the yearbook asking about anything that could be embarrassing but making no connection to the purpose of the hearing—Christine Blasey Ford's allegations. He asked about "Devil's Triangle," and Kavanaugh explained it was a drinking game similar to quarters, in which players try to bounce a coin into a cup, typically a shot glass. The senator then asked whether notations that Kavanaugh did not know the outcome of an Orioles baseball game and a Georgetown basketball game meant that he was so inebriated that he could not remember what had happened. Kavanaugh answered that he was at a party and did not watch the game, but Democrats were not satisfied. Senator Patrick Leahy of Vermont, a former Judiciary Committee chairman, had already cross-examined Kavanaugh at length about the yearbook before Whitehouse started.

Senators Dick Durbin of Illinois and Amy Klobuchar of Minnesota implored Kavanaugh to stop the hearing by asking for an FBI investigation of Ford's allegations, although they did not make clear precisely what remained to be investigated. Klobuchar then asked Kavanaugh five times whether he ever drank so much that he could not remember something. Senator Cory Booker asked which specific days of the week he drank alcohol in high school. And on and on it went. As Democrats quizzed Kavanaugh about his yearbook and his adolescent drinking habits, Republicans were growing frustrated with Rachel Mitchell's methodical approach. Senator Durbin was expounding upon on the necessity of an FBI investigation when Senator Lindsey Graham of South Carolina finally had enough.

Graham erupted in rage. He noted that the Democrats could have had another FBI investigation if they had approached the Republicans when Senator Feinstein came into possession of Ford's accusation. "When you see [Justices Sonia] Sotomayor and [Elena] Kagan, tell them Lindsey said hello, because I voted for them," Graham said of the Supreme Court justices appointed by President Obama, a Democrat. "I would never do to them what you've done to this guy. This is the most unethical sham since I've been in politics. And if you really wanted to know the truth, you sure as hell wouldn't have done what you've done to this guy."

Graham then turned to Kavanaugh and asked if he was a "gang rapist," to which Kavanaugh replied that he was not. The indignant senator concluded by addressing his Democratic colleagues: "Boy, y'all want power. God, I hope you never get it. I hope the American people see through this sham. That you knew about it and you held it. You had no intention of protecting Dr. Ford. None," Graham said, before looking to Kavanaugh. "She's as much a victim as you are. God, I hate to say it because these have been my friends, but let me tell you, when it comes to this, you're looking for a fair process? You came to the wrong town at the wrong time, my friend."

CHAPTER 7

Time to Fill or Kill

Senate Republicans had stayed preternaturally quiet throughout the controversy over Christine Blasey Ford's accusation. The eleven Republicans on the Judiciary Committee sat silently through the long hours of testimony as the Democrats first championed Ford and then cross-examined Kavanaugh. Then Senator Lindsey Graham ended the silence.

Graham was on deck to succeed Chuck Grassley as the chairman of the Judiciary Committee in 2019 if Republicans held the Senate in the midterm elections one month after the Kavanaugh hearings. Grassley, a proud Iowan farmer, was not a lawyer. Graham was. He entered the U.S. Air Force after law school and served in the Judge Advocate General's Corps.

The safe bet for a politician up for reelection in 2020, as Graham was, would have been not to rock the boat, but Graham could not help himself. He not only took Democrats to task for politicizing the court, but he also issued a public warning to any lily-livered Republican afraid to buck them. "To my Republican colleagues," he said, "if you vote no [on Kavanaugh], you're legitimizing the most despicable thing I have seen in my time in politics." Then he trained his fire on the Democrats. "You want this seat? I hope you never get it."

During the fight over the vacancy left by Justice Antonin Scalia's death one year earlier, Republicans had followed a simple strategy: select a jurist in the mainstream who was respected by his colleagues and whose judicial philosophy mirrored Scalia's—that is to say, an originalist and textualist interpretation of the Constitution. They tried to follow the same strategy when Justice Kennedy's seat opened up, but Kavanaugh's nomination threatened to tip the high court's balance. Christine Blasey Ford's allegation allowed the Democrats to undermine the Republicans' strategy for vetting a nominee and filling a vacancy. Graham's remonstrance forced Republicans to consider the allegation on its merits in light of the available evidence.

For weeks, pundits debated the proper standard for judging the unsubstantiated allegations against Kavanaugh. Was the accused innocent until proven guilty? And must guilt be demonstrated beyond a reasonable doubt by a preponderance of the evidence? Or was the standard simply #BelieveTheWoman? The Senate Democrats promptly declared that they would #BelieveTheWoman, leaving the fate of Kavanaugh's confirmation in the hands of the Republicans and a handful of Democrats up for reelection in states that Trump had carried in 2016. There were no Trump-state Democrats among the twenty-one members of the Judiciary Committee. Graham's diatribe, ostensibly addressed to all ten of his Republican colleagues on the committee, was aimed at one in particular—Jeff Flake of Arizona.

Flake now sought to have the last word, offering a rebuttal of sorts: "I would just urge my colleagues to recognize that, in the end, we are twenty-one very imperfect senators trying to do our best to provide advice and consent. And in the end, there is likely to be as much doubt as certainty going out of this room today." Flake did not get the last word at the hearing, however. That distinction went to John Kennedy of Louisiana, the committee's newest Republican, who assured Kavanaugh he was "100 percent certain" that the accusations against him were untrue.

Jeff Flake was a casualty of Trump's rise in the Republican Party. Unable to reconcile himself to the direction in which the president was taking his party, Flake had decided not to seek reelection in 2018 after a single term in the Senate. He was not going quietly, however. He promised to block all of Trump's judicial appointments until Republican leaders brought legislation aimed at restricting the president's trade agenda to the floor for a vote. As soon as Justice Kennedy announced his retirement, however, Flake backtracked, saying he would not block a vote on the coming Supreme Court appointment. Critics viewed him as a country club Republican who was more concerned with decorum than with conservative principles. The Ford-Kavanaugh hearing had not challenged any conservative principle Flake deemed important, but it offended his sense of what was appropriate.

The day after the hearing, as he was on his way to the Judiciary Committee vote on advancing Kavanaugh's nomination to the full Senate, Flake was ambushed by protestors as he stepped into an elevator. Ana Maria Archila, a professional activist surrounded by cameras, screeched at the cornered senator that he was "allowing someone who actually violated a woman to sit in the Supreme Court." Archila told Flake that she had been sexually assaulted previously and that his vote on Kavanaugh would harm her children. "I have two children. I cannot imagine that for the next fifty years they will have to have someone in the Supreme Court who has been accused of violating a young girl," she said. "What are you doing, sir?"

A second protester, Maria Gallagher, said that she too had been sexually assaulted, but no one had believed her. "Don't look away from me!" she shouted. "Look at me and tell me that it doesn't matter what happened to me, that you will let people like that go into the highest court of the land and tell everyone what they can do with their bodies."

Flake, clearly distressed, answered only with, "Thank you" and "I need to go to the hearing."

The video of the confrontation went viral. Archila told reporters that she was in Washington for the confirmation hearings and happened to spot Flake in the hallway. She did not mention that she was co-executive director of the Center for Popular Democracy, part of the Demand Justice coalition that was committed to stopping President Trump's appointment of *anyone* to the Supreme Court. As a reward for her disruption, Congresswoman Alexandria Ocasio-Cortez invited Archila to be her guest at the 2019 State of the Union Address.

Flake had announced that he would vote for Kavanaugh before his close encounter with Archila and Gallagher, but after he found out that progressives were making him a symbol of Republican insouciance about sexual assault, Flake flaked again. This time however he did not completely back-track on his public pledge. He voted to send the nomination out of committee on the condition that the FBI spend another week investigating what he called the "current and credible" allegations. Jeff Flake had his final say.

Washington's center-left pundit class and the mainstream press hailed the "Kavanaugh compromise" crafted by Flake and Senator Chris Coons of Delaware, a Democrat. The terms of the compromise were that Coons got a delay of the confirmation vote and yet another FBI investigation of Kavanaugh's background in return for...nothing. Flake got glowing press coverage (followed by a gig with CBS News after he left the Senate) and the political cover to vote with his party without being demonized by the political establishment he did not want to offend.

"Friday, as the Senate descended into chaos, one Republican and one Democrat found a way forward with an old technique that seemed long forgotten: compromise," intoned Scott Pelley on CBS's *60 Minutes*. "It was Republican Flake who forced his party to accept a one-week FBI investigation into the assault allegations against Judge Kavanaugh."

At the time of the interview, Flake was considering a challenge to President Trump for the GOP nomination in 2020, but he had given up on running for reelection to the Senate. He eventually decided not to challenge Trump, and he said his decision to roll over for the Democrats would not have been possible if he were having to face the voters again. "There's no value to reaching across the aisle," he complained on CBS. "There's no currency for that anymore. There's no incentive."

For all his posturing, Flake had been intimidated—not only by the women on the elevator, but also by threats of violence, some of which were not revealed to the public—as the Senate wrestled with Kavanaugh's nomination. One such threat came from court proceedings involving James Dean Blevins, a Chicago man who had left a voicemail message threatening to kill Flake and his family. "I am tired of him interrupting our president, and I am coming down there to take him and his family out," Blevins said, according to court documents.

A year earlier, Flake had been at the Republican congressional baseball practice during which a politically motivated gunman yelled "This is for healthcare!" and opened fire. Simply being Republican and in Washington during the Trump era was enough to put a target on your back, but the threats increased during the Kavanaugh confirmation battle.

Senator Ted Cruz of Texas and his wife were chased out of a Washington restaurant by rowdy protesters yelling, "We believe survivors!" Senator Rand Paul's home address was posted online by malicious critics, terrifying his wife. "I now keep a loaded gun by my bed," she wrote in a letter published on the date of Kavanaugh's confirmation. "Our security systems have had to be expanded. I have never felt this way in my life."

Senator Chuck Grassley, the chairman of the Judiciary Committee, and Senator Susan Collins of Maine received more than ten voicemail messages threatening assault and murder from Ronald DeRisi of Long Island, who wanted to retaliate for their failure to ruin Kavanaugh. "It's a nine-millimeter. Side of your... skull," DeRisi said in a message left on the day of Christine Blasey Ford's testimony. He ended the call, "Yeah, Kavanaugh—I don't think so." On the day of the final vote on Kavanaugh's confirmation, DeRisi called again. "You better pray this guy don't get in." And then he called again, saying, "I'm gonna get you." These threats, Grassley acknowledged, were "pretty unusual," and the authorities took them seriously. Grassley said he had faced only three or four similar threats in his thirty-eight years in the Senate. But, Grassley said, when it came time for him and his staff to proceed with Kavanaugh's nomination, they were unfazed. "It didn't bother us," he said. DeRisi was eventually sentenced to eighteen months in prison for threatening to murder two U.S. senators.

Other threats were more sophisticated. Jackson Cosko, a twenty-seven-year-old former staffer for Democrat senator Maggie Hassan from New Hampshire, used the knowledge he acquired on the Hill to target and intimidate Republican senators. A computer systems administrator in Hassan's office until approximately two months before Kavanaugh's nomination, Cosko repeatedly burglarized his former boss's office in a computer fraud and data-theft scheme. Furious about Kavanaugh's appointment, he decided during the Ford hearings to post the home addresses and telephone numbers of three Judiciary Committee Republicans—Lindsey Graham, Mike Lee, and Orrin Hatch—on their Wikipedia pages. He then shared news of his attempts to intimidate the Republicans on Twitter. As word of Cosko's antics spread, Senator Paul called for an investigation into how the material became public. Cosko responded by posting the home addresses and phone numbers of Paul and Senate Majority Leader Mitch McConnell online.

"He dares call for an investigation of ME?!?!?!?" Cosko wrote on a Wikipedia page for Paul. "I am the Golden God!... Also it's my legal right as an American to post his info.... We are malicious and hostile...send us bitcoins."

On Wednesday, October 3, a few days before the final confirmation vote, Cosko threatened to post more private information, but he was arrested before he could continue. The night before his arrest, someone spotted him in Senator Hassan's office. He threatened to leak the private communications of senators, medical information about senators' children, and Social Security numbers of senators if he was reported. The "Golden God" pleaded guilty in April 2019 to committing a slew of crimes to stop Kavanaugh's confirmation and was sentenced to four years in prison.

The ferocity of the controversy surrounding Kavanaugh's appointment not only affected Congress, but also troubled some in the judicial branch, as well. Reggie Walton, a senior judge on the U.S. District Court for the District of Columbia, told an American Bar Association national security group, "I think the confirmation hearings that we just went through further will give some people the perception that the judges are nothing but politicians also, who make decisions based upon political considerations as compared to the rule of law. I think obviously that's very destructive to the credibility that the system has because our judicial process relies upon the citizenry believing in the process, and they're only going to believe in the process if they think and believe it operates fairly."

The public's confidence in its institutions was falling before the 2016 elections and has plumbed new depths since then. The presumption that government officials are acting in good faith was under attack in the first year of the Trump administration. From the special counsel's Russia probe to the administration's travel ban, political opportunists and media agitators insisted that the government was not acting in the interests of the American people and that the executive branch harbored a secret animus. The public's confidence in the FBI to conduct its additional inquiry into Kavanaugh's past thoroughly and honestly was critical to the public's willingness to accept his eventual confirmation.

Kavanaugh's allies were confident that they knew how the FBI's additional investigation would turn out. In the past twenty-five years, he had been through six FBI background investigations, which included interviews of nearly 150 people. Democratic and Republican congressional investigators who reviewed those reports indicated that nothing hinted at sexual misconduct or alcohol abuse. The additional FBI inquiry, lasting nearly a week, produced a report of about fifty pages, including findings from interviews with approximately ten people with relevant testimony and incorporating Ford's and Kavanaugh's sworn testimony to the Judiciary Committee.

In May 2019, the FBI released more than five hundred pages of its "supplemental background investigation and related tip records" regarding Justice Brett Kavanaugh. The records showed the FBI investigated queries and allegations arriving in field offices far from Washington, D.C., throughout the fall of 2018. The Louisville field office received one particularly dramatic allegation the day after Ford revealed her identity in the *Washington Post*. The unstable accuser, whose name was redacted in files released by the FBI, said Kavanaugh raped Ford at a house party in Palo Alto, California, in what "could have been around 1983," when both Kavanaugh and Ford were teenagers living in suburban D.C.:

> I recall hearing Ford's name spoken and seeing her in the room where and soon before she was assaulted. I also recall Kavanaugh's face and hearing his name attached to his face. I think I left the room to use the bathroom and was walking down the hall when I was told a woman is being assaulted. I think we opened the locked upstairs room (or tried to) using the bobby pin trick. We called the police. I saw Kavanaugh race down the stairs and out of the house. I think we tried to file a police report upon the incident. Inside the house where the party was held I heard a person say Kavanaugh has done that before (sexual assault/rape).
>
> I don't yet recollect the entire party event perfectly but I will swear that I saw Christine Blasey Ford (she has a distinctive face I recognize) and Brett Kavanaugh at a Palo Alto party in the early 80's and that we tried to get Ford to make a police report upon the assault which was an attempted rape charge against Kavanaugh. Someone at the party said Brett Kavanaugh has attempted and/or committed rape before. Although Wikipedia dates the assault 1982 I think it may have occurred in the summer of 1983. This is because I think I spoke to someone at the party about my Ultra Deep Dive and that could not have occurred in 1982.
>
> I saw Brett Kavanaugh inside the Austin, TX bar around March 10, 2015. He was talking to Donald Trump. Trump has asked him something which led him to say: yeah, I've raped. After hearing that Trump offered him a place on his team. Sometime later Kavanaugh said that he wanted the

Supreme Court Justice appointment. I was unable to discern all of the conversation between Trump and Kavanaugh. I think I heard a person in the bar on the same night say Kavanaugh's going to need an alibi.

I am currently and repeatedly being harmed by wireless radiation especially energy which is being emitted from the man who lives in the apartment above mine. The energy can keep me from remembering past events clearly. The energy has and continues to cause my brain injury: migraine with aura, soreness, tiredness, damage to neurons. Please refer to 80 page document I mailed in mid July 2018 for details upon connections to Apt 304.

Less than thirty minutes after the Louisville office received that allegation, the San Francisco office received an allegation that Kavanaugh was part of a "child rape ring":

Sir I am concerned about the Supreme Court nominee Brett Kavanaugh. I currently have an active case with the Special Council regarding a pedophile human trafficking organized crime organization and the judge presents the same way using their license plates to identify with the crimes they commit. His license plate says that [he] committed crimes of rape against at least one of his children. I say this because he shouldnt be allowed to serve on the supreme court if he is in a child rape ring. you should open a new investigation on this judge before he is confirmed.

The FBI's documents labeled both the Louisville and San Francisco cases closed, but that did not stop the allegations and queries from flooding into the FBI. Some allegations appeared to be facetious, intended to distract the FBI from its actual business. On the day of Ford's hearing before the Senate Judiciary Committee, FBI headquarters received a message from someone appearing to joke about Kavanaugh and the late Justice Antonin Scalia committing a crime together:

> Dear FBI,
>
>   I have credible information regarding the fact that Brett Kavanaugh and Anthony [sic] Scalia were enforcers for John Gotti; They were the ones who cut the head off the horse of that Hollywood Producer. 9 or 10 drunk high school girls will confirm this.
>
>   Just trying to help.

Before such FBI records saw the light of day, the Democrats took issue with the scope of the FBI's investigation, and as soon as it was completed, they denounced it as insufficient. Senate Minority Leader Chuck Schumer complained that it was "not a thorough investigation" and said Republicans "engaged in a giant Kabuki game."

> We Democrats had many fears that this would be an all-too-limited process that would constrain the FBI from getting the facts. Having received a thorough briefing a few minutes ago, our fears have been realized.... The White House and the Republican side here in the Senate has attempted to rush this through regardless of the facts. It's wrong. It jaundices relationships between the sides in this body, which we all want to be better. It hurts the agencies involved, the reputation of the FBI, and above all it hurts the Supreme Court and the American people.

Schumer added, "Ultimately, Dr. Ford came forward and won America's hearts, and our Republican colleagues were upset because that might derail their headlong rush to put Judge Kavanaugh on the Supreme Court."

Senator Dianne Feinstein rushed to the cameras to criticize the FBI's investigation, saying, "The most notable part of this report is what's not in it." She then admitted she did not actually know the scope of the report because she had not read it in full. "Candidly, what we reviewed today in a very limited time, uh, I was there, I had to leave, the report is in parts, and I had the opportunity to read some, but not all of it," Feinstein said.

She had more time to review what the FBI was investigating than any other senator, since she waited approximately six weeks after receiving Ford's letter to deliver it to the FBI—not to the criminal investigation component, but to the background investigation division. Ford's letter did not describe a federal crime, and the BI division would not refer concerns about the alleged conduct to a criminal division because the statute of limitations had expired long ago and Kavanaugh was under age eighteen at the time of the alleged incident. Had Feinstein given Ford's letter to the FBI when she received it, the FBI probably would have finished its investigation much sooner. The allegations would have been less likely to become public before law enforcement had reviewed them, and the investigation would not have slowed down the Senate's consideration of Kavanaugh's nomination.

Senator Feinstein's incuriosity about the final FBI report matched her fello Democratic senators' lack of interest in Christine Blasey Ford's background. They had asked her a mere thirty-four questions in the hearing, using the rest of their time to talk themselves. Ford's responses to questions from Democrats took up ten minutes and twenty-four seconds. Her answers to the Republicans' 175 questions, by contrast, took up nearly thirty minutes.

Now that the FBI investigation was concluded, there was little the Senate Democrats could do to slow Kavanaugh's confirmation, so the #Resistance intensified its efforts. Two days before the Ford-Kavanaugh hearing, Senator Kamala Harris's staff turned over to Senate investigators an undated letter from "Jane Doe" of Oceanside, California, alleging that Kavanaugh had repeatedly raped her. On the day the Senate received the FBI's final report, Judy Munro-Leighton sent an email to the Judiciary Committee with the subject line "I am Jane Doe from Oceanside CA— Kavanaugh raped me." Her email reproduced the text of the handwritten letter she had sent to Senator Harris on September 19, which read:

Dear Senator Grassley, et al

The current situation regarding the allegations made by Dr. Ford against Brett Kavanaugh have prompted me to write you today.

I have moved on with my life since he forced himself on me as well. The times were so different and I didn't expect to be taken seriously, embarrass my family be believed at all.

I was at a party with a friend. I had been drinking. She left with another boy leaving me to find my own way home. Kavanaugh and a friend offered me a ride home. I don't know the other boys name. I was in his car to go home. His friend was behind me in the back seat. Kavanaugh kissed me forcefully I told him I only wanted a ride home, Kavanaugh continued to grope me over my clothes, forcing his kisses on me and putting his hand under my sweater. "No!" I yelled at him.

The boy in the back seat reached around putting his hand over my mouth and holding my arm to keep me in the car. I screamed into his hand.

Kavanaugh continued his forcing himself on me. He pulled up my sweater and bra exposing my breasts and reached into my panties inserting his fingers into my vagina.

My screams were silenced by the boy in the back seat covering my mouth and groping me as well.

Kavanaugh slapped me and told me to be quiet and forced me to perform oral sex on him. He climaxed in my mouth.

They forced me into the backseat and took turns raping me several times each.

They dropped me off two blocks from my home. "No one will believe you if you tell. Be a good girl." He told me.

Watching what has happened to Anita Hill and Dr Ford has me petrified to come forward in person or even provide my name. A group of white men powerful senators who wont believe me will come after me

Like Dr Ford. Im a teacher. I have an education. A family. A child. A Home.

I have credibility. Just because something happens a long time ago because a rape victim doesn't want to personally come forward does not mean something cant be true!

Jane Doe

Oceanside CA

Senate Majority Leader Mitch McConnell had heard enough. On Thursday, October 4, hours after Munro-Leighton sent her email to the Judiciary Committee, McConnell scheduled a vote to end debate on Kavanaugh's confirmation. It was time to bypass the noise and "uncorroborated mud," McConnell said, and actually vote on Kavanaugh:

> This is now the seventh time the FBI has thoroughly reviewed Judge Kavanaugh's background.... What do the facts and evidence tell us after seven FBI investigations? The fact is that these allegations have not been corroborated. None of the allegations have been corroborated by the seventh FBI investigation. Not in the new FBI investigation, not anywhere. So none of these last-minute allegations have been corroborated, as is confirmed by the seventh and latest FBI investigation.

McConnell, who had been speaking in his typically solemn and slow cadence, now grew uncharacteristically impassioned:

> For goodness sake, this is the United States of America! Nobody is supposed to be guilty until proven innocent in this country! Nobody is supposed to be guilty until proven innocent in the United States of America! The Senate should not set a fundamentally un-American precedent here. Judge Kavanaugh's right to basic fairness does not disappear just because some disagree with his judicial philosophy. Our society is not

a place where uncorroborated allegations of misconduct from nearly forty years ago—allegations which are vigorously disputed—can nullify someone's career or destroy their reputation. Is that what the Senate's going to be known for? Your nomination comes up here and we destroy your reputation. That's what the Senate is going to participate in?

So, above the partisan noise, beyond this shameful spectacle, which is an embarrassment to the Senate, what will endure are the actual facts before us. The actual facts. Upon reviewing them, only one question is left for us to answer: Is Judge Brett Kavanaugh qualified to serve on the Supreme Court? Well, Mr. President, there's a good reason the political opponents of this nomination have never wanted to litigate that issue. Oh no. They don't want to talk about that. There's a good reason why they let the politics of personal destruction run away ahead of the facts, in an effort to dodge that very good question. Because Judge Brett Kavanaugh is stunningly and totally qualified for this job.

Senate investigators found many holes in Munro-Leighton's story. She was several decades older than Kavanaugh. She lived in Kentucky, not Oceanside, California, or Washington, D.C. She was a liberal activist. And she proved difficult to reach. When the investigators were finally able to talk to her, in early November, she insisted that she was not "Jane Doe." Asked whether she knew Kavanaugh, she answered, "Oh Lord, no." She explained that she "just wanted to get attention" and labeled her efforts a "ploy" and a "tactic" to stop Kavanaugh's confirmation. Senator Grassley referred the matter to the FBI and Justice Department, as he had done with Julie Swetnick's and Michael Avenatti's misrepresentations.

The day after McConnell's speech—Friday, October 5—the Senate voted to close the debate on Kavanaugh's nomination and proceed to a vote on the Senate floor. One year earlier, Senate Democrats had attempted to thwart the cloture vote on Neil Gorsuch's confirmation with the first filibuster of a Supreme Court nominee along strictly partisan lines. The Republican majority responded by changing the Senate's rules to eliminate the filibuster in Supreme Court confirmations. Therefore, the cloture vote appeared to kill any remaining Democratic hope of averting Kavanaugh's appointment. But the Senate votes on Kavanaugh's confirmation were not cast strictly along partisan lines. Five Democrats up for reelection in states that Trump carried in 2016 had a difficult decision to make. They knew what was at stake and their challengers did, too.

CHAPTER 8

Survival of the Fittest

In late September, the attorney general of Missouri, Josh Hawley, stood on a stage next to President Trump, who had come to the Ozarks to boost the thirty-eight-year-old's challenge to Senator Claire McCaskill in her bid for reelection. The race was neck and neck for much of the summer. Two days before Trump's visit, McCaskill announced that she would vote against Brett Kavanaugh's confirmation. Christine Blasey Ford had revealed herself as Kavanaugh's accuser a week earlier, and it was not yet clear whether she would agree to talk to the Senate. Kavanaugh's nomination was on shaky ground.

When Trump turned the microphone over to Hawley, the candidate complimented the president on the size of the crowd, remarking that "twenty thousand people or something" were turned away. He then ran through the Trump résumé, which all Republican candidates had been citing—new jobs, lower taxes, and a commitment to delivering big for the American people. When Hawley came to Trump's record of putting "pro-Constitution judges on the bench," the crowd went wild. Before he could utter Kavanaugh's name, the crowd yelled it for him, chanting "Ka-va-naugh! Ka-va-naugh!" The applause had roared for about twenty seconds, and Hawley decided against trying to shout over the crowd.

"That's right, wow," he said, taking a step back and looking over at Trump. The president responded to the chants with two thumbs up and a couple of fist pumps. "That's pretty good," Trump said to Hawley with a look of surprise. Hawley repeated, "That's pretty good," cocked his head in astonishment, and searched for his place in the teleprompter. Finding he was mid-sentence, he raised his voice over the crowd: "Judges who love the Constitution, judges who love our country, judges like Brett Kavanaugh," and the crowd erupted again.

Hawley was happy to tie himself to Kavanaugh, whom he knew personally. They were members of the same caste—graduates of Yale Law School and Supreme Court clerks. After practicing appellate litigation in Washington, D.C., Hawley returned to his home state to teach at the University of Missouri Law School and was elected state attorney general in 2016.

Hawley appreciated the power of Supreme Court appointments to galvanize conservative voters. The issue helped Trump win in 2016, and Hawley took advantage of it in 2018. Soon after Justice Anthony Kennedy retired, he set up the website "supremeclaire.com" to spotlight the differences between the judges he wanted and those McCaskill favored. The message was clear and concise: "McCaskill supported Obama's judicial nominees, yet obstructs President Trump." She had voted to confirm 100 percent of President Obama's judicial nominees but voted against confirming Neil Gorsuch.

McCaskill, however, had gone further than simply voting for all of Obama's judges and against Trump's Supreme Court picks. She also opposed federal appellate court nominees who were on Trump's Supreme Court shortlist or who were likely to be added to it, voting against Amul Thapar and Don Willett and declining to vote on the nominations of Amy Coney Barrett, Joan Larsen, and Allison Eid, who filled Gorsuch's seat on the Tenth Circuit. Each "no" vote or failure to vote made Hawley's case stronger, and the Republican was intent on forcing a reckoning with her votes on judges.

However astute Hawley was in sizing up McCaskill's vulnerability, many Trump voters were leery of his establishment résumé. So in the late fall, Trump rode into the Show Me State to convince his followers to get behind Hawley. It worked. Trump's campaigning and the Kavanaugh bump lifted Hawley's support, and Trump noticed.

Campaigning in Indiana, Trump charged the incumbent Democratic senator, Joe Donnelly, of joining the "Democratic mob" against Kavanaugh. "A vote for Joe [Donnelly]," he declared, "is a vote to put Schumer in charge of the Senate and to put Dianne Feinstein in charge of Senate Judiciary."

In North Dakota, Trump leveled the same attacks against Senator Heidi Heitkamp. "Democrats want judges who will rewrite the Constitution any way they want to do it and take away your Second Amendment, erase your borders, throw open the jailhouse doors, and destroy your freedoms," he warned voters in Fargo. "We must elect more Republicans. We have to do that."

By the time Trump got to Southaven, Mississippi, a suburb of Memphis, on October 2, he knew his voters enthusiastically stood with his nomination of Brett Kavanaugh. He had refined his message and was moving public opinion in support of Kavanaugh. He told the crowd, "They've been trying to destroy Judge Kavanaugh since the very first second he was announced because they know Judge Kavanaugh will follow the Constitution as written." Pointing to the accusations of gang rape against Kavanaugh, he said he accepted the Democrats' standard of "guilty until proven innocent" as "part of the job description" of the president, but judicial nominees, he said, should not be subject to that injustice.

Then Trump did what no other Republican was willing to do. He recounted Christine Blasey Ford's testimony before the Senate Judiciary Committee, pointing out her inconsistencies without ever criticizing her personally: "How did you get home? I don't remember. How'd you get there? I don't remember. Where is the place? I don't remember. How many years ago was it? I don't know. I don't know. I don't know. I don't know. What neighborhood was it in? I don't know. Where's the house? I don't know. Upstairs, downstairs, where was it? I don't know. But I had one beer, that's the only thing I remember!"

The applause grew after each "I don't know" until the crowd was in a frenzy. The president drove his point home, charging that Kavanaugh's life was "shattered" and "in tatters" because of "evil people" who wanted to "destroy" him. Trump identified each of the villains on the Judiciary Committee, starting with "Da Nang Richard Blumenthal," the Connecticut senator whom Trump criticized for misleading the public about his military service during the Vietnam War. The president pointed to New Jersey's Cory Booker, "a guy who destroyed, practically by himself, the city of Newark," urged the crowd to google "Patrick Leahy" and "drink," and solicited boos at the mention of Dianne Feinstein's name, mocking her performance at the hearings. Not limiting his criticism to senators, the president also took aim at Michael Avenatti, a "sleazebag lawyer."

What had happened to Brett Kavanaugh, Trump suggested, could happen to anyone in the society Democrats were trying to build:

> This is a time when your father, when your husband, when your brother, when your son could do great. "Mom, I did great in school, I've worked so hard. Mom, I'm so pleased to tell you I just got a fantastic job with IBM, I just got a fantastic job with General Motors. I'm so proud. Mom, a terrible thing just happened. A person who I've never met said I did things that were horrible, and they're firing me from my job, Mom. I don't know what to do. Mom, what do I do? What do I do, Mom? What do I do, Mom?" It's a damn sad situation, okay? And we better start, as a country, getting smart and getting tough and not letting that stuff right back there, all those cameras, tell us how to live our lives because they are really dishonest people. Not all of them. But damn well most of them. That I can tell you. Fake news.

Trump had portrayed Kavanaugh as a victim, Ford as unreliable, Democrats and liberals as villains, and the press coverage that fueled the controversy as "fake news." His rally thrilled his audience, but the press reported it through a different filter. The *New York Times* accused Trump of "taunting" Ford, while CNN, CBS, the *Washington Post*, and numerous other outlets reported that he "mock[ed]" her. Despite the hostile framing, Trump had reached his intended target and was building support for the decision he wanted senators to make.

As President Trump amassed support for Kavanaugh with GOP voters in front of the cameras, another Republican president, George W. Bush, worked behind the scenes to secure the necessary votes in the Senate for his former aide. Among those receiving calls from Bush were Joe Manchin, Jeff Flake, Lisa Murkowski, and Susan Collins. Bush's phone call with Collins may have contributed to her decision, but his influence was not decisive. No one's was.

The effort to intimidate Susan Collins into voting against Kavanaugh started as soon as he was nominated. Before Christine Blasey Ford ever appeared on camera, some three thousand coat hangers were delivered to her office—a macabre symbol of the choice Kavanaugh supposedly would leave women seeking an abortion. As the controversy heated up, attempts to persuade Collins were mingled with threats of violence. Three days before Ford testified, scores of protesters swarmed the hallway outside her office on Capitol Hill and forty-six protesters were arrested. Fifty of their counterparts marched on Collins's office in Maine. In the three months following Kavanaugh's nomination, protesters had followed her everywhere, including to her houses in Maine and Washington. One man ambushed her late at night as she made her way home, and she sprinted to her house clutching her dry cleaning and a briefcase.

Then threats of poison, violence, and death began to flood in. She received a fax from someone promising to cut her throat and tear off her limbs if she voted for Kavanaugh. One Collins staffer assigned to assisting constituents with Social Security problems received a phone call from a man who said he hoped the staffer would be raped and impregnated if Collins voted for Kavanaugh. In October, the senator's husband opened a letter that purported to be "coated in Ricin" and read "Good luck to you and Susan in the next life." A hazardous-materials response team found no ricin or other poisons, but her husband and dog were temporarily quarantined as a precaution. The U.S. Postal Service then assigned a postal inspector to hand-check all mail to the Collins residence. Within days, the inspector discovered an envelope that was leaking white powder. Inside was a note reading "AnthRAX!! HA HA HA!!!" and a drawing of a stick figure with its tongue out and X's for eyes. The sender wrote "You" and drew an arrow to the stick figure.

Collins temporarily retreated from her home, but not from her convictions. Sources close to her say thuggish efforts to strong-arm her have always failed, but she is always open to arguments based upon reason. She bucked her party by voting against President Bill Clinton's impeachment and supporting the repeal of the military's "Don't Ask Don't Tell" policy. As the vote on Kavanaugh approached, she sought advice from many lawyers, advisers, and colleagues over several months and then made her decision known on the Senate floor.

Collins's speech ahead of the cloture vote was carried live across the cable news networks. She called attention to the special interest groups opposed to Kavanaugh's appointment that were marshaling protesters at her home and offices. Then she explained her view of the advice and consent for which the Senate is responsible under the Constitution and how she tries to fulfill that duty. It was a master class in civics, instructing viewers in the procedure and role of the world's greatest deliberative body.

"Informed by Alexander Hamilton's Federalist 76, I have interpreted [advice and consent] to mean that the president has broad discretion to consider a nominee's philosophy, whereas my duty as a senator is to focus on the nominee's qualifications as long as that nominee's philosophy is within the mainstream of judicial thought," Collins said. "I have always opposed litmus tests for judicial nominees with respect to their personal views or politics, but I fully expect them to be able to put aside any and all personal preferences in deciding the cases that come before them." She explained that this approach led her to vote for two justices nominated by President George W. Bush, Chief Justice John Roberts and Justice Samuel Alito; two justices selected by President Barack Obama, Justices Elena Kagan and Sonia Sotomayor; and President Trump's first Supreme Court pick, Justice Neil Gorsuch.

Focusing on qualifications and not philosophy, Collins had researched Kavanaugh's more than three hundred opinions with the help of nineteen attorneys, including some from the Congressional Research Service, who briefed her regularly throughout the confirmation process. Collins interviewed Kavanaugh in private for two hours and spent another hour talking to him on the phone. She was satisfied with what she learned about him, though some of the views that she now attributed to Kavanaugh were the very ones that worried conservatives.

Contrary to progressives' assertion that Kavanaugh was likely to be hostile to Obamacare, Collins pointed to his dissent in the *Seven-Sky* case as the basis for Chief Justice Roberts's opinion saving Obamacare. In other words, the Kavanaugh opinion that most troubled skeptical conservatives was a major reason Collins was voting for him.

Collins cast doubt on the assumption that Kavanaugh was opposed to the decision in *Obergefell v. Hodges*, which required the legal recognition of same-sex marriage in every state, and she challenged the suggestion that he would be a rubber stamp for President Trump, noting, "That Judge Kavanaugh is more of a centrist than some of his critics maintain is reflected in the fact that he and Chief Judge Merrick Garland [President Obama's unsuccessful nominee to fill Scalia's seat] voted the same way in 93 percent of the cases that they heard together. Indeed Chief Judge Garland joined in more than 96 percent of the majority opinions authored by Judge Kavanaugh, dissenting only once."

Kavanaugh was unlike any originalist or textualist ever nominated to the Supreme Court, Collins indicated, in that he viewed adherence to precedent not as a jurisprudential goal but as a requirement evident in the original public meaning of Article 3 of the Constitution. Collins said Kavanaugh told her that following precedent is not simply a goal or aspiration, but also is a constitutional mandate that "has to be followed" to provide stability, predictability, reliability, and fairness. With Kavanaugh's understanding of precedent in mind, Collins then turned to *Roe v. Wade.*

Collins had tried to find out if Kavanaugh's deference to precedent changed when the underlying question was abortion—probably the issue of greatest importance to both his allies and his opponents. Kavanaugh told her that long-established precedent ought not to be trimmed, discarded, or overlooked. *Roe v. Wade* was decided forty-five years before Kavanaugh's nomination, and *Planned Parenthood v. Casey*, which relied upon it, had been on the books for a quarter of a century. Kavanaugh explained that honoring longstanding precedent "is essential to maintaining public confidence." And when Collins asked him if five justices should overturn such a long-established precedent if they thought it had been wrongly decided, Kavanaugh "emphatically said no." In other words, *Roe v. Wade* should be overturned only with the votes of more than the five Republican appointees.

For months, Democrats and liberal activists had portrayed Kavanaugh as not to be trusted. Anticipating that such groups would contradict her assessment of Kavanaugh's approach to *Roe* by pointing to President Trump's campaign promise to nominate only justices who would overturn *Roe*, Collins observed that the same pledge had appeared in every Republican platform since at least 1980, but that Republican presidents had appointed three justices—Sandra Day O'Connor, David Souter, and Anthony Kennedy—who joined the *Casey* decision reaffirming *Roe*. Collins recalled the same liberal groups that opposed Kavanaugh sporting "Stop Souter or Women Will Die" badges when Souter was nominated in 1990, two years before he joined the majority in *Casey*. Lest Democrats think Collins was the lone prominent pro-choice woman supporting Kavanaugh, she cited Lisa Blatt's public endorsement at Kavanaugh's hearings.

After poking holes in the portrayal of Kavanaugh as the next Scalia or as beholden to pro-lifers, Collins acknowledged that the scope of the Senate's advice and consent function changed when Christine Blasey Ford emerged on the scene. Collins waited until she was more than twenty minutes into her floor speech before raising Ford's allegations. When she did address the flood of sexual harassment allegations, she chose not to play the prosecutor and instead tried to determine the judge's fitness.

> The confirmation process now involves evaluating whether or not Judge Kavanaugh committed sexual assault and lied about it to the Judiciary Committee. Some argue that, because this is a lifetime appointment to our highest court, the public interest requires that doubts be resolved against the nominee. Others see the public interest as embodied in our long-established tradition of affording to those accused of misconduct a presumption of innocence. In cases in which the facts are unclear, they would argue that the question should be resolved in favor of the nominee.
>
> Mr. President, I understand both viewpoints. This debate is complicated further by the fact that the Senate confirmation process is not a trial. But certain fundamental legal principles about due process, the presumption of innocence and fairness do bear on my thinking, and I cannot abandon them. In evaluating any given claim of misconduct, we will be ill-served in the long run if we abandon the presumption of innocence and fairness, tempting though it may be. We must always remember that it is when passions are most inflamed that fairness is most in jeopardy. The presumption of innocence is relevant to the advice-and-consent function when an accusation departs from a nominee's otherwise exemplary record. I worry that departing from this presumption could lead to a lack of public faith in the judiciary and would be hugely damaging to the confirmation process moving forward.
>
> Some of the allegations levied against Judge Kavanaugh illustrate why the presumption of innocence is so important.

I am thinking in particular not of the allegations raised by Professor Ford, but of the allegation that when he was a teenager, Judge Kavanaugh drugged multiple girls and used their weakened state to facilitate gang rape. This outlandish allegation was put forth without any credible supporting evidence and simply parroted public statements of others. That such an allegation can find its way into the Supreme Court confirmation process is a stark reminder about why the presumption of innocence is so ingrained in our American consciousness.

Mr. President, I listened carefully to Christine Blasey Ford's testimony before the Judiciary Committee. I found her testimony to be sincere, painful, and compelling. I believe that she is a survivor of a sexual assault and that this trauma has upended her life. Nevertheless, the four witnesses she named could not corroborate any of the events of that evening gathering where she says the assault occurred. None of the individuals Professor Ford says were at the party has any recollection at all of that night. Judge Kavanaugh forcefully denied the allegations under penalty of perjury. Mark Judge denied under penalty of felony that he had witnessed an assault. P. J. Smyth, another person allegedly at the party, denied that he was there under penalty of felony. Professor Ford's lifelong friend Leland Keyser indicated that under penalty of felony she does not remember that party. And Ms. Keyser went further. She indicated that not only does she not remember a night like that, but also that she does not even know Brett Kavanaugh.

In addition to the lack of corroborating evidence, we also learned some facts that raised more questions. For instance, since these allegations have become public, Professor Ford testified that not a single person has contacted her to say I was at the party that night. Furthermore, the professor testified that although she does not remember how she got home that evening, she knew that because of the distance she would have needed a ride, yet not a single person has come forward to say that they were the one who drove her home or were in the car with her that night. And Professor Ford also indicated that, even though she left that small gathering of six or so people abruptly and without saying good-bye, and distraught, none of them called her the next day or ever to ask why she left, is she okay? Not even her closest friend, Ms. Keyser.

Mr. President, the Constitution does not provide guidance on how we are supposed to evaluate these competing claims. It leaves that decision up to each senator. This is not a criminal trial, and I do not believe that the claims such as these need to be proved beyond a reasonable doubt. Nevertheless, fairness would dictate that the claims at least should meet a threshold of more likely than not as our standard. The facts presented do not mean that Professor Ford was not sexually assaulted that night or at some other time, but they do lead me to conclude that the allegations fail to meet the more-likely-than-not standard. Therefore, I do not believe that these charges can fairly prevent Judge Kavanaugh from serving on the court.

Collins's defense of the presumption of innocence and her insistence on a standard of more likely than not, which she said Ford had not met, undermined the Democrats' case against Kavanaugh. But the senator made it clear that she was not attacking Ford. Indeed, she thought those who wanted to engineer Kavanaugh's defeat cared little about Ford, as evidenced by Ford's testimony and the handling of her allegations by Kavanaugh's opponents. Collins ended her remarks by expressing her hope that Kavanaugh would work to bring about fewer five-to-four decisions and work to instill public confidence in the judiciary.

Collins's pledge to vote for Kavanaugh all but ensured his confirmation. Every Trump-state Democrat pledged to vote against

Kavanaugh except Joe Manchin—who, unlike Donnelly, Heitkamp, and McCaskill, won reelection to the Senate a month later. Jeff Flake, having voted for Kavanaugh in the Judiciary Committee, did not flake again; he voted for confirmation. Collins's, Flake's, and Manchin's votes gave Senator Lisa Murkowski of Alaska cover to break with her party without defeating confirmation.

There was one complication, however. After the vote to end debate on Kavanaugh's nomination, Senator Steve Daines of Montana, a Republican and a vote for Kavanaugh's confirmation, was headed home to walk his daughter down the aisle at her wedding on October 6—the day of the final vote. If Daines went home and Murkowski defected, Kavanaugh would no longer have the votes for confirmation. The problem was quickly solved with Murkowski's cooperation. Reviving an old Senate tradition of "paired votes," she agreed to vote "present" instead of "no" so that Daines could be at his daughter's wedding. On Saturday, the U.S. Senate—with Vice President Pence presiding in case a tie-breaking vote was necessary—voted fifty to forty-eight to confirm Kavanaugh.

Liberal activists and opportunistic lawyers, who had remained publicly hopeful until the end, were apoplectic. As senators cast their votes, protesters in the gallery and in the halls began shrieking, "Shame!" and chanting, "I did not consent."

"That was a difficult day," Debra Katz later told law students at the University of Wisconsin. "I remember pulling up to the Capitol, and the lawyers also needed security. And we pulled up to the Capitol through a secret entrance, and I saw throngs—gorgeous, gorgeous throngs—of mostly young people who were there with signs saying, 'I believe Dr. Ford.' I think the world believed Dr. Ford. Unfortunately fifty members of the Senate did not care."

While Katz's clan mourned, Kavanaugh's supporters celebrated in the one spot in the "swamp" where it was safe to do so in public—the Trump International Hotel in the Old Post Office building. Since its opening in 2016, the hotel has been a favorite haunt for Trump administration officials and Republicans. No angry mob of progressives would chase them out. After Kavanaugh's Saturday afternoon confirmation, officials from the Justice Department, White House, and staffers from several Republican senators took refuge in the hotel to celebrate Kavanaugh's win.

The Benjamin Bar and Lounge, the hotel's inner sanctum named after Benjamin Franklin, was teeming with Trump supporters sporting red MAGA hats and Trump pins, side by side with Republican aides to Collins, Graham, and Grassley. Gina Loudon, a member of the Trump campaign's media advisory board, rounded up Trump fans to pose for photos behind a blue and white "Trump 2020" flag. As Loudon's crew burst into sporadic cheers and chants of "Trump!" the representatives of Republican officialdom kept their distance, careful to stay out of the photos that would be splashed across Instagram and Facebook. The mood was that of a Trump campaign rally, but this time the hero was Kavanaugh. The Republican staffers attributed Kavanaugh's success in large part to Michael Avenatti's antics and the personal attacks against Kavanaugh that were easily refuted. "Sunlight is the best disinfectant," they agreed.

The Left's coalition of angry protesters woke early the next morning. While Chief Justice Roberts administered the oath of office to Kavanaugh in a private ceremony in the Supreme Court building, protesters outside pushed past a police line and stormed the steps. Pounding on the massive bronze doors, they yelled, "Brett Kavanaugh, not my judge!" The demonstration was unlawful, but the actual threat of a breach of the building was small. The eighty-year-old doors weigh thirteen tons and stand seventeen feet high and nine and a half feet wide. The side doors through which lawyers, the press, and visitors enter would have been easier to breach, but not nearly as dramatic. Images of shrieking protesters slapping the doors and climbing into the lap of the marble statue *Contemplation of Justice* were broadcast on cable news throughout the day, inspiring demonstrations in cities across the country and encouraging an army of protesters to join Katz's crusade.

CHAPTER 9

Collateral Damage

Christine Blasey Ford's decision to come forward was a costly one, particularly for her supporters. Her fans sent her nearly $650,000 through the crowdfunding platform GoFundMe. The initial appeal described Ford as "a Palo Alto mom" who was "scared" by the "right wing smear machine" and needed your money to survive. She told the Senate Judiciary Committee in her hearing that she was aware of the ongoing fundraisers but had not yet decided how to manage them. When the hearings ended, she posted regular updates on the fundraising page to keep the cash coming.

"I feel like all of you who have made a contribution are on this journey with me, which is very heartening," Ford wrote in an update on October 3, 2018. "And some journey it has been and continues to be." She then explained that the costs she was incurring—"security, housing, transportation and other related expenses"—were greater than she expected, so she needed to raise more funds to take on Brett Kavanaugh. She finally closed the GoFundMe account on the day before Thanksgiving.

"Because of your support, I feel hopeful that our lives will return to normal," Ford wrote to her 13,969 donors. "The funds you have sent through GoFundMe have been a godsend." Part of the donations had gone to "reasonable" expenses such as physical and home security, and the rest would cover future security or would be donated to various groups she deemed worthy of her support, such as "organizations that support trauma survivors." She added that she would post additional updates on how she was spending her donors' money. Six months later, she had posted no updates.

Never far from the limelight during those six months, Ford hit the awards circuit in California. Elected officials, the mass media, special-interest groups, scientists, and academics acclaimed her as a hero worthy of honor, media attention, and large cash donations. She recorded a video message presenting *Sports Illustrated*'s Inspiration of the Year award to former Michigan State University gymnast Rachael Denhollander. State Assemblyman Marc Berman had her named California's "Woman of the Year," and Congresswoman Jackie Speier nominated her for the annual John F. Kennedy Profile in Courage Award. Ford was a finalist for *Time*'s "Person of the Year" feature and was one of the magazine's "100 most influential pioneers, leaders, titans, artists, and icons of 2019." The accompanying tribute, composed by Senator Kamala Harris, a future Democratic presidential candidate, noted that she "shook Washington and the country" and celebrated her courage "in the face of those who wished to silence her."

Faculty members, students, and graduates of the University of North Carolina nominated Ford for the Distinguished Alumna and Alumnus Award in recognition of the "courage it took for her to take the moral and ethical stand that she did in testifying about her sexual assault experience in front of the world." Raliance, a "national partnership dedicated to ending sexual violence in one generation" founded with a multimillion-dollar investment from the National Football League, named Ford its Person of the Year because of the "global impact" of her testimony against Kavanaugh.

The American Psychological Association established a grant in Ford's honor as the result of a GoFundMe campaign by Heidi Li

Feldman, a law professor at Georgetown University. "Watching Christine Blasey Ford testify, I realized her professional skills as a collaborator and educator bolstered her ability to participate effectively," Feldman wrote. "I also feared that she would not be recognized, remembered and valued for her keen professional achievements as well as her keen sense of civic responsibility."

Perhaps the only person to emerge from the Kavanaugh battle with as much acclaim as Ford was Debra Katz. After the hearing, Katz received the *Washington Business Journal's* C-Suite award, and the legal rating service Super Lawyers named her a top D.C. laywer. The Women's Bar Association gave Katz its "Dare to Make an Impact" award. U.S. News–Best Lawyers designated her firm one of 2019's "best," Law360 named her a "Titan of the Plaintiffs Bar" in 2019, and *Ms.* magazine gave Katz its Wonder Woman award.

The accolades were not universal, however. Judicial Watch, a conservative legal organization, filed a complaint with the Board on Professional Responsibility for the District of Columbia Court of Appeals alleging that Katz and her co-counsel, Lisa Banks and Michael Bromwich, deliberately disregarded Ford's stated aversion to traveling to Washington to appear before the Senate: "Their failure to inform their client of the offer to have Committee staff investigate Dr. Ford in California was dishonest at worst and careless at best. Either way, it is inexcusable, and raises substantial questions about their character and fitness to practice law. It warrants a full investigation by the Office of Disciplinary Counsel."

The D.C. bar seems unlikely to distance itself from the attorneys, however, as its president-elect, Susan Hoffman, hosted Katz and Bromwich for an uncritical conversation about their work with the Washington Lawyers Committee. Katz became a mainstay of the academic and liberal activist speaking circuit in the months after Ford's testimony, using her appearances to shape the enduring public perception of what happened. No longer obliged to masquerade as an apolitical lawyer at the service of the U.S. Senate, Katz has been furious. She told an audience at the University of Baltimore's "Applied Feminism and #MeToo" feminist legal theory conference, "You bet we were angry," and, "Fighting is much better than feeling depressed."

Katz is angry with men, particularly white men, insisting that it is "really important that we consider issues of class and race and privilege when we think about how and why we got as far as we did in demanding that Dr. Ford be given an opportunity" to take down Kavanaugh:

> We must ponder the very real possibility that had Dr. Ford not come from the same background, and the same race, and the same class, and the same country club as Brett Kavanaugh, had she not had an impeccable academic record, and stellar professional credentials, if she was not on the faculty of Stanford with seventy publications to her name, if she wasn't married to a man with two children, would she have been given the opportunity? Or would Senator Grassley and others have made the political calculation that she was expendable and we could bury her?...When I think about her role in history, I don't think about the white men on the Judiciary Committee, I think of the diverse young people outside the Capitol, standing up for her with their bodies and their words. That is the lasting impact of her bravery.

Katz argued that Ford "cooperated fully, even though the process was fixed and the result was a foregone conclusion," while Kavanaugh "was belligerent; he oozed with rage, and contempt for the process." She praised the anti-Kavanaugh activists: "Had there not been strong forces, organized forces, people in the street like you all, they would have figured out a way to bury her." The Trump administration, she charged, was motivated by "relentless cruelty," and the consequences of Kavanaugh's making it to the Supreme Court will "haunt us for generations."

Then for the first time, Katz revealed something about Christine Blasey Ford's motive in airing her last-minute allegations that had not yet been made public. Before the confirmation, Ford had maintained that she came forward out of a sense of civic duty to provide information that she thought senators needed to know before voting on Kavanaugh. Among friends at the "Applied Feminism and #MeToo" conference, however, Katz admitted that Ford came forward, in part, to taint any Supreme Court decision altering *Roe v. Wade* by undermining Kavanaugh's authority:

> In the aftermath of these hearings, I believe that Christine's testimony brought about more good than the harm misogynist Republicans caused by allowing Kavanaugh on the Court. We were going to have a conservative [justice]...elections have consequences, but he will always have an asterisk next to his name. When he takes a scalpel to *Roe v. Wade*, we will know who he is, we know his character, and we know what motivates him, and that is important; it is important that we know, and that is part of what motivated Christine.

Ford's audience was not the Senate, as Katz had previously suggested, but the American people. If they could be persuaded that Justice Kavanaugh was a predator, then they might not accept a future ruling by the five Republican-appointed justices altering the right to obtain an abortion established by *Roe v. Wade*. Had the Senate understood Ford's real motivation, as described by Katz, it might have appreciated more fully the pressure that "organized forces" were applying.

The presumption that Kavanaugh is a threat to *Roe* is not supported by his public or private comments before or after his confirmation. In her speech explaining her vote to confirm him, Senator Susan Collins reported that he had "emphatically said no" when asked in private whether long-established precedents, such as *Roe*, ought to be overturned by five of the current justices.

Unlike President Trump's previous Supreme Court appointee, Justice Neil Gorsuch, Justice Kavanaugh declined to speak at the Federalist

Society's national lawyers' convention in Washington, D.C., one month after his confirmation. Gorsuch had used the occasion in 2017 to respond to criticism of himself and to lampoon the idea that the Federalist Society was a secretive group taking over the federal judiciary. In 2018, Justice Kavanaugh attended the convention and posed for pictures, but he sat silent.

Kavanaugh offered his first post-confirmation public remarks in May 2019 on stage with Justice Kennedy, his former boss, at a judicial conference of the Seventh Circuit. The new justice explained that he hoped to follow Kennedy's approach to judging and to continue his "legacy of civility." Before signing off on an opinion or asking a question during an oral argument, Kavanaugh said that he asks himself, "What would Justice Kennedy...think about this?" When it came to *Roe*, Kennedy thought it ought not to be overturned—as he made clear in his decision in *Planned Parenthood v. Casey*. If Kavanaugh really meant what he said, then he is no threat to the rights created in *Roe*.

Such considerations, however, have not altered the animosity of Kavanaugh's opponents who point to his emotional self-defense before the Senate as evidence that he is incapable of fairly administering justice. More than nine hundred law professors signed a letter to the Senate arguing that his testimony "displayed a lack of judicial temperament that would be disqualifying for any court, and certainly for elevation to the highest court of this land." The retired justice John Paul Stevens, appointed by President Gerald Ford, reinforced their case when he told an audience of retirees in Boca Raton, Florida, that while he initially thought Kavanaugh "should be selected" as the justice to replace Kennedy, he had changed his view after watching Kavanaugh's "performance in the hearings."

Recognizing the damage being done to his reputation, Kavanaugh penned a rebuttal that was published in the *Wall Street Journal* just before the vote on his nomination:

> I might have been too emotional at times. I know that my tone was sharp, and I said a few things I should not have said. I

hope everyone can understand that I was there as a son, husband and dad. I testified with five people foremost in my mind: my mom, my dad, my wife, and most of all my daughters.

Going forward, you can count on me to be the same kind of judge and person I have been for my entire 28-year legal career: hardworking, even-keeled, open-minded, independent and dedicated to the Constitution and the public good. As a judge, I have always treated colleagues and litigants with the utmost respect. I have been known for my courtesy on and off the bench. I have not changed.

As the vote on Kavanaugh's nomination approached, Justice Stevens's words increased the political pressure but were not going to prevent confirmation. Some of Kavanaugh's colleagues in the federal judiciary then joined the effort to halt his confirmation. Judge Karen LeCraft Henderson, who sat on the same federal appellate court as Kavanaugh, referred miscellaneous complaints against him filed by members of the general public to the chief justice of the United States hours before the Senate's vote on confirmation. "The complaints do not pertain to any conduct in which Judge Kavanaugh engaged as a judge," she wrote. "The complaints seek investigations only of the public statements he has made as a nominee to the Supreme Court of the United States."

Chief Justice Roberts did not act before Kavanaugh's confirmation. Afterward, he referred the complaints to a judicial council formed from the U.S. Court of Appeals for the Tenth Circuit—a court with no ties to Kavanaugh. Those judges dismissed the eighty-three ethics complaints on the grounds that they did not have jurisdiction over a justice of the Supreme Court. While the press hyped the complaints as pertaining to "judicial misconduct," Tenth Circuit chief judge Tim Tymkovich wrote that they dealt with "some miscellaneous assertions" and with allegations that Kavanaugh "made inappropriate partisan statements that demonstrate bias and a lack of judicial temperament; and treated members of the Senate Judiciary Committee with disrespect." The "judicial misconduct" complaints had nothing to do with Kavanaugh's judicial record or, for that matter, the allegations of sexual misconduct lodged against him. Much as Tymkovich and his colleagues may have wanted to rule on the merits of the complaints, they were obliged to dismiss them because Kavanaugh was "no longer a judge covered by the [Judicial Conduct and Disability Act]."

When Tymkovich was nominated for the Tenth Circuit by President George W. Bush, Kavanaugh worked in the White House Counsel's Office. In a separate opinion, Judge Tymkovich addressed the question of whether Kavanaugh's role in his appointment compromised his impartiality. Kavanaugh's involvement, Tymokovich wrote, amounted to an email "proposing a press release about numerous judicial nominees, one of whom was me." Kavanaugh's opponents smelled collusion, however, and took issue with Tymkovich's presence on President Trump's shortlists for future vacancies on the Supreme Court. Two men appealed Tymkovich's decision to dismiss the complaints—Jeremy Bates, a member of the New York City Bar's professional ethics committee and a former aide to retired Democratic senator Byron Dorgan, and Paul Horvitz, a former journalist from Massachusetts who regularly tweets anti-Trump and anti-Kavanaugh messages.

Bates's appeal charged that Tymkovich's decision was "unlawful, inequitable, and wrong," while Horvitz's appeal argued that the judicial council selected by Chief Justice Roberts should be disqualified from ruling on any appeals because it ruled against the original complaints. More appeals flooded in, and Tymkovich dismissed them for the same reason that he had dismissed the complaints—Kavanaugh's conduct as a nominee was not reviewable after the Senate confirmed him. Bates and Horvitz, however, would not give up their desire to see investigations of Kavanaugh continue in perpetuity. After losing repeatedly through the normal review process, the duo turned to a committee of the Judicial Conference of the United States and asked it to rule in their favor because other federal judges had repeatedly told them no.

The ongoing battle over the ethics complaints was intended to reinforce the organized Left's assertion that the allegations against Kavanaugh were never fully investigated—despite the Senate's investigation and the FBI's multiple background investigations. Throughout his career as a federal judge, Kavanaugh had spoken at conferences and taught at universities. After his confirmation to the Supreme Court, he made plans to teach a two-week class on constitutional history for George Mason University's Antonin Scalia Law School in the summer of 2019. GMU is located in Fairfax, Virginia—a Washington, D.C., suburb outside the beltway—and the Scalia Law School is in Arlington, Virginia, which is a suburb of D.C. and is located adjacent to the district, separated by the Potomac River. Kavanaugh's course, titled "Creation of the Constitution," was scheduled to be offered to students abroad in Runnymede, England, for two weeks as the 2019 calendar turned from July to August. Such courses are commonplace for Supreme Court justices—Justice Neil Gorsuch, who replaced the Scalia School of Law's namesake on the high court, taught a similar course in 2018 in Italy. When Justice Kennedy skipped his annual trek to Salzburg, Austria, for a University of the Pacific summer program in 2016, it set off a frenzy of questions about his potential retirement. Kennedy returned to the school and was teaching his 28th year in Austria in July 2018 when President Trump named Kavanaugh as Kennedy's successor at the White House. The left, however, was bound and determined to deny Kavanaugh the same opportunity that all of his colleagues had. Demand Justice began running attack ads on Facebook aimed at students, parents, alumni, and anyone else with a connection to George Mason University online. The ads featured an image of Kavanaugh with eyes covered by a black bar next to the words, "TELL GEORGE MASON UNIVERSITY: FIRE KAVANAUGH." The ads linked to a petition saying, "#CancelKavanaughGMU," and demanded that the university sever all ties with Kavanaugh and issue a "formal apology from administration to survivors." Nearly fourteen thousand people signed the petition more than two months before the course was scheduled to begin, and many were not affiliated with George

Mason University. The law school's total enrollment was 525, according to its website, and students began signing up for the study abroad course with Kavanaugh by the time Demand Justice had gotten wind of the school's plans in the spring. The class, which served only as an elective credit, was made available to law students in February and was oversubscribed by the following month.

Undergraduate students did not care. Egged on by Demand Justice, protesters carried hand-made signs and Demand Justice's professionally printed ones to a "teach-in" on campus. The protesters flooded administration meetings and the College Fix captured a video of female students at one administration meeting telling the university's leadership that "the hiring of Kavanaugh threatens the mental wellbeing of all survivors on campus." Members of the faculty senate called for a new investigation of Kavanaugh. GMU's president, Ángel Cabrera, declined to question the judgment that placed Kavanaugh on the Supreme Court. "This is not a crazy appointment," he told the faculty on video, which was captured by the College Fix. "This is a Supreme Court justice who is going to be teaching about the United States Constitution."

The Scalia Law School did not cower before the organized mob. Other institutions with a more personal connection to Kavanaugh underwent an entirely different level of scrutiny and reacted differently. The student body at Yale, Kavanaugh's undergraduate and law school alma mater, was largely against Kavanaugh's appointment from the beginning, but it became more aggressive as his confirmation became more likely. Two hundred and fifty law students, faculty, and alumni joined to declare, "People will die if he is confirmed." When the sexual assault allegations were lodged months later, the students and some faculty lost their minds. More than three hundred of them swarmed the law school for a sit-in, classes were canceled, and posters emblazoned with the slogans #IBelieveChristineBlaseyFord and #IStillBelieveAnitaHill littered the hallways. The dean, Heather Gerken, had initially praised the nomination of Kavanaugh, but she quickly became silent and then changed her tune as fifty of her colleagues wrote to the U.S. Senate seeking to delay his confirmation.

"As dean, I cannot take a position on the nomination, but I am so proud of the work our community is doing to engage with these issues, and I stand with them in supporting the importance of fair process, the rule of law, and the integrity of the legal system," Gerken said before Christine Blasey Ford's hearing.

On the day of the Ford hearing, hundreds of Yale Law students and faculty gathered in the Sterling Law Building that had hosted the anti-Kavanaugh demonstrations to watch the event on television together. They were not prepared to change their minds. "We are watching the collapse of the judicial nomination process in the era of extreme partisan ideological polarization," said law professor John Fabian Witt to Yale's campus newspaper during the Ford watch party. "I still stand behind the law school professors' letter."

The Yale faculty members were far from alone in having made up their minds about fact and fiction, innocence and guilt, in the Kavanaugh controversy before the Senate and FBI concluded their work. Projecting their own teenage grievances and high school traumas onto the controversy, they cast Kavanaugh as the villain in their own tragedies. For example, Issac J. Bailey, an award-winning journalist a decade younger than Kavanaugh, attended not Yale, but Davidson College in North Carolina where he somehow acquired special insight into Kavanaugh's behavior. In "I Went to College with Men Like Kavanaugh. That's Why I Know He's Probably Lying about His Drinking," which was published in the online journal the Root, Bailey wrote:

> At Davidson, I saw men of privilege, just like Kavanaugh, get disgustingly drunk during parties on the weekends to the point of passing out or almost passing out, or stumbling back to their dorm room with equally drunk women on their arms—and get up on Monday morning and attend classes as though the weekend never happened.... And they found time

to make it to the chemistry lab and spent several hours in the library, sometimes after a sports practice. That's not a practice unique to privileged white men, but it is telling that Kavanaugh used his status as a privileged white man—because he got into Yale—as a reason to believe he never could have behaved in such a manner.

Bailey regarded himself as an unimpeachable narrator with "a near-perfect view of such behavior in college because I never got drunk and could watch it all while sober." He also interviewed his classmates about what Kavanaugh might have done:

> Since the Kavanaugh story began galvanizing the country, I've heard from some of my former classmates who tell me, in no uncertain terms, that that kind of drinking was prevalent in colleges like ours and that many people who are upstanding citizens and leaders today participated when we were in college.... They are not proud of these moments but are willing to own up to them and say that they are better people today. Why couldn't Kavanaugh simply do the same? Probably because it would give more credence to his primary accuser's claim that he tried to rape her in high school when he was drunk. That's the heart of Christine Blasey Ford's allegation. At this point, it is reasonable to say that Blasey Ford is telling the truth and Kavanaugh could have done something he can't even remember because he was too drunk.

Bailey does not mention that Kavanaugh plainly acknowledged his alcohol consumption, repeating "I like beer" so frequently that it became an Internet meme. This journalist—a recipient of a prestigious Nieman Fellowship at Harvard—believed he had everything he needed to conclude that Kavanaugh "was probably lying." As for the accuser, whom he had not investigated, "I have zero questions of Ford's credibility—zero."

Bailey's willingness to judge Kavanaugh on the basis of people he knew who were supposedly just like him was shared by many other commentators, viewers, and writers. Typecasting Kavanaugh as the villain in one's own tragedy became a popular pastime for progressives. People who had no direct connection to Kavanaugh but were acquainted with private single-sex high schools in the Washington area jumped at the opportunity to take potshots at their own or rival school. Writing for Slate, Alexandra Lescaze produced one of the more notable examples of professing knowledge without relying on evidence or experience: "We Didn't Call It Rape: I know what happened at prep school parties in the 1980s. The Brett Kavanaugh and Mark Judge allegations are upsettingly familiar."

Lescaze, who attended the National Cathedral School in Washington a few years after Christine Blasey Ford left Holton-Arms, did not know Ford, but Ford's allegations set off a flurry of "fraught emails and chats" among Lescaze's high school friends.

"A large part of my high school experience were [sic] the parties at cavernous houses with multiple bedrooms, huge dark basements with enormous sofas and yards, and lots and lots of beer," Lescaze wrote. "No parents—thinking back on it now, as a parent myself—were ever around. We traveled in groups and knew never to leave a friend alone at a party, but there was so much drinking that we sometimes lost track of each other. It could be difficult to know where your friends were and—if they were in a room with a boy—what was going on in there."

Ford described a small gathering of between four and six persons; the number varied in her different accounts. She first suggested that the assault took place in 1983, and Kavanaugh produced a calendar from that year documenting his whereabouts. Kavanaugh's calendar contained a notation for "Beach Week"—when teenagers partied at beach houses during the summer. Lescaze's own unhappy memories of Beach Week included her ex-boyfriend heroically forestalling boys "presumably" getting ready to have sex with a drunk woman and "a campfire circle that could have started as a game of spin the bottle" but escalated from kissing to groping.

"[I]t was often like this: a solitary girl who found herself helpless against the power of a group of boys," Lescaze wrote. "It's why Ford's description of her alleged attack sounded so plausible to me—two drunk boys who had cornered her and were egging each other on. We went through years of parties like this intimidated, afraid, and horrified. And yet it was also just the way things were."

Lescaze did not explain why she frequented parties that terrified her but wrote that the absence of boys at her all-girls' high school was "part of why every encounter became sexualized."

"Now it's clear to me how powerless I felt throughout high school," Lescaze wrote. "The entire time I attended NCS, we had a male head-master. We were a school for girls, which was presumably meant to empower us, but the boys were still in charge. High school is where we learned to put up with it. And now, as the prep-school boys are running the country and a kind of masculine backlash has taken hold of our democracy, it feels like we're back in high school again."

One institution in particular suffered from its association with Kava-naugh's youth: Georgetown Preparatory School. The day before Ford's Senate hearing, the school issued a statement explaining that the *Washington Post*, *New York Times*, and other outlets, "in pursuit of their own agenda, have published articles about and including Georgetown Preparatory School without seeking comment or response from the School."

The statement labeled disparaging depictions of the school as demon-strably false and touted the school's reputation as the oldest Catholic high school in the United States—founded in 1789—with a mission of "form-ing men of conscience, competence, courage, and compassion; men of faith and men for others."

"It is all too easy to paint malicious stereotypes about a group of people based on assumptions about their gender, ethnicity, or their sta-tion in life," the Georgetown Prep statement read. "Part of our educa-tional foundation is the continued evaluation of everything that we do, personally and institutionally, that we may live most fully the command-ment to love God and neighbor. The core of our mission is to be men for and with others. Our students take that call to service seriously and give of their own time and effort to stand with and serve others in our nation and in the world, broadening their understanding about the reality of poverty and oppression."

The day Senator Feinstein elevated Ford's private allegation by acknowledging its existence and referring it to federal investigators, the Georgetown Prep community was overrun with reporters looking for dirt on Kavanaugh. Patrick Coyle, Georgetown Prep's spokesman, wrote in *National Review* about the reporters' deception:

> On the afternoon of Thursday, September 13, as parents arrived at our school to pick up students, a journalist from a major network camouflaged herself among them, avoiding identification at our front gate. She was subsequently found snooping around the halls of our main building and was escorted off campus. She later apologized. But others soon followed. One reporter from a national newspaper deceived his way into our library so that he could rummage through old yearbooks. Some of our alumni had news crews staked out in front of their houses. Reporters were even harassing their elderly parents, tracking down home addresses and banging on doors, demanding interviews.

More than sixty articles involving Georgetown Prep appeared in the *Washington Post*, which labeled the school as "a troubled, morally questionable symbol of a snobby elite" and charged that "disregard or mistreatment of women [was] widely accepted." The *Post* erroneously reported that because of the bad press relating to Kavanaugh, the institution was hunting for a new director of alumni relations—even though Georgetown Prep had posted the job months earlier in July. The paper acknowledged its error only after Coyle pressed it. The attacks continued as more than sixty Georgetown Prep alumni stepped forward to dispute Julie Swetnick's allegations against Kavanaugh.

"Instead of presenting a three-dimensional view of culture at George-town Prep and the type of young men it produces, reporters took up amateur cryptology, attempting [to] decode the obscure meanings of yearbook citations from 35 years in the past," Coyle wrote.

> It is hard not to wonder what has motivated all this deep indifference and indeed deep antipathy from the press. And it is harder still to avoid the conclusion that many simply sought an expedient narrative that would bolster the arguments made by their ideological allies, tipping the scales toward their preferred political outcome.... If there has been any self-reflection from the press in the aftermath of their barrage, it has been hard to find.

Evgenia Peretz, a contributing editor at *Vanity Fair* and an adjunct professor of journalism at New York University, prowled about the bowling alley to which some of Kavanaugh's classmates repaired for a class reunion. Her anthropological analysis of the gathering was printed as a feature for *Vanity Fair* under the title "'Men for Others, My Ass': After Kavanaugh, Inside Georgetown Prep's Culture of Omertà." ("Omertà" is the Mafia's code of silence.) Peretz evidently could not penetrate the inner sanctum of the bowling alley and therefore wrote her observations of the "all white" crowd's clothing and trips to the bathroom:

> Most are dressed in suburban dad wear: there are a lot of pleated khakis, some fleece, and brown Eddie Bauer–style shoes for the active, middle-aged bro. When they step outside the private room to use the restroom or meander, they do American Guy stuff. They take out their phones and type importantly. They check the score of Game Four of the World Series. They mutter skeptically about putting any hope in the Redskins this year. They order better drinks than what's apparently available inside. A handful of them have brought

their wives, who look like they wouldn't mind calling it a night. Up at the bar, one of the wives asks her husband what he wants to drink. "An Artois," he snaps at her. *Duh.*

Peretz followed the same formula as the *New York Times*' Kate Kelly and Robin Pogrebin: name and shame the attendees, eavesdrop on nameless white men whom you stereotype as belonging to a "bro" culture, and label the event as a "victory celebration" for Kavanaugh—even though he was not there. But Peretz took a more conspiratorial slant: the Georgetown Prep alumni were "bonded together by a shared history of mischief" and a secret code that was aimed at "preserving a certain world order." The conspirators, Peretz wrote, "aren't just Prep's alumni and students, but the school's network of Catholic priests, teachers, wives, and family members." The women who knew Kavanaugh in high school and supported him in 2018 were deliberately misleading the public, Peretz said anonymous women told her.

Peretz wrote that allegations of abuse occurring two decades after Kavanaugh's graduation were kept quiet because of the secret code Kavanaugh helped establish as a teenager. He was responsible not only for a single accuser's trauma, but also for anything unpleasant that happened later to anyone in the Prep orbit. By opposing Kavanaugh and the Catholic all-boys institution that produced him, you too could get revenge on bullies from your high school years.

"Kavanaugh and many of his friends were known to take their privilege as license to act with obnoxious abandon," Peretz wrote. "This type of group wasn't unique in the history of Georgetown Prep. Every senior class had a version—a band of bros, usually football players, who staked their claim as kings of the school. Indeed, anyone who's gone to any high school in America, or watched a John Hughes film, inherently gets the world order."

The collateral damage of the Kavanaugh controversy reached every corner of Washington, D.C., and his most vehement opponents knew it and did not care. In May 2019, former president Bill Clinton argued that the attacks on Kavanaugh were fitting, given Kavanaugh's work on Ken Starr's investigation of Clinton in the late 1990s.

"He didn't have any problem making Vince Foster's wife and children put up with three years of what he knew was a total charade," Bill Clinton said in Las Vegas while on stage with his wife, Hillary, for a speaking-tour stop titled "An Evening with the Clintons." The former president's comments echoed the lingering animosity Chelsea Clinton expressed during her "Rise Up for Roe" appearances. When Kavanaugh, in his opening statement at the hearing on Ford's accusations, attributed the attacks on his reputation in part to "revenge on behalf of the Clintons, and millions of dollars in money from outside left-wing partisan opposition groups," he was criticized for partisanship. Former president Clinton's comments lent credence to Kavanaugh's comments, but the same news organizations that raised questions about Kavanaugh's temperament and partisanship saw nothing to question in the president's vindictive view of Kavanaugh's predicament.

Those familiar with the inner workings of the Starr investigation, however, think Clinton had the wrong culprit. Reviewing a book on the scandals of the Clinton presidency for the *Wall Street Journal*, the journalist Quin Hillyer wrote that Kavanaugh helped him to separate fact from fiction at the direction of his superiors. Hillyer wrote a column saying Kavanaugh shared already-public information and walked him through information that "tended more to absolve the Clintons (on the specific issues at hand) than condemn them."

"Under instructions from Starr and others outranking him, Kavanaugh also privately walked several journalists through the public evidence as his report was being released," Hillyer wrote of his own experience for the *Washington Examiner*. "In doing so, he was particularly likely to emphasize little-noticed information that further exonerated, or cast an innocence on, the Clintons and their close associates."

None of this mattered to the attack dogs at Demand Justice led by the Clinton veteran Brian Fallon. In its first year of existence, it became the most influential progressive group focused on the federal judiciary, playing an indispensable role in altering the Senate's advice and consent function on Supreme Court nominations and changing the Democrats' calculus on judicial confirmations.

Fallon's stated reason for opposing anyone Trump nominated for the Supreme Court was to "build the muscle memory to organize around the courts." He succeeded, and Senate Democrats took notice. When Democrats and Republicans were poised to reach a compromise in April 2019 on how soon after the end of debate the full Senate could vote on a judicial confirmation, the Democrats' spines suddenly stiffened, and they forced Republicans to act unilaterally. When Majority Leader Mitch McConnell, with no Democratic support, shortened the time between debate and a vote on judicial nominees, he reportedly blamed Minority Leader Chuck Schumer, who was "scared of Brian Fallon."

Having failed to kill Kavanaugh's confirmation, Fallon set his sights on diluting the voting power of the justices appointed by President Trump by increasing the number of seats on the Supreme Court. In partnership with the group Pack the Courts, Demand Justice announced in February 2019 that it had raised five hundred thousand dollars and would press the Democratic presidential candidates in 2020 to support its cause. Many of these candidates quickly took notice. Pete Buttigieg, the mayor of South Bend, Indiana, was among the first to embrace the idea. "In some ways, it's no more a shattering of norms than what's already been done to get the judiciary to where it is today," he said.

A slew of other Democratic candidates expressed openness to changing the number of justices, which has stood at nine since 1869. Senators Cory Booker, Kirsten Gillibrand, Kamala Harris, and Elizabeth Warren, as well as former congressman Robert "Beto" O'Rourke, have all indicated an openness to remaking the Supreme Court. Gillibrand also vowed that she would "only nominate judges who will uphold *Roe v. Wade*." Harris and other candidates have made similar promises. Such progressive promises were no coincidence. In April 2019, Demand Justice issued report cards grading Democratic senators' "response to the far-right capture of our courts during Trump's first two years in office."

Warren got an A, Booker got an A-, and Gillibrand and Harris scored B+. Two Democratic presidential candidates flunked, namely, Minnesota's Amy Klobuchar and Colorado's Michael Bennet. Fallon denounced Bennet's bipartisan gesture of introducing his fellow Coloradan Neil Gorsuch at the Judiciary Committee hearings on his nomination and his votes to confirm some of Trump's nominations to the federal appellate bench. Demand Justice's hostility was so strong that in May 2019 it paid approximately ten thousand dollars for anti-Bennet television ads in New Hampshire, despite Bennet's failure to register any detectable support in several polls there.

A five-figure ad buy against a presidential candidate polling at 0 percent in New Hampshire might seem excessive, but Fallon's message was clear: if you fail to conform, you will get whacked. Demand Justice's political approach to judicial appointments has been cast as an answer to the right-leaning Federalist Society, but Demand Justice is a participant in an entirely new arena. The days of decorum in the judicial selection process ended with the Kavanaugh fight. They were replaced by no-holds-barred fighting and ruthless politicking.

Mike Davis, the nominations counsel to former Judiciary Committee chairman Chuck Grassley, formed the Article III Project as the conservative answer to Demand Justice. "A3P will punch back," Davis announced, "and help confirm President Trump's judicial nominees, defend these new judges from left-wing attacks once confirmed, defend the integrity of the confirmation process, and fight back against the assaults on judicial independence—including radical court-packing, term-limit, and even impeachment schemes."

Before A3P, the right had made the left's campaign against Kavanaugh an effective issue in state judicial elections. The Republican State Leadership Committee spent more than one million dollars on ads in support of Brian Hagedorn's campaign for the Wisconsin Supreme Court. They tied attacks on Hagedorn to out-of-state special interest groups trying to do to Hagedorn what Kavanaugh's critics did in the fall of 2018. Hagedorn narrowly won his race in April 2019, showing that courts remained a critical issue to Wisconsin's conservative voters.

The aftermath of the Kavanaugh fight was painful for Democrats in Senate races in states that Trump had carried in 2016. Democrats who voted against Kavanaugh's confirmation lost their seats in Indiana, North Dakota, Missouri, and Florida. The controversy changed the midterm dynamics in each of those states, narrowing the enthusiasm gap between liberals hoping to retake Congress and conservatives seeking revenge for the anti-Kavanaugh votes.

Indiana provided a good test of what the electorate would look like for Trump-state Democrats. The home of both Vice President Mike Pence and South Bend *Wunderkind* Pete Buttigieg, Indiana turned blue for Obama and red for Trump. ABC News exit polls in 2018 showed that Senator Joe Donnelly's vote against Kavanaugh was an important factor for 53 percent of Indiana voters. Of that majority, 54 percent voted for the Republican challenger, Mike Braun. By comparison, those for whom health care was the most important issue voted for Donnelly by an overwhelming margin of 74 to 22 percent. Donnelly lost the election by a margin of nearly 6 percent to a political novice who presented himself as an outsider and tied himself to Trump. The vanquished Donnelly took a job at the nation's highest-grossing federal lobbying firm, Akin Gump, where he joined another victim of Kavanaugh's revenge: Heidi Heitkamp of North Dakota.

ABC News exit polls showed that Heitkamp's vote against Kavanaugh was a decisive factor in the votes of 47 percent of North Dakotans in 2018, and they voted nearly two-to-one in favor of her Republican challenger, Kevin Cramer. As North Dakota's only member of the U.S. House of Representatives, Cramer had experience getting votes statewide, but his 55 to 44 percent victory surprised Democrats expecting the "blue wave" of 2018 to save Heitkamp.

If not for her vote against Kavanaugh's confirmation, Claire McCaskill of Missouri might still reside in Washington. Her Republican opponent, Josh Hawley, the Show Me State's attorney general, campaigned shoulder to shoulder with Trump when the race was in a dead heat and made the Kavanaugh vote a major issue. Hawley pulled away after McCaskill's vote against Kavanaugh, winning by nearly 6 percent and more than 140,000 votes. ABC News exit polling showed that McCaskill's vote against Kavanaugh was a top factor for the majority of voters. Among those voting on Kavanaugh, Hawley won 52 to 46 percent. Hawley's victory was in large part attributable to suburban voters who had voted for McCaskill six years earlier. Suburban voters broke for Hawley 52 to 46 percent. Hawley won suburban men's votes by 11 points and suburban women's votes by 1 point.

In Montana and Florida, Democratic incumbents faced electorates that were less concerned about the Kavanaugh vote. Just 38 percent of Floridians and 45 percent of Montanans thought their senators' votes against Kavanaugh were important, as compared with a majority of voters in Indiana and Missouri and nearly half of voters in North Dakota. ABC News exit polling in Montana revealed that the majority's chief concern was that a candidate "shares my view of government." Floridians cited healthcare as a top issue, and more Floridians thought the Kavanaugh controversy did not matter at all than thought that it mattered most. The Democrat Jon Tester kept his seat in Montana, while Florida's Bill Nelson lost to his Republican challenger, Governor Rick Scott.

The one Democratic senator who voted to confirm Kavanaugh—West Virginia's Joe Manchin—may not have gotten the same lift for doing so as his Republican counterparts did. He did get the same reward, however, and returned to the Senate having neutralized the issue in the minds of Republican voters who would have otherwise ditched him for the state's attorney general, Patrick Morrisey. Approximately 40 percent of West Virginia voters in ABC News exit polling said they cared about Manchin's vote to confirm Kavanaugh, while more than a third said it did not matter at all. Far more critical to Manchin's success was his wonky opponent's abysmal favorability ratings. Manchin was viewed favorably by 49 percent of West Virginians and unfavorably by 47 percent. Morrisey's favorable/unfavorable ratings were under water at 40 to 55 percent.

While House seats were flipping from Republican to Democrat across the country, the blue wave never reached the Senate, and its momentum was reversed in vulnerable deep-red states such as Tennessee and Texas. Both the Republican and the Democratic candidates for Tennessee's open Senate seat said they would have voted for Kavanaugh. Both candidates had above-water approval ratings, but neither was as high as President Trump, and a plurality of Tennesseans in ABC News exit polling said they voted to put Republican Marsha Blackburn in the Senate as a sign of support for Trump.

In Texas, Senator Ted Cruz held off the media darling "Beto" O'Rourke, a Democratic congressman from El Paso. Fifty-nine percent of Texans said Cruz's vote to confirm Kavanaugh mattered, and Cruz won the pro-Kavanaugh voters by a margin of 60 to 40 percent. The narrowness of Cruz's margin of victory, 2.5 percent, or approximately 215,000 votes, suggested that without the Kavanaugh fight Cruz might have been a one-term senator.

When the dust settled on the midterm elections, Democrats were cheering their victories in the House as the culmination of a #MeToo reckoning and an anti-Kavanaugh backlash. The Anita Hill–Clarence Thomas controversy of 1991 yielded the "Year of the Woman" in the minds of Democratic voters. Following the Kavanaugh controversy, CNN's commentators sought to appropriate the label and declared, "It's not the 'Year of the Woman.' It's the 'Year of the Women.'" In the Senate, however, the winning women were Republican. Claire McCaskill and Heidi Heitkamp lost, Marsha Blackburn won, and Martha McSally was appointed to the Arizona seat held by the late John McCain and then, briefly, by Jon Kyl, who retired.

As a result of the Kavanaugh controversy and the 2018 election, the Republicans' Senate majority had grown by two seats when the new Congress convened in 2019. The Judiciary Committee gained two new women members, Republicans Marsha Blackburn of Tennessee and Joni

Ernst of Iowa, replacing Jeff Flake of Arizona and Orrin Hatch of Utah, who had both retired. The addition of Senator Josh Hawley expanded the Republican majority on the committee to two. The committee's new chairman was Lindsey Graham, as Chuck Grassley moved on to chairing the Finance Committee. The day after Christine Blasey Ford's hearing, Graham had warned his Democratic counterparts about what to expect:

> If I am chairman, next year, if we keep the majority and Sena-
> tor Grassley moves over—and I hope he doesn't because I
> think he's done a great job—I'm gonna remember this....
> There's the process before Kavanaugh and the process after
> Kavanaugh. If you want to vet the nominee, you can. If you
> want to delay things for the next election, you will not. If you
> try to destroy somebody, you will not get away with it.

However effectively a new Chairman Graham might restrain the character assassins among the senators, it has become clear that the media can do the job almost instantaneously. This reality has changed how judges on President Trump's Supreme Court shortlists have interacted with the public in the months since Kavanaugh's confirmation. After going through a federal appellate court nomination hearing in which Democratic senators displayed Texas judge Don Willett's tweets on printed placards—such as "I could support recognizing a constitutional right to marry bacon"—the judiciary's Twitter laureate stopped publishing on social media. He has said the lifetime appointment to the U.S. Court of Appeals for the Fifth Circuit meant there was no reelection nudge to participate online as there had been when he faced partisan judicial elections in Texas. Following his confirmation, Willett considered being an effective member of his court more important than the educational component of his social media usage.

Others embraced the public's attention. Judge Amy Coney Barrett was relatively unknown when she finished as the runner-up to Kavanaugh for Kennedy's seat. In the months since Kavanaugh's confirmation,

Barrett has spoken at law schools across the country, with several pit stops in Washington. Before the close of the Supreme Court's term in 2019, Barrett had spoken at Villanova University, near Philadelphia, the University of Virginia, and a Notre Dame alumni gathering at the Washington office of Jones Day, a firm President Trump has relied on since the days of his 2016 campaign. Her speeches have allowed her to introduce herself in private without the filter of the press or others hostile to her work and philosophy.

While Barrett has embraced her newfound celebrity, she has made it clear to audiences that she is not out to win a popularity contest. Speaking at Hillsdale College's Kirby Center in Washington in mid-May 2019, she emphasized that federal judges need "the courage of Robert Jackson" in their willingness to rule against the presidents who appointed them. Justice Jackson, she explained, dissented from the majority's opinion in *Korematsu v. United States*, which permitted the internment of Japanese Americans during World War II. By voting with the minority, Jackson had bucked the policy preference of his patron, President Franklin Roosevelt, who had appointed him solicitor general, attorney general, and eventually justice of the Supreme Court. Barrett told her audience at the Kirby Center:

> You are not there to decide cases as the public or as the press may want you to.... You're not there to win a popularity contest. You are there to do your duty and to follow the law wherever it may take you. Justice Scalia used to say that a judge who likes every result that she reaches is not a very good judge; in fact, she's a very bad judge. The law simply does not align with a judge's political preference or personal preference in every case. And so it will be the case that judges have to make hard decisions and that they have to decide cases in ways that yield outcomes that are not the outcomes that they would prefer. I've been at this only for about a year and a half, and I can attest that that has happened to me many times already.

Barrett said she approaches opinion-writing as though she were ruling against her own children or loved ones, and therefore strives never to be harsh. During a question-and-answer session, she rejected the idea that the Supreme Court has become more politicized and she shot down the suggestion that a judicial nominee's faith is relevant to his fitness for any court. She also discussed her solo dissent in a Second Amendment case that was sure to endear her to proponents of originalism and make gun-control advocates shake with rage. In *Kanter v. Barr*, two of Barrett's Seventh Circuit colleagues ruled that a man convicted of Medicaid fraud lost his Second Amendment right to possess a firearm because of his felony conviction. Barrett disagreed:

> That sounds kind of radical to say that felons can have firearms, but I think it's because what the longstanding prohibitions were and, in fact, had been, even under federal law until more recently.... What the history showed me was that there's a longstanding practice of saying that those who have, who pose a threat of violence to the community cannot have a firearm. And that makes sense, right? History is consistent with common sense. Those who would be risky with guns, those who would pose danger with guns, then the state can take guns away, but in the instance of someone who has not, the state has not shown that the person has demonstrated any risk. The mere status of having committed a felony—I found no historical support for saying that the state was then justified [in] taking it away.

By describing her own opinion as "radical," Barrett might have written a future Demand Justice attack ad against herself. The group had already drawn up plans to oppose her if Kavanaugh had withdrawn and if Trump had chosen her as his replacement. Her statement on her Second Amendment decision is sure to give progressives new ammunition against "Judge Dogma." President Trump's previous Supreme Court nominees,

Kavanaugh and Gorsuch, were at pains to depict their own judicial philosophy as well within the "mainstream" of American legal thought.

If Barrett was aware that her comments would likely incite new antagonists, she did not show any signs of caring, and her overflow audience responded enthusiastically. Her 2019 "originalism tour" continued at Georgetown Law School, where she delivered the keynote address at the Originalism Summer Seminar. The top draw at the weeklong originalism "boot camp" was Justice Gorsuch, and other Supreme Court hopefuls participated, including Justice Thomas Lee of the Utah Supreme Court, the brother of Utah's senior senator; Judge Diane Sykes of the U.S. Court of Appeals for the Seventh Circuit, one of two judges Trump referred to by name in a presidential debate with Hillary Clinton in 2016; and Judge Amul Thapar of the U.S. Court of Appeals for the Sixth Circuit, who is as active as Barrett on the legal speaking circuit. After Kavanaugh's nomination, Thapar told the Federalist Society's law school chapters that he would accept invitations to speak about originalism that came with the promise of more than twenty undergraduates in the audience. In the months thereafter, Thapar spoke at Brigham Young University, Notre Dame, and Georgetown Law School, where attendees were promised free Chick-fil-A.

To be clear, Georgetown's originalism boot camp and similar events are fundamentally different from the cattle calls of presidential candidates in New Hampshire and Iowa. The judges who come are interested in building the farm system of future originalists for the federal bench. The organizers prefer applicants who express an interest in a judicial clerkship over their less ambitious counterparts. The judges' jockeying for increased visibility in the legal community suggests that the brutality of Justice Kavanaugh's journey to the Supreme Court has not deterred Trump's shortlist members from pursuing a seat there for themselves.

Sources close to the jurists on Trump's shortlist and to those who compiled it have indicated that no one has removed himself from consideration since Kavanaugh's confirmation. But members of the younger generation of lawyers—law review editors, judicial clerks, government officials, and associates at leading law firms—have privately expressed to mentors and peers their growing unease about facing a campaign like the one mobilized against Kavanaugh. The Kavanaugh controversy's lasting effect on the judicial nominations process will be apparent when the next Supreme Court vacancy occurs, but its effect on the field of public servants from which presidents fill such vacancies may never be fully known.

Acknowledgments

F irst and foremost, I'm grateful to the sources, mentors, colleagues, and others who made this book possible. Given the subject and nature of this book, many sources risked personal and professional harm to ensure the facts reported here became public. Several mentors have provided the guidance and instruction necessary to know how to report and write *Search and Destroy* at a time when facts have hardly mattered more and been valued less. I will not identify these people here out of an abundance of caution.

This book would not have been possible without the dedication of Dylan Colligan and his team at Javelin. Dylan provided expert assistance throughout every stage of development for *Search and Destroy* and helped ensure that the adversity facing the project never morphed from pressure into stress.

It was an honor to work with Regnery Publishing, whose uncommon courage and devotion to truth is unmatched. Regnery does not scare easily, and an author could ask for nothing more.

Lastly, I'm thankful for my family and friends for putting up with me—and without me—throughout this process. Thanks for your love, patience, and support.

A Note on Sources

S earch and Destroy is the product of the author's original reporting on the Supreme Court, White House, Congress, and the judicial selection process from the earliest days of President Trump's 2016 presidential campaign to the present. Interviews were conducted on the record and on background with sources who work in all three branches of the federal government, in law and lobbying firms, in think tanks, schools, and universities, in nonprofit organizations, in private businesses, and elsewhere. Sources were granted varying degrees of anonymity in limited circumstances to enable them to provide details about ongoing criminal proceedings and to speak about the Kavanaugh confirmation without fear of retribution by their employers, colleagues, or others.

The primary source documents I have relied on include, but are not limited to, emails, text messages, encrypted messages, official transcripts of congressional investigators, legal complaints, FBI complaints, and numerous other relevant documents. Some names of persons and entities provided in such documents were withheld from publication when doing so was necessary to prevent harm to sources' safety and wellbeing.

Debra Katz, lawyer for Christine Blasey Ford, did not agree to an interview for this book and did not make her client available for an interview. Katz asked to read passages of the book in advance to "fact check" it instead of speaking with the author, and she was not provided prior review. Katz's private email correspondence with Senate Democrats and with Senate Republicans that is quoted in the text of this book is reproduced here in context with personal identifying information from the messages removed.

The following is a chapter-by-chapter accounting of sourcing for individual facts and comments included in *Search and Destroy*. Citations for specific facts and relevant context for the material of this book are provided hereafter. Any comment or fact not presented in the following notes was made directly to the author for use in this book.

Chapter 1

Led by Mitch McConnell, the Republicans responded by exercising the "nuclear option"....
Ryan Lovelace, "How Will the 'Nuclear Option' Affect Future Supreme Court Selections?," *Washington Examiner*, April 10, 2017, https://www. washingtonexaminer.com/how-will-the-nuclear-option-affect-future-supreme-court-selections.

Senator Jeff Merkley of Oregon complained that Gorsuch occupied a "stolen" seat....
Jeff Merkley, "Five #SCOTUS Justices—including Neil Gorsuch in a stolen seat—believe deliberate voter suppression is just fine in a democratic republic," *Twitter*, June 11, 2018, https://twitter.com/senjeffmerkley/status/1006258265229910016?lang=en.

...while former Vice President Joe Biden declared the appointment the "single most damaging thing" Trump had done as president.
Jason Devaney, "Biden: Gorsuch Appointment 'Single Most Damaging Thing' of Trump Presidency," *Newsmax*, March 29, 2018, https://www.newsmax.com/newsfront/joe-biden-neil-gorsuch-supreme-court-trump-presidency/2018/03/29/id/851536/.

Earlier in 2018, Congress had allocated seven hundred thousand dollars more for the Supreme Court than it has requested. The extra funds went toward security.

U.S. House of Representatives, lead sponsor: Rep. Ed Royce, "H.R. 1625-Consolidated Appropriations Act, 2018," March, 23, 2018, https://www.congress.gov/bill/115th-congress/house-bill/1625/text; the Administrative Office of the U.S. Courts, "The Judiciary FY 2018 Congressional Budget Summary Revised," June 2017, https://www.uscourts.gov/sites/default/files/fy_2018_congressional_budget_summary_0.pdf.

One Nation ... began running ads the next day....

One Nation, "SCOTUS," YouTube, June 28, 2018, https://www.youtube.com/channel/UCGjMWdz_BiE7QI39ejdsKyA/videos.

But neither Kavanaugh nor Gorsuch was on the list that Trump published during the campaign.

Donald Trump 2016 presidential campaign, "Donald J. Trump Finalizes List of Potential Supreme Court Justice Picks," donaldjtrump.com, September 23, 2016, https://www.donaldjtrump.com/press-releases/donald-j.-trump-adds-to-list-of-potential-supreme-court-justice-picks.

In March, Malcolm had included Kavanaugh in his first draft....

John Malcolm, "The Next Supreme Court Justice," The Daily Signal, March 30, 2016, https://www.dailysignal.com/2016/03/30/the-next-supreme-court-justice/.

...Malcolm recalled in July 2018.

Ryan Lovelace, "This Legal Scholar Put Brett Kavanaugh on President Trump's Radar in 2016," *National Law Journal*, July 31, 2018, https://www.law.com/nationallawjournal/2018/07/31/hold-this-legal-scholar-put-brett-kavanaugh-on-president-trumps-radar-in-2016/?slreturn=2 0190601150101.

"it's called the *Seven-Sky* case"....

Seven Sky v. Holder, 661 F.3d 1 (D.C. Cir. 2011).

But there were signs in his dissent that he might have upheld the mandate for the same reasons that Chief Justice Roberts eventually did.
National Federation of Independent Business v. Sebelius, 567 U.S. 519 (2012).

"The dogma lives loudly within you," Feinstein scolded.
Senator Dianne Feinstein, "Nominations: Amy Coney Barrett to be United States Circuit Judge for the Seventh Circuit," *U.S. Senate Judiciary Committee hearing*, September 6, 2017.

"Judge Dogma is on the list."
Donald F. McGahn, "17th Annual Barbara K. Olson Memorial Lecture," the Federalist Society, November 17, 2017.

Vice President Mike Pence's office ... approached Nicole Garnett of Notre Dame Law School. She was not interested, however, and directed Pence's office to her colleague Amy Coney Barrett.
Nicole Garnett referred questions about such conversations with Pence's office to her husband, Rick Garnett, who said in an email, "I don't think it would be appropriate for me to comment on any conversations that my wife may, or may not, have had."

Judge Barrett spoke about her decision to accept the job in a May 2019 speech to Hillsdale College in D.C. Barrett said her interest in taking the job was about "our tradition of judges upholding the rule of law" and that she "would have had no interest in the job if the job was about policy-making."

... Kavanaugh's name was floated to the *New York Times*....
Adam Liptak, "How President Trump Chose His Supreme Court Nominee," *New York Times*, February 6, 2017, https://www.nytimes.com/2017/02/06/us/politics/neil-gorsuch-trump-supreme-court-nominee.html.

America Rising ... worked with Republican officials and external conservative groups to secure Gorsuch's confirmation....

Ryan Lovelace, "Supreme Court confirmation week: Neil Gorsuch's game plan," *Washington Examiner,* March 20, 2017, https://www.washingtonexaminer.com/supreme-court-confirmation-week-neil-gorsuchs-game-plan.

America Rising…was quietly directed to begin vetting Kavanaugh in the summer of 2017.
At the same time, America Rising also began researching Judge Amul Thapar, now a judge on the U.S. Court of Appeals for the Sixth Circuit, and Justice Thomas Lee, the associate chief justice of the Utah Supreme Court and brother of Senator Mike Lee, who were both already on Trump's shortlist.

"…I know what's under Brett's bed, I know what's in his closets."
John Yoo, "Judging Brett Kavanaugh and the Supreme Court with John Yoo," Hoover Institution, August 28, 2018, https://www.hoover.org/research/judging-brett-kavanaugh-and-supreme-court-john-yoo.

When Kavanaugh worked in the White House counsel's office, he advocated for the nomination of Yoo to the Court of Appeals for the Ninth Circuit.
Brett M. Kavanaugh, "Re: More Parsky," email to White House colleagues, November 29, 2001.

But Ian Samuel … wrote about his interview for the *New York University Journal of Law & Liberty.*
Ian Samuel, "The Counter-Clerks of Justice Scalia," *New York University Journal of Law & Liberty,* Vol. 10., No. 1, 2016, https://papers.ssrn.com/sol3/papers.cfm?abstract_id=2760442.

After a half-hour with the candidate, the justice sent [Samuel] to meet with his quartet of clerks for another interrogation.
Samuel succeeded, completed his clerkship, and later became a law professor at Indiana University. He vehemently opposed Kavanaugh in major media outlets, writing for the *Guardian* that Kavanaugh would help bring "decades of misery" unless liberals acted quickly to pack the

Supreme Court with additional justices to negate Kavanaugh. Samuel, a self-identified #MeToo champion, was then reportedly placed on leave from Indiana University in December 2018 as the school opened a Title IX investigation—which protects students against sexual discrimination, harassment, and violence—involving Samuel. Samuel resigned from his professorship in May 2019.

Prior administrations had interviewed potential judicial nominees by telephone or not at all, but the Trump administration took a more hands-on approach. Robert Luther, McGahn's former deputy, writes in the *University of Pittsburgh Law Review*....
Robert Luther, "Two Years of Judicial Selection in the Trump Administration," *University of Pittsburgh Law Review Vol. 80*, 2019, https://lawreview.law.pitt.edu/ojs/index.php/lawreview/article/view/636/427.

... Kavanaugh's next stop on Monday, July 2 was a meeting with Trump.
Brett M. Kavanaugh, "Questionnaire for Nominee to the Supreme Court," *United States Senate Committee on the Judiciary*, July 21, 2018, https://www.judiciary.senate.gov/imo/media/doc/Brett%20M.%20Kavanaugh%20SJQ%20(PUBLIC).pdf.

Three other candidates met with Trump that day, according to White House press secretary Sarah Huckabee Sanders, and word began to leak out about the candidates moving up Trump's shortlist.
Sarah Sanders, "Sarah Sanders Remarks to Reporters at White House," *C-SPAN*, July 3, 2018, https://www.c-span.org/video/?447915-1/sarah-sanders-speaks-reporters-supreme-court-north-korea.
    Trump ultimately met with seven potential nominees, and his emphasis on considering multiple women nominees came after a meeting with Republican senators Susan Collins of Maine and Lisa Murkowski of Alaska.

Exit polls from the 2016 election showed that Trump's voters...had been strongly influenced by his promise....
NBC News, "NBC News Exit Poll: Future Supreme Court Appointments Important Factor in Presidential Voting," NBC News, November 8,

2016, https://www.nbcnews.com/card/nbc-news-exit-poll-future-supreme-court-appointments-important-factor-n680431.

...including Leonard Leo, the executive vice president of the Federalist Society.
To advise Trump on judicial nominations and Supreme Court matters, Leo took leave from the Federalist Society.

"Kavanaugh brings with him all the baggage of the George W. Bush administration, including millions of pages of records," a source with knowledge of the judicial selection process said before Kavanaugh met Trump.
Ryan Lovelace, "Kavanaugh Allies Muster 'Army' of Lawyers to Back Potential SCOTUS Pick," *National Law Journal*, July 2, 2018, https://www.law.com/nationallawjournal/2018/07/02/kavanaugh-allies-muster-army-of-lawyers-to-back-potential-scotus-pick/.

Instead, conservative talk radio hosts amplified the Kavanaugh skepticism.
Rush Limbaugh, "The Latest Rumors on Trump's SCOTUS Search," *The Rush Limbaugh Show*, July 2, 2018.

At the top of Bopp's long list of concerns about Kavanaugh, according to sources inside and outside of government, was the judge's views on campaign finance law.
Ryan Lovelace, "Conservative Lawyer Bopp Urges Trump to Pass on Kavanaugh for SCOTUS," *National Law Journal*, July 3, 2018, https://www.law.com/nationallawjournal/2018/07/03/conservative-lawyer-bopp-urges-trump-to-pass-on-kavanaugh-for-scotus/.
    When asked about his letter, Bopp answered, "I don't discuss communications with government officials." He declined to discuss specific nominees with me at the time, but his letter was not nearly as bashful about boosting Barrett.

Judge Amul Thapar...was known to be a favorite of Senate Majority Leader Mitch McConnell, who admitted as much to the Associated Press.

Bruce Schreiner, "McConnell touts Thapar for Supreme Court seat," Associated Press, June 30, 2018, https://www.apnews.com/f2aeee6 88c3f4f68afd58fee26439115.

...the judge's father reportedly told the *Louisville Courier-Journal* that Amul "nearly wouldn't speak to me after I voted for Barack Obama."
Andrew Wolfson, "KY Judge on Trump's Short List for High Court," *Louisville Courier-Journal*, December 9, 2016, https://www.courier-journal.com/story/news/politics/2016/12/09/ky-judge-trumps-short-list-high-court/95139578/.

Hardiman was well-connected in the Senate, having enjoyed a close relationship with the late Arlen Specter of Pennsylvania and benefitting from former senator Rick Santorum's unrelenting support.
Ryan Lovelace, "Get to know Supreme Court short lister Thomas Hardiman," *Washington Examiner*, January 26, 2017, https://www.washingtonexaminer.com/get-to-know-supreme-court-short-lister-thomas-hardiman.

[Kethledge] earned the moniker "Gorsuch 2.0" from Hugh Hewitt....
Hugh Hewitt, "Here's Who Trump Should Pick for the Supreme Court," *Washington Post*, July 2, 2018, https://www.washingtonpost.com/opinions/why-trump-should-nominate-raymond-kethledge/2018/07/02/e13e0540-7e37-11e8-b660-4d0f9f0351f1_story.html.

Quin Hillyer...lauded Kethledge in the *Washington Examiner*....
Quin Hillyer, "For Supreme Court writing, give Raymond Kethledge the edge," *Washington Examiner*, July 3, 2018, https://www.washingtonexaminer.com/opinion/for-supreme-court-writing-give-raymond-kethledge-the-edge.

Justin was employed for more than a decade at Deutsche Bank, where he worked directly with Trump on financing his real estate projects.
Justin Kennedy formerly led Deutsche Bank's commercial real estate group, and Justice Kennedy reportedly visited his Deutsche Bank offices on occasion. After his first address to Congress in 2017, Trump

stopped to shake Justice Kennedy's hand and said, "Say hello to your boy. Special guy."

"There is an army of people who stand ready and prepared to spring to action to support him," Travis Lenkner said before Kavanaugh's July nomination.
Lovelace, "Kavanaugh Allies Muster 'Army' of Lawyers to Back Potential SCOTUS Pick."

"We will vote to confirm Justice Kennedy's successor this fall," McConnell promised in June....
New York Times staff, "Anthony Kennedy Retires from Supreme Court, and McConnell Says Senate Will Move Swiftly on a Replacement," *New York Times*, June 27, 2018, https://www.nytimes.com/2018/06/27/us/politics/anthony-kennedy-supreme-court-live-briefing.html.

The longest vacancy, 841 days, ended with the confirmation of Robert C. Grier to take Justice Henry Baldwin's seat in 1846.
Drew DeSilver, "Long Supreme Court vacancies used to be more common," Pew Research Center, February 26, 2016, https://www.pewresearch.org/fact-tank/2016/02/26/long-supreme-court-vacancies-used-to-be-more-common/.

A Pew Research Center analysis of the fifteen Supreme Court vacancies immediately preceding Kennedy's retirement, dating back to 1970, found that vacancies were filled within an average of fifty-five days.
Ibid.

Democrats Joe Donnelly of Indiana, Heidi Heitkamp of North Dakota, and Joe Manchin of West Virginia met with Trump that night, according to Sarah Huckabee Sanders.
Sarah Huckabee Sanders, @PressSec, Twitter, June 28, 2018, https://twitter.com/PressSec/status/1012506179350777856.

...the president called the looming announcement "exciting" and was uncharacteristically coy about his shortlist....

Philip Rucker, 'Trump Says He Is Considering 2 Women for Supreme Court, Will Announce Pick July 9," *Washington Post*, June 29, 2018, https://www.washingtonpost.com/politics/trump-says-he-is-considering-two-women-for-supreme-court-will-announce-pick-july-9/2018/06/29/7 54288be-7be1-11e8-80be-6d32e182a3bc_story.html.

…Trump formally extended the offer and Kavanaugh accepted it.
Kavanaugh, "Questionnaire for Nominee to the Supreme Court."

The Heritage Foundation's John Malcolm explained, "I received the invitation about three hours beforehand and I was delighted to get it. I wasn't even sure at that point who the nominee was going to be."
Lovelace, "This Legal Scholar Put Brett Kavanaugh on President Trump's Radar in 2016."

Chapter 2

They notified reporters that activists would descend on the Supreme Court one hour after Trump announced a nominee to replace the late Justice Antonin Scalia.
Ryan Lovelace, "Left-leaning Groups to Demonstrate Outside Supreme Court after Trump Selects a Nominee," *Washington Examiner*, January 30, 2017, https://www.washingtonexaminer.com/left-leaning-groups-to-demonstrate-outside-supreme-court-after-trump-selects-a-nominee.

The *Weekly Standard*'s Haley Byrd spotted [the signs] within thirty minutes of Trump uttering Kavanaugh's name.
Haley Byrd, "Begun the Kavanaugh Wars Have," the *Weekly Standard*, July 10, 2018, https://www.weeklystandard.com/haley-byrd/protests-against-brett-kavanaugh-start-at-the-supreme-court.

…Demand Justice, which was formed in May 2018 to "prod Democrats to show more guts when it comes to opposing Trump's extreme nominees," according to Brian Fallon.…
Brian Fallon, "Demand Justice: Saving Courts from Donald Trump," *USA Today*, July 23, 2018, https://www.usatoday.com/story/

opinion/2018/07/23/demand-justice-saving-courts-from-donald-trump-editorials-debates/37075645/.

...Fallon chided a progressive *New York Times* columnist....
David Leonhardt, "The Nominee Is Coming. What Then?," *New York Times*, July 9, 2018, https://www.nytimes.com/2018/07/09/opinion/trump-supreme-court-midterms.html.

In May 2018, Demand Justice began its efforts to "change minds and sensitize rank-and-file progressives to think of the courts as a venue for their progressive activism and a way to advance the progressive agenda."
Carl Hulse, "After Garland Defeat, New Group Hopes to Draw Democrats to Judicial Battlefield," *New York Times*, May 3, 2018, https://www.nytimes.com/2018/05/03/us/politics/merrick-garland-judicial-trump.html.

Board member Cristóbal Alex....
Cristóbal Alex, deleted Latino Victory Fund profile and his LinkedIn profile, accessed June 2019.

Board member Eric Kessler....
Eric Kessler, Friends of the Global Fight Against AIDS, Tuberculosis, and Malaria profile and LinkedIn profile, accessed June 2019.

...the New Venture Fund...[is] the beneficiary of at least $150,000 from George Soros's Open Society Foundations.
Deleted webpage from Open Society Foundations' list of awarded grants.

Board member Monica Dixon....
Monica Dixon, Georgetown Day School profile of vice chair Monica Dixon, accessed June 2019.

...[Senator Kamala] Harris replied, "As far as possible—I don't know how you define that."
Elana Schor, "Dems Wrestle with Hardball Tactics in Supreme Court Battle," *Politico*, June 28, 2018, https://www.politico.com/story/2018/06/28/supreme-court-democrats-fight-683537.

"[T]he right of privacy, as defined or undefined by Justice Douglas, was a free-floating right that was not derived in a principled fashion from constitutional materials," Bork said at his Senate Judiciary Committee hearings....

Robert H. Bork, "Nomination of Robert H. Bork to be Associate Justice of the Supreme Court of the United States," U.S. Senate Judiciary Committee, 1987.

Culvahouse admitted that he was "surprised" by Senator Kennedy's attack on Bork and the ferocity of Bork's enemies.

A.B. Culvahouse, "A.B. Culvahouse Oral History, White House Counsel," University of Virginia's Miller Center, April 1, 2004, https://millercenter.org/the-presidency/presidential-oral-histories/ab-culvahouse-oral-history-white-house-counsel.

"My father taped [the hearings] on a VHS player and made me watch them, and it was fascinating because I was inspired and it made me go to law school."

Donald F. McGahn, "Keynote Address to Federalist Society Western Chapters Conference at the Ronald Reagan Presidential Library," broadcast by C-SPAN, January 26, 2019, https://www.c-span.org/video/?457107-2/don-mcgahn-judicial-selection.

Culvahouse seemed sickened by the state of judicial nomination battles when we talked in July 2018.

Ryan Lovelace, "Lifetime Achiever: A.B. Culvahouse Jr., O'Melveny & Myers," *American Lawyer*, August 22, 2018, https://www.law.com/americanlawyer/2018/08/22/lifetime-achiever-a-b-culvahouse-jr-omelveny-myers/.

...*The Hill*'s "Fifty Most Beautiful" people list in 2017....

"50 Most Beautiful," *The Hill*, July 26, 2017, https://thehill.com/50-most-beautiful/2017/343749-zina-bash.

Brian Fallon...charged that Kavanaugh...must have known about the sexual harassment of which Kozinski was accused in 2017.

Brian Fallon, "Cuomo Prime Time," CNN, July 10, 2018.

Chapter 3

Lori Lodes of Demand Justice told ABC that the women in red trained their sights on Kavanaugh because "he represents the greatest threat to legal abortion since *Roe* was decided."

Cheyenne Haslett, "'*The Handmaid's Tale*' Protesters Target Kavanaugh," ABC News, September 4, 2018, https://abcnews.go.com/Politics/handmaids-tale-protesters-target-kavanaugh/story?id=57592706.

A group of Texas doctors waiting in line for the hearings made a video saying they saw people accept cash to enter the hearing room and protest by yelling and screaming.

Tim Hains, "Three Texas Doctors: We Saws Protesters Paid In Cash To Disrupt Brett Kavanaugh Hearing On Line To Enter," RealClearPolitics, September 4, 2018, https://www.realclearpolitics.com/video/2018/09/04/texas_doctor_i_saw_people_handing_out_cash_to_protesters_in_the_line_for_kavanaugh_hearing.html.

Dr. Chris Dundas of Corpus Christi said some of the women who made it through the hearing room were disappointed they were not arrested. "When they were arrested, they were keeping a record and celebrating who got arrested without any regard for open discussion or even the possibility of being convinced of anything," added Dr. Burton Purvis of Arlington, Texas.

Ibid.

Megaphone Strategies, a self-described "social justice media strategy firm" co-founded by the progressive activist Van Jones....

Megaphone Strategies website, megaphonestrategies.com; Corinne Grinapol, "CNN Contributor Van Jones and Molly Haigh Start New Social Justice PR Firm," *AdWeek*, July 22, 2016, https://www.adweek.com/digital/cnn-contributor-van-jones-and-molly-haigh-start-new-social-justice-pr-firm/.

A couple of months later, [Haaland] was one of two Native American women elected to Congress.

Amanda Becker, "Deb Haaland becomes one of first two Native American congresswomen," Reuters, January 7, 2019, https://www.

reuters.com/article/us-usa-congress-haaland/deb-haaland-becomes-one-of-first-two-native-american-congresswomen-idUSKCN1P11D1.

Deputy Attorney General Rod Rosenstein reportedly directed all ninety-three U.S. Attorney offices around the country to deploy as many as three prosecutors, as warranted, to assist the Justice Department with its document review.
Katie Benner, "Rosenstein Asks Prosecutors to Help With Kavanaugh Papers in Unusual Request," *New York Times*, July 11, 2018, https://www.nytimes.com/2018/07/11/us/politics/rosenstein-kavanaugh-document-review-prosecutors.html.

Candice Wong, a former Kavanaugh clerk and an assistant U.S. attorney in the District of Columbia, was moved to the Justice Department's Office of Legal Policy to help with the confirmation effort, a source with knowledge of the move said at the time.
Ryan Lovelace, "Kavanaugh Confirmation Team Takes Shape, Boosted By Former Clerks," *National Law Journal*, July 11, 2018, https://www.law.com/nationallawjournal/2018/07/11/kavanaugh-confirmation-team-takes-shape-boosted-by-former-clerks/.

Sarah Isgur Flores, a Justice Department spokeswoman, said that moves like Wong's were not "unusual in the slightest."
Ibid.

Hearron told the *National Law Journal* that one noticeable difference between his work as a litigator and his work on judicial nominations was the absence of a judge who "is going to decide who's right and is going to issue a ruling."
Marcia Coyle, "Why Dianne Feinstein's Lead Counsel for Nominations Isn't Returning to Big Law," *National Law Journal*, January 17, 2019, https://www.law.com/nationallawjournal/2019/01/17/why-dianne-feinsteins-lead-counsel-for-nominations-isnt-returning-to-big-law/.

While Feinstein raged in public, the Senate's top-ranking Democrat, Chuck Schumer, leaned on Ferriero in private, imploring him over the telephone "to do the right thing."

Chuck Grassley, "Letter to President George W. Bush," Senate Judiciary Committee, July 31, 2018.

[Schumer] also made a private, written appeal to former President Bush, but the Democrats were too late.
Chuck Schumer, "Letter to President George W. Bush," U.S. Senate, July 26, 2018.

Little more than an hour into the hearings, Harris blasted out an email solicitation that read, "I am prepared to do everything in my power to stop this nomination," and asked recipients to sign a petition during the hearings.
Aryssa Damron, "Democratic Senators Send Fundraising Emails During Kavanaugh Hearing," *Washington Free Beacon*, September 4, 2018, https://freebeacon.com/politics/dem-senators-fundraise-kavanaugh-hearing/.

Those who supported Kavanaugh, [Booker] said, were "complicit to that evil."
Tim Hains, "Sen. Cory Booker: Supporters Of Judge Kavanaugh Are 'Complicit' in 'Evil'," RealClearPolitics, July 25, 2018, https://www.realclearpolitics.com/video/2018/07/25/sen_cory_booker_supporters_of_judge_kavanaugh_are_complicit_in_evil.html.

Finding no adversary among the Republicans to act as a foil for his heroism, Booker turned instead to cable news for approbation and applause.
Cory Booker, *All In with Chris Hayes*, MSNBC, September 2018; Cory Booker, *Anderson Cooper 360*, CNN, September 2018.

In private, [Blatt] faced much worse.
Emails containing images of coat hangers as a means of abortion and verbal attacks on Blatt's children were sent her way simply because she was a woman who supported Kavanaugh.

She and her R Street Institute colleague Anthony Marcum compiled a searchable and sortable database of the text of the confirmation hearings for every Supreme Court nominee since Lewis Powell and William Rehnquist....

The R Street Institute's database excludes the Anita Hill hearings for Justice Clarence Thomas, since Shoshana Weissmann and Marcum wanted to focus on legal issues instead of scandal.

Soon after Kavanaugh's first hearings, Justice Clarence Thomas was asked at a Federalist Society event about what preserves the legitimacy of the Supreme Court.

Clarence Thomas, Gregory S. Coleman Memorial Lecture Series at the Texas Chapters of the Federalist Society, broadcast by C-SPAN, September 8, 2018, https://www.c-span.org/video/?450905-1/justice-clarence-thomas-speaks-federalist-society.

Chapter 4

The *Washington Post*'s Ruth Marcus...appeared on MSNBC that morning to assess which Supreme Court candidate was, in her view, "the biggest danger to abortion rights."

Ruth Marcus, "The Trump Supreme Court Pick Who'd Pose the Biggest Danger to Abortion Rights," *Washington Post*, July 4, 2018, https://www.washingtonpost.com/opinions/the-trump-supreme-court-pick-whod-pose-the-biggest-danger-to-abortion-rights/2018/07/04/401a8aa0-7fa2-11e8-b0ef-fffcabeff946_story.html.

Ford told the receptionist that "someone on the president's shortlist attacked me."

Christine Blasey Ford, "Senate Judiciary Committee Hearing on the Nomination of Brett M. Kavanaugh to be an Associate Justice of the Supreme Court," broadcast by C-SPAN, September 27, 2018, https://www.c-span.org/video/?451895-1/professor-blasey-ford-testifies-sexual-assault-allegations-part-1.

First [Ford's] encrypted message to the *Washington Post* said "mid 1980s"....
See Appendix, Figure 1.

...later [Ford] wrote to Senator Feinstein that [the alleged assault] occurred in the "early 1980's."
See Appendix, Figure 2.

She then told the *Washington Post* that it happened precisely in the "summer of 1982"....
Emma Brown, "California professor, writer of confidential Brett Kavanaugh letter, speaks out about her allegation of sexual assault," *Washington Post*, September 16, 2018, https://www.washingtonpost.com/investigations/california-professor-writer-of-confidential-brett-kavanaugh-letter-speaks-out-about-her-allegation-of-sexual-assault/2018/09/16/46982194-b846-11e8-94eb-3bd52dfe917b_story.html.

...before ultimately testifying, "I can't give the exact date."
Ford, "Senate Judiciary Committee Hearing."

Ford testified that on the day she first submitted the allegations to the *Washington Post*, she "had a sense of urgency to relay the information to the Senate and the president as soon as possible." "I felt like the best option was to try to do the civic route," she testified. "I wasn't interested in pursuing the media route, particularly."
Ibid.

Later that night, Ford testified, she received a return call from Congresswoman Eshoo's office.
Ibid.

Early the next morning, Ford again submitted an anonymous message to the *Washington Post* through the encrypted app. "Been advised to contact senators or *NYT*," she wrote, before pointedly adding that the

Post had not responded.... Within ninety minutes of threatening to go to the *Washington Post*'s competition, Ford received a reply: "I will get you in touch with a reporter."
See Appendix, Figure 1.

That reporter was Emma Brown, a graduate of Stanford University and former seventh-grade teacher.
Emma Brown, "LinkedIn profile," LinkedIn, https://www.linkedin.com/in/emma-brown-93322b8.

She began at the *Post* in 2009 writing obituaries before moving to the education beat, where her work on the accomplishments of Arne Duncan, President Obama's secretary of education, won plaudits from fellow journalists. She also was a finalist for an award from fellow education journalists for her reporting on sexual assaults at colleges.
Alexander Russo, "How former education reporter Emma Brown broke the Christine Blasey Ford story," *Phi Delta Kappan*, October 3, 2018, https://www.kappanonline.org/russo-how-former-education-reporter-emma-brown-broke-the-christine-blasey-ford-story/.

(She would take a leave from the *Post* in 2019 to write a book about raising boys after the #MeToo reckoning.)
Emma Brown, "@emmersbrown," Twitter, https://twitter.com/emmersbrown?lang=en.

"She really wanted to tell somebody her story," the reporter later told CNN, "but she also didn't want to have her life upended, and she was terrified of what would happen if she came forward. She struggled with that all summer long."
John Berman and Emma Brown, *New Day*, CNN, September 17, 2018.

To assure the *Post* that her allegation against Kavanaugh pre-dated his emergence as a candidate for Kennedy's seat on the Supreme Court, Ford provided the newspaper with details that she never gave the Senate Judiciary Committee—the "therapy records" from 2012, which she cited in her first encrypted message.

Brown, "California professor, writer of confidential Brett Kavanaugh letter, speaks out about her allegation of sexual assault."

In March 2012, Jeffrey Toobin wrote in the *New Yorker*, "If a Republican, any Republican, wins in November, his most likely first nominee to the Supreme Court will be Brett Kavanaugh."
Jeffrey Toobin, "Holding Court," *New Yorker*, March 19, 2012, https://www.newyorker.com/magazine/2012/03/26/holding-court.

Ford attributed her 2012 allegation in therapy to a disagreement over a "very extensive, very long remodel" of her home in her testimony to the Senate Judiciary Committee.
She said the discussion of doors related to memories of her assault because she said she had claustrophobia in addition to her panic attacks and bouts of anxiety. Ford wanted the door, but her husband did not. Ultimately, she got her door. Now, she testified, the couple is able to host Google interns.
    Ford, "Senate Judiciary Committee Hearing on the Nomination of Brett M. Kavanaugh to be an Associate Justice of the Supreme Court."

She left work as director at Corcept Therapeutics, a pharmaceutical company....
See Appendix, Figures 3.1–3.3

Corcept Therapeutics' only drug is Korlym, which may be dispensed in the United States only to treat patients with Cushing Syndrome, an illness in which the body produces too much cortisol.
Corcept Therapeutics, "Korlym (Mifepristone)," Corcept Therapeutics, https://www.corcept.com/product/.

Mifepristone was approved by the U.S. Food and Drug Administration for use in abortions in 2000.
U.S. Food and Drug Administration, "Mifeprex (Mifepristone) Information," U.S. Food and Drug Administration, https://www.fda.gov/drugs/postmarket-drug-safety-information-patients-and-providers/mifeprex-mifepristone-information.

At that time, Stanford University Medical School's psychiatry department began studying the use of mifepristone as a cortisol-blocker to treat depression and psychosis.

J. W. Chu, D. F. Matthias, J. Belanoff, A. Schatzberg, A. R. Hoffman, D. Feldman, "Successful Long-term Treatment of Refractory Cushing's Disease with High-dose Mifepristone (RU 486)," *The Journal of Clinical Endocrinology and Metabolism*, via U.S. National Library of Medicine National Institutes of Health, August 2001.

The Stanford researchers formed Corcept Therapeutics in 1998, shortly before Ford became a research psychologist at that university in 1999.

Corcept Therapeutics, "About Corcept," Corcept Therapeutics, https://www.corcept.com/about/.

Dr. Alan Schatzberg, a co-founder of Corcept Therapeutics and the former chairman of the psychiatry department at Stanford, said in 2002 that the drug he was developing "may be the equivalent of shock treatments in a pill" for patients with major depression.

Stanford University, "Stanford Researchers Study Controversial Drug as Treatment for Psychotic Major Depression," August 1, 2002, https://med.stanford.edu/news/all-news/2002/08/stanford-researchers-study-controversial-drug-as-treatment-for-psychotic-major-depression.html.

A drug usually goes through several phases of clinical trials before the manufacturer applies to the FDA for permission to market it.

U.S. Food and Drug Administration, "Step 3: Clinical Research; Step 4: FDA Drug Review," January 4, 2018, https://www.fda.gov/patients/drug-development-process/step-3-clinical-research.

Following the completion of a Phase 3 trial in 2006, Corcept Therapeutics did not publish the results at the U.S. National Library of Medicine online.

U.S. National Library of Medicine, "A United States Study of Corlux for Psychotic Symptoms in Psychotic Major Depression," U.S. National

Library of Medicine ClinicalTrials.gov, https://www.clinicaltrials.gov/
ct2/show/results/NCT00130676?view=results.

**This failure to publish results led critics to label the work of Corcept
Therapeutics and Stanford as "experimercials"—that is, medical
research undertaken to produce publicity for a specific drug.**
Paul Jacobs, "Science Critics Make Issue of Financial Ties," Mercury
News via Alliance for Human Research Protection, July 10, 2006, https://
ahrp.org/harvard-stanford-psychiatrists-financial-ties-to-industry/.

**Schatzberg was particularly susceptible to such criticism because he
owned millions of shares of Corcept Therapeutics stock while researching
the only drug Corcept Therapeutics produced with funding from the
federal government.**
Alan Schatzberg, "Schedule 13G Filed Under Rule 13d-1(d)," U.S.
Securities and Exchange Commission, 2007-2008, https://www.sec.gov/
Archives/edgar/data/1088856/000119312508016481/dsc13ga.htm.

**In 2008, the curious arrangement piqued the interest of Senator Chuck
Grassley, then the ranking member of the Finance Committee.**
Senator Charles Grassley, "Letter via electronic transmission to Dr. John
L. Henderson, President of Stanford University," United States Senate
Committee on Finance, June 23, 2008.

**According to a 2008 letter from Stanford's general counsel, Schatzburg
forfeited his responsibility for Stanford's research into mifepristone
because of Grassley's investigation.**
Debra L. Zumwalt, "Letter to Dr. Jane Steinberg, Director of the Division
of Extramural Activities at the National Institute of Mental Health,"
Stanford University general counsel, July 31, 2008.

**The Project on Government Oversight, a nonprofit watchdog, later
uncovered internal emails from the U.S. National Institutes of Health
revealing that the federal government wanted the clinical trial**

component of its grant to Stanford to be "terminated immediately and permanently."
Project on Government Oversight, "Concerns About Potential Conflicts of Interest, Patient Safety Cited in Shut Down of Stanford Clinical Trial, According to Emails," POGO press release, January 13, 2011, https:// www.pogo.org/press/release/2011/concerns-about-potential-conflicts-of-interest-patient-safety-cited-in-shut-down-of-stanford-clinical-trial-according-to-emails/.

But Corcept Therapeutics secured FDA approval under the Obama administration in 2012—the year Ford left the company—for the specific use of treating Cushing Syndrome in a select set of patients.
Mary H. Parks, M.D., "Approval Letter," U.S. Department of Health and Human Services, 2012.

The Southern Investigative Reporting Foundation discovered in 2019 that the pharmaceutical company undertook a pay-to-play plot to induce physicians to prescribe the drug.
Roddy Boyd, "Corcept Therapeutics: The Company That Perfectly Explains the Health Care Crisis," Southern Investigative Reporting Foundation, January 25, 2019, http://sirf-online.org/2019/01/25/ corcept-therapeutics-the-company-that-perfectly-explains-the-health-care-crisis/.

Blue Orca Capital, a self-described "activist investment firm," then revealed that Corcept Therapeutics used an undisclosed specialty pharmacy and distributor of its drug that appeared to be a component of Corcept Therapeutics designed "to boost sales, hide losses or engage in other financial shenanigans."
Blue Orca Capital, "Blue Orca Short Corcept Therapeutics Report," *Blue Orca Capital*, February 5, 2019, https://www.blueorcacapital.com/ terms-of-service-corcept.

Corcept Therapeutics responded that its critics were motivated by short-sellers looking to enrich themselves at the expense of the company, an answer that did not satisfy all of its investors.

Charles Robb, "Some Important Facts about Corcept, Physicians and Patients," Corcept Therapeutics, 2019, https://www.sec.gov/Archives/edgar/data/1088856/000119312519027646/d625461dex991.htm.

The fraud allegedly perpetrated by Corcept Therapeutics spawned a class action lawsuit by the company's investors, filed on March 14, 2019, which threatened to dismantle the entire operation. The investors alleged that the company "aggressively promoted Korlym for off-label uses," paid doctors "improperly" to promote the drug, and artificially inflated its revenue and sales figures through "illicit sales practices," all while keeping the company's investors in the dark.
Nicholas Melucci and all others similarly situated, "Class action complaint for violations of the federal securities laws by Nicholas Melucci, individually and on behalf of all others similarly situated, v. Corcept Therapeutics Incorporated, Joseph K. Belanoff, and Charles Robb," *United States District Court for the Northern District of California 19-cv-01372*, March 14, 2019.

Ford is not a medical doctor. She obtained a Ph.D. in psychology from the University of Southern California in 1996, where she specialized in marriage and family therapy. She trained as a clinical psychologist at Pepperdine University, graduating with a master's degree in 1991.
See Appendix, Figures 3.1–3.3.

On July 6, Ford had told the Post that the assault occurred in the "mid 1980s," but in her letter to Feinstein, she said it was "in the early 1980s." The number of people present had changed too.
See Appendix, Figures 1 and 2.

She said she had spotted Judge once at a Safeway, however, and knew that "he was extremely uncomfortable seeing me."
Ford, "Senate Judiciary Committee Hearing on the Nomination of Brett M. Kavanaugh to be an Associate Justice of the Supreme Court."

When Jeff Sessions was confirmed as attorney general one month later, ABC's *Good Morning America* featured Katz, identified only as a "protester," pledging to "fight back."
George Stephanopoulos, *Good Morning America*, ABC, 2017.

"Paula Jones' suit is very, very, very weak," Katz told CNN in 1998. "She's alleged one incident that took place in a hotel room that, by her own testimony, lasted ten to twelve minutes. She suffered no repercussions in the workplace."
Alex Pappas, "Lawyer for Kavanaugh accuser downplayed sexual misconduct allegations against Clinton, Franken," Fox News, September 17, 2018, https://www.foxnews.com/politics/lawyer-for-kavanaugh-accuser-downplayed-sexual-misconduct-allegations-against-clinton-franken.

Jones ultimately collected an $850,000 settlement from Clinton, while the Clintons collected thousands of dollars in campaign contributions from Katz in the ensuing decades.
Neil A. Lewis, "Clinton Settles Jones Lawsuit With a Check for $850,000," *New York Times*, January 13, 1999, https://www.nytimes.com/1999/01/13/us/clinton-settles-jones-lawsuit-with-a-check-for-850000.html.

Katz raised money for the Clintons too, raking in twenty-nine thousand dollars for Hillary Clinton's 2016 campaign a full year before the election, according to an internal campaign memo revealed by WikiLeaks.
Amanda McTyre, Angelique Cannon, and Amanda Renteria, "Memorandum for Hillary Rodham Clinton," WikiLeaks, November 30, 2015, https://wikileaks.org/podesta-emails/fileid/55842/15333.

[Katz's] clients have included victims of such high-profile defendants as Harvey Weinstein and former New York attorney general Eric Schneiderman.
Ryan Lovelace, "#MeToo Whistleblower Makes Waves in Washington," *National Law Journal*, September 14, 2018, https://www.law.com/nationallawjournal/2018/09/14/metoo-whistleblower-lawyer-makes-waves-in-washington/.

Katz's practice benefitted from the attention of Ronan Farrow in the *New Yorker*. The former State Department official and adviser to Secretary of State Hillary Clinton wrote about Weinstein and Schneiderman and other sexual misconduct cases involving Katz's clients, sometimes naming Katz as a source.

Ronan Farrow, "Les Moonves and CBS Face Allegations of Sexual Misconduct," *New Yorker*, July 27, 2018, https://www.newyorker.com/magazine/2018/08/06/les-moonves-and-cbs-face-allegations-of-sexual-misconduct.

Jodi Kantor and Megan Twohey of the *New York Times* wrote articles about Weinstein that, in Katz's view, "should have won [them] the Nobel Prize" for activism instead of the Pulitzer Prize they won for journalism.

Debra Katz, "UWLawTalks," University of Wisconsin Law School, November 29, 2018, https://www.facebook.com/watch/?v=2260747217526796.

In an admiring profile in the alumni magazine of the University of Wisconsin in August 2018, she explained that the #MeToo movement had forced cases to end "more quickly and for higher dollar amounts than before," acknowledging that she turns to the press to win cases that would never reach a courtroom.

Karen Koethe, "#MeToo Advocate Debra Katz '84: Empowering Stories, Changing Lives," *Gargoyle: Alumni Magazine of the University of Wisconsin Law School*, August 9, 2018, https://gargoyle.law.wisc.edu/2018/08/09/metoo-advocate-debra-katz-84-empowering-stories-changing-lives/.

Ford did not recall where she took the test or where she was beforehand or afterward. The name of the hotel, however, is the Hilton BWI Baltimore Airport Hotel on 1739 West Nursery Road in Linthicum Heights, Maryland. Jeremy P. Hanafin, a polygraph examiner from a Virginia suburb of Washington, administered the test on August 7, 2018, identifying the subject as "Christine Blasey."

See Appendix, Figures 4.1–4.3.

An attorney from the Katz firm, Lisa Banks, accompanied Ford into the room for the test and asked Hanafin to leave the room while they composed a handwritten statement, signed "Christine Blasey," that would serve as Ford's account for the polygraph test.

See Appendix, Figures 4.1–4.3.

Ford's story had changed again; indeed, it appeared to change as she was writing it. She first wrote that the assault took place in the "early 80's" before scratching out the word "early." She wrote that "4 people" had been present and then crossed out the word "people" and wrote that "4 boys and a couple of girls" were present.

See Appendix, Figure 5.

Chapter 5

A frustrated Debra Katz told a meeting of the bipartisan Congressional Caucus for Women's Issues on Wednesday, September 12, 2018, that she was worried about the "Weinstein effect—if you haven't assaulted eighty people, it doesn't count.... If you haven't raped people and done the most egregious things, it's more of a 'huh.' It's not even worthy of the *Washington Post* anymore."

Ryan Lovelace, "#MeToo Whistleblower Makes Waves in Washington," *National Law Journal*, September 14, 2018, https://www.law.com/nationallawjournal/2018/09/14/metoo-whistleblower-lawyer-makes-waves-in-washington/.

...Holiday explained how he concocted falsehoods which he got major news organizations to report as fact.

Most news organizations acknowledged they had been fooled after Holiday made his deceptions public. A correction in the 2012 *New York Times* noted that Holiday had "lied," but the paper expressed no remorse for failing to verify what it printed before misleading its readers. The *Times* now publishes Holiday directly, albeit mostly in its opinion section.

His work became the stuff of legend, and by the time President Trump took office, Holiday wrote in the *New York Times* that he had fielded a

job offer as a "communications director for a cabinet member," which he turned down.
Ryan Holiday, "How to Serve a Deranged Tyrant, Stoically," *New York Times*, April 2, 2018, https://www.nytimes.com/2018/04/02/opinion/stoicism-political-tyrants.html.

...Ryan Grim reported in the Intercept that Senator Dianne Feinstein was refusing to share a "Brett Kavanaugh–related document" with her fellow Democrats on the Judiciary Committee....
Ryan Grim, "Dianne Feinstein Withholding Brett Kavanaugh Document from Fellow Judiciary Committee Democrats," the *Intercept*, September 12, 2018, https://theintercept.com/2018/09/12/brett-kavanaugh-confirmation-dianne-feinstein/.

One former staffer turned to a rival, *Politico*, to dismiss the Intercept as "where journalism goes to die."
Ken Silverstein, "Where Journalism Goes to Die," *Politico Magazine*, February 27, 2015, https://www.politico.com/magazine/story/2015/02/ken-silverstein-the-intercept-115586_full.html.

...Grim ran Strong Arm Press, an anti-Trump publishing house that relies on crowdfunding and solicits cash in return for mentions in its books.
Benjamin Freed, "How Can a Small Progressive Publisher Keep Up With the Trump Administration? Via Crowdfunding. And Speed," *Washingtonian*, February 21, 2018, https://www.washingtonian.com/2018/02/21/ryan-grim-strong-arm-press-trump-administration-books/.

Grim's initial report was riddled with inaccuracies (the letter was not "relayed to someone affiliated with Stanford University," for example) and ambiguities (such as Feinstein's harboring a "document" that "purportedly describes an incident"). His account was refuted by its very subjects as Democrats flocked to CNN to say that the allegations "caught [Judiciary] committee Democrats by surprise."
Manu Raju, "Why Dianne Feinstein Waited to take the Brett Kavanaugh allegations to the FBI," CNN, September 18, 2018, https://www.cnn.com/2018/09/17/politics/dianne-feinstein-brett-kavanaugh-allegations/index.html.

As he had done before, Farrow published Katz's client's anonymous allegations on the *New Yorker* website. His article was co-authored by Jane Mayer.

Ronan Farrow and Jane Mayer, "A Sexual-Misconduct Allegation Against the Supreme Court Nominee Brett Kavanaugh Stirs Tension Among Democrats in Congress," *New Yorker*, September 14, 2018, https://www.newyorker.com/news/news-desk/a-sexual-misconduct-allegation-against-the-supreme-court-nominee-brett-kavanaugh-stirs-tension-among-democrats-in-congress.

[Mayer's] effort to sink Justice Clarence Thomas's nomination thirty years earlier had failed, but now she had a second chance to take a Republican judicial scalp.

Jane Mayer and Jill Abramson, *Strange Justice: The Selling of Clarence Thomas*, (Boston: Houghton Mifflin Harcourt, 1994).

...Katz publicly refused to say she was representing the accuser, as the Intercept had reported, telling BuzzFeed, "There's nothing to say."

Lissandra Villa and Paul McLeod, "Senate Democrats Have Referred A Secret Letter About Brett Kavanaugh To The FBI," BuzzFeed, September 13, 2018, https://www.buzzfeednews.com/article/lissandravilla/senate-democrats-have-sent-a-secret-letter-about-brett.

...Katz had gone on CNN and *CBS This Morning* on Monday.

Alisyn Camerota and Debra Katz, *New Day*, CNN, September 17, 2018; Norah O'Donnell and Debra Katz, *CBS This Morning*, CBS, September 17, 2018.

Emma Brown's Sunday *Washington Post* story focused not on Ford's allegations against Kavanaugh, but on her decision to speak out.

Emma Brown, "California Professor, Writer of Confidential Brett Kavanaugh Letter, Speaks Out About Her Allegation of Sexual Assault," *Washington Post*, September 16, 2018, https://www.washingtonpost.com/investigations/california-professor-writer-of-confidential-brett-kavanaugh-letter-speaks-out-about-her-allegation-of-sexual-assault/2018/09/16/46982194-b846-11e8-94eb-3bd52dfe917b_story.html.

CNN's Alisyn Camerota, for example, said to Katz, "[A]s we know the story, she really did not want to come forward, she wrote a confidential letter, so tell me the trajectory of her willingness now to go to such a public forum." Alisyn Camerota and Debra Katz, *New Day*, CNN, September 17, 2018.

Katz charged the Republicans with playing "hardball," though she had not talked to them directly, and Ford's legal team would not do so until the following day on Tuesday, September 18.
See Appendix, Figures 6.1–6.2.

The next day, Thursday, September 20, Katz sent an email to Jennifer Duck, a lawyer for Feinstein's staff:
"From: Debra Katz
Sent: Thursday, September 20, 2018 6:29 PM
To: Duck, Jennifer (Judiciary-Dem)
Subject: RE: Dr. Christine Blasey Ford
Importance: High
Dear Ms. Duck:
    We authorize Senator Feinstein to provide Sen. Grassley's staff with the unredacted letter to Senator Feinstein dated July 30, 2018 provided that Senator Grassley's staff agrees not to publish or disseminate the letter.
    Please do not transmit the letter electronically, Ms. Duck.
Sincerely,
Debra S. Katz"

Willey sent a lengthy email to Katz and her law partner Lisa Banks before three o'clock in the afternoon:
"From: Willey, Katharine (Judiciary-Rep)
Date: Friday, September 21, 2018 2:33 PM
To: Lisa Banks; Debra Katz
Subject: RE: Dr. Christine Blasey Ford
Ms. Banks—below is the response.
Dear Ms. Katz and Ms. Banks:
    I am writing in response to your conditions under which your client, Dr. Christine Blasey Ford, is willing to testify as to her allegations of sexual assault by Judge Brett Kavanaugh while the two individuals were

in high school more than 35 years ago. On behalf of Chairman Chuck Grassley, I want to reiterate that the Senate Judiciary Committee considers these serious allegations and wants to honor Dr. Ford's request to testify. We are committed to providing a secure and respectful setting for her testimony. The Chairman fully agrees with Dr. Ford that we cannot have another "media circus." The Chairman has offered the ability for Dr. Ford to testify in an open session, a closed session, a public staff interview, and a private staff interview. The Chairman is even willing to fly female staff investigators to meet Dr. Ford and you in California, or anywhere else, to obtain Dr. Ford's testimony.

Sometime before last Sunday, September 16, your client described her allegations to a reporter for the *Washington Post*, which published the allegations that Sunday. This was the first time that the Chairman or his staff learned of Dr. Ford's identity. Dr. Ford had made these allegations privately to her elected representatives, including Senator Feinstein, who was aware of these allegations since July. Neither Senator Feinstein nor her staff asked Judge Kavanaugh about these allegations despite having numerous opportunities to do so, including in a closed-door meeting between the senator and the nominee, during confidential phone calls with Judge Kavanaugh regarding his background, during three days and more than 32 hours of testimony at his public confirmation hearing two weeks ago, during a closed session of that hearing when sensitive information could be discussed—which Senator Feinstein did not attend—or when senators issued Judge Kavanaugh nearly 1,300 written questions after his confirmation hearing, more written questions submitted than were submitted to all previous Supreme Court nominees combined. Senator Feinstein also could have referred these allegations anonymously and confidentially to the FBI when she was made aware of them. That would have protected her anonymity, as Dr. Ford requested.

These actions were profoundly unfair to both parties. Judge Kavanaugh has unequivocally denied Dr. Ford's allegations. He should have been given the opportunity to say so directly to Senator Feinstein had he been made aware of serious allegations against him. And 64 other senators met with Judge Kavanaugh before his hearing. If Senator Feinstein had made them aware of these serious allegations, those senators could have also questioned Judge Kavanaugh. Dr. Ford requested that her allegations remain confidential. Instead, this confidential information leaked due to the actions of Democratic offices on the Judiciary Committee, and the allegations are now in the public arena, contrary to Dr. Ford's wishes. The media circus and eleventh-hour intrigue could have been avoided if my colleagues and their staff treated these allegations seriously and responsibly. I'm afraid their actions have undermined the dignity of these proceedings.

Chairman Grassley, when he became aware of Dr. Ford's allegations last Sunday, instructed his staff to begin an immediate investigation. The next day, Ms. Katz went on morning shows asking that the Committee hold a public hearing so that Dr. Ford may offer her testimony. The Committee immediately honored that request, scheduling a hearing for one week later. Chairman Grassley informed you that the hearing could be public or private and that Dr. Ford could also choose to have a public or private staff interview with Democratic and Republican staff.

The next day, you withdrew your request for a hearing until the FBI conducted an investigation. The FBI, however, issued a statement that it considered the matter closed. The Senate does not have the authority to direct an Executive Branch department to conduct further investigation. Moreover, the Senate has a constitutional obligation to conduct its own investigations. Chairman Grassley's staff has tried to work with Democratic staff to conduct an investigation, but they have so far refused to participate. On Monday, September 17, Chairman Grassley's staff interviewed Judge Kavanaugh under penalty of felony. Democratic staff was invited to participate, and they could have asked any question they wanted to, but they declined. Judge Kavanaugh was forthright and emphatic in his testimony. He fully answered all questions. Chairman Grassley's staff also contacted three alleged witnesses named by Dr. Ford and obtained two statements under penalty of perjury. These witnesses directly contradict Professor Ford's allegations against Judge Kavanaugh.

Yesterday, you issued ten demands to us regarding the conditions under which Dr. Ford is willing to testify. Consistent with our sincere desire to hear Dr. Ford's testimony in her preferred setting—while, at the same time, respecting fundamental notions of due process and Committee practice—we are willing to meet you halfway. You demanded that we not hold the hearing on Monday because Dr. Ford needs time to prepare her testimony. Because Dr. Ford's testimony will concern only her personal knowledge of events, events which she already described to the *Washington Post*, holding a hearing more than one week after she aired these allegations is more than reasonable. We will nevertheless reschedule the hearing for later in the week, as you requested. The Committee will take Dr. Ford's and Judge Kavanaugh's testimony on Wednesday, September 26.

We deplore that Dr. Ford has faced serious threats and harassment over the past week, and we will make every effort to guarantee her safety. At the same time, Judge Kavanaugh and his family, including his two young daughters, have also faced serious death threats and vicious assaults as a result of these allegations. And they're getting worse each day. Judge Kavanaugh unequivocally and categorically denied these allegations. He was willing to testify last week after the allegations were made publicly, and he already accepted our invitation to testify on Monday. It is not fair to him or to his family to allow this situation to continue without a resolution and without an opportunity for him to clear his name. Holding the hearing on Wednesday honors your request for a later hearing date while recognizing that Judge Kavanaugh is entitled to due process. It is the fairest option for both parties.

We also accept some of your other demands. You demanded that Judge Kavanaugh not be in the hearing room during Dr. Ford's testimony. We have no objection to that.

You demanded that only one camera be permitted in the hearing room and that there be limited press access. We have no objection to that.

You demanded that the number of rounds and minutes per round of questions be equal for all senators. We have no objection to that.

You demanded that Dr. Ford be given adequate breaks during her testimony. We of course have no objection to that.

You also expressed concerns about Dr. Ford's safety and that the Senate provide adequate security. This, of course, we will do. The Capitol Police offers more than adequate security. The Senate hosts the President, Vice President, Cabinet secretaries, heads of state, and other prominent public figures all the time with the necessary precautions.

Some of your other demands, however, are unreasonable and we are unable to accommodate them. You demanded that Judge Kavanaugh be the first person to testify. Accommodating this demand would be an affront to fundamental notions of due process. In the United States, an individual accused of a crime is entitled to a presumption of innocence. And, further, the accused has the right to respond to allegations that are made about him. Judge Kavanaugh cannot be expected to respond to allegations that have been made to the press. He is entitled to hear the full, detailed testimony of Dr. Ford before he testifies. You have indicated that Dr. Ford has allegations that she would like to make in public and under oath. She will have the opportunity to do so before we give Judge Kavanaugh the opportunity to respond.

You also demanded that only senators be permitted to ask questions of the witnesses. We are also unable to accommodate this demand. There is no rule of the Senate or the Committee that precludes staff attorneys from asking witnesses questions. We reserve the option to have female staff attorneys, who are sensitive to the particulars of Dr. Ford's allegations and are experienced investigators, question both witnesses. We believe this will allow for informed questioning, will generate the most insightful testimony, and will help de-politicize the hearing.

You demanded that the Committee issue subpoenas for the testimony of Mark Judge and other unidentified witnesses. The Committee is unable to accommodate this demand. The Committee does not take subpoena requests from witnesses as a condition of their testimony. You went on television earlier this week and said Dr. Ford wants the chance to tell her story in public and under oath. This is the opportunity we have given her. We don't need to subpoena additional witnesses to do that.

You demanded that the Committee call additional witnesses that Dr. Ford requests. We are unable to accommodate this demand. The Committee does not take witness requests from other witnesses. Mark Judge and one other alleged witness to the events Dr. Ford has described have already denied the allegations under penalty of felony to the Committee. We can obtain additional testimony through staff interviews, obtaining statements, or other means that are subject to penalties of felony, if necessary.

This Committee has been extremely accommodating to your client. We want to hear Dr. Ford's testimony and are prepared to accommodate many of your demands, including further delaying a hearing that is currently scheduled for Monday. We are unwilling to accommodate your unreasonable demands. Outside counsel may not dictate the terms under which Committee business will be conducted.

Please respond by 5:00 pm to accept the invitation for Dr. Ford to testify on Wednesday according to the terms outlined above. We will have to issue various Committee notices soon after, so timeliness is extremely important."

The committee moved the deadline to ten o'clock in the evening, and Katz finally sent a reply to Willey and Davis at about a quarter past nine:

"From: Debra Katz
Date: 9/21/18 9:12 PM (GMT-05:00)
To: Willey, Katharine (Judiciary-Rep), Davis, Kolan (Judiciary-Rep)
Subject: RE: Dr. Christine Blasey Ford
Dear Ms. Willey and Ms. Davis:

I am writing to respond to your emails from earlier today. I was stunned to see that the Judiciary Committee noticed Judge Kavanaugh's vote for Monday morning, in the midst of our ongoing discussions regarding the terms and conditions under which Dr. Christine Blasey Ford could testify before the Committee. Incredibly, you did so well before the 10:00 p.m. deadline you had arbitrarily imposed just hours before. The imposition of aggressive and artificial deadlines regarding the date and conditions of any hearing has created tremendous and unwarranted anxiety and stress on Dr. Ford. Your cavalier treatment of a sexual assault survivor who has been doing her best to cooperate with the Committee is completely inappropriate.

Yesterday, we had what I thought was a productive dialogue about the conditions Dr. Ford would find acceptable to be able to testify before the Senate Judiciary Committee about her allegations of sexual assault involving Judge Brett Kavanaugh. Rather than continuing that dialogue, Senator Grassley today conveyed a counterproposal through the media, insisting that she appear for a hearing on a date I had expressly told you was not feasible for her. Hours after those media accounts first appeared, you sent me a response to the proposals that we had conveyed in good faith yesterday. You rejected a number of the proposals that are important to Dr. Ford to ensure that the process would be a fair one, including subpoenaing Mark Judge to testify. Instead, you spent much of your email making points that distorted the requests we had made and the sequence of events. It would be fruitless to review each of those misstatements as it is now abundantly clear that regardless of the assurances Senator Grassley has made, you have been tasked with pressuring Dr. Ford to agree to conditions you find advantageous to the nominee and also with denying Democratic members of the Senate Judiciary Committee any input about how this hearing would proceed. When I urged you to include them in our discussions today, you rejected my request outright, accusing them of being the source of leaks. Even more disturbing, while you took almost a full day to consider our proposal, you demanded a 5:00 p.m. response to your proposal this evening.

By email sent today at 4:01 p.m., I advised you that Dr. Ford had traveled to meet with the FBI for several hours about the death threats she had been receiving, and we would need until tomorrow to confer with her and to be able to provide you with a well-considered response. Rather than allowing her the time she needs to respond to the take-it-or-leave-it demand you conveyed, you sent us an email at 5:47 p.m. – which you again gave to the media first – insisting that we accept your "invitation" for a Wednesday hearing by 10:00 p.m. tonight. I now have learned that Senator Grassley has scheduled the Committee's vote for this Monday.

The 10:00 p.m. deadline is arbitrary. Its sole purpose is to bully Dr. Ford and deprive her of the ability to make a considered decision that has life-altering implications for her and her family. She has already been forced out of her home and continues to be subjected to harassment, hate mail, and death threats. Our modest request is that she be given an additional day to make her decision.

Sincerely,

Debra S. Katz

A lawyer with extensive political and prosecutorial experience, [Bromwich] had testified before Congress forty times, himself.

Marcia Coyle, "Michael Bromwich Looks Back—and Ahead—After Kavanaugh-Ford Hearings," *National Law Journal*, October 24, 2018, https://www.law.com/nationallawjournal/2018/10/24/michael-bromwich-looks-back-and-ahead-after-kavanaugh-ford-hearings/.

A member of the independent counsel team investigating the Iran-Contra affair, he had prosecuted Lieutenant Colonel Oliver North and served as inspector general of the Justice Department in the Clinton administration.

Michael Isikoff, "Justice Dept. to Merge Two Internal Watchdog Units," *Washington Post*, December 1, 1993, https://www.washingtonpost.com/archive/politics/1993/12/01/justice-dept-to-merge-two-internal-watchdog-units/49e75721-5419-4f6e-8bae-4d2fb75967c1/.

A late addition to the legal team, joining just one week before the hearings, Bromwich had not helped formulate the legal strategy that

Ford had followed throughout the summer, such as the decision to take the polygraph.

Coyle, "Michael Bromwich Looks Back—and Ahead—After Kavanaugh-Ford Hearings."

Ricki Seidman, an investigator for Senator Edward Kennedy during the Clarence Thomas confirmation hearings and an aide in the Clinton White House, had helped guide Sonia Sotomayor to the nation's highest court. Now she was preparing Ford for the hearings.

Annie Karni, "Kavanaugh accuser leans on Democratic operative for advice," *Politico*, September 20, 2018, https://www.politico.com/story/2018/09/20/kavanaugh-accuser-democratic-operative-advice-833013.

Ford's advisers also included Kendra Barkoff, a consultant at the PR firm SKDKnickerbocker and a former press secretary to Vice President Biden.

SKDKnickerbocker is a large public relations company owned by a private equity firm run by former Clinton pollster Mark Penn, and it regularly gets involved in contentious Supreme Court fights. SKDKnickerbocker worked directly with Jim Obergefell to coordinate a "unified strategy and message" with progressive groups to secure public support for same-sex marriage ahead of the *Obergefell v. Hodges* decision, which legalized same-sex marriage.

Alex Pappas, "Kavanaugh accusers enlist high-powered lawyers, Dem operatives," Fox News, September 24, 2018, https://www.foxnews.com/politics/kavanaugh-accusers-enlist-high-powered-lawyers-dem-operatives.

When Bromwich resigned on the Saturday before the hearings, the firm released a statement saying he had been planning to leave and that Ford's allegations did not cause his departure, but did "accelerate" his exit.

Marcia Coyle and Tony Mauro, "Veteran Prosecutor Michael Bromwich Joins Kavanaugh Accuser's Legal Team," *National Law Journal*, September 25, 2018, https://www.law.com/nationallawjournal/2018/09/22/veteran-prosecutor-michael-bromwich-joins-kavanagh-accusers-legal-team/.

Bromwich made the most of the week before the hearings, demanding that photographers from certain news organizations be allowed in the

hearing room, seeking to determine the number of television cameras, and requesting that only a handful of wire services be present.

"From: Michael R. Bromwich
Date: Tuesday, September 25, 2018 2:16 PM
To: Davis, Mike (Judiciary-Rep)
Cc: Debra Katz; Duck, Jennifer (Judiciary-Dem); Lisa Banks; Joseph Abboud; Sawyer, Heather (Judiciary-Dem); Willey, Katharine (Judiciary-Rep); Covey, Jason (Judiciary-Rep)
Subject: Re: Dr. Christine Blasey Ford
    A correction and an addition to what we specified below:
    We want the three cameras to be the CSPAN TV pool, we also request a radio pool.
    Thanks.
MRB"

"On Sep 25, 2018, at 12:50 PM, Michael R. Bromwich wrote:
Mike,
Here are the specifics we request:
Three robocams for TV pool coverage
Three still photographers from wire services pooled (AP, Reuters, one other)
Pooled print press: Congressional Correspondents Association chooses who is next in the rotation
Three print wire services (AP, Reuters, Bloomberg)
    We look forward to your responses to this and the other outstanding issues.
    Thank you.
MRB"

The Republicans also hired a female sex-crimes prosecutor from Arizona, Rachel Mitchell, to question Ford on their behalf, although they did not share the news immediately. Katz and Bromwich were livid.
"From: Debra Katz
Date: Monday, September 24, 2018 10:54 PM
To: Davis, Mike (Judic   iary-Rep)
Cc: Duck, Jennifer (Judiciary-Dem); Lisa Banks; Joseph Abboud; Sawyer, Heather (Judiciary-Dem); Willey, Katharine (Judiciary-Rep); Covey, Jason (Judiciary-Rep); Michael Bromwich; Debra Katz

Subject: RE: Dr. Christine Blasey Ford
Importance: High
Dear Mr. Davis,

Are there reasons — other than strategic advantage and unfair surprise — that you will not tell us the name of the experienced sex crimes prosecutor Senator Grassley hired to question our client? Please send us her name and cv immediately. It is impossible to square the Chairman's promise of a fair hearing with his staff's refusal to provide us with this most basic of information or to speak with us about the outstanding issues we raised on Sunday. We would like to have a call with the staff from both the Majority and Ranking Member tomorrow morning. I propose 11:00 a.m.

Please confirm that you will make yourself available to speak then.
Best regards,
Debbie Katz"

"When we entered the Capitol that day," Katz said afterward, "we had powerful tailwinds—activists and everyday people, of unions and other organized groups, and of those who were so moved by [Ford's] courage, they just wound up at the Capitol. And a lot of people have congratulated the lawyers for prepping Dr. Ford so well, but what you see is Dr. Ford. What we did was we made it safe for her to talk."
Debra Katz, "Feminist Legal Theory Conference Lunch Keynote," University of Baltimore, April 12, 2019.

"I have no more information to offer the Committee and I do not wish to speak publicly regarding the incidents described in Dr. Ford's letter."
Judge penned a memoir of his battle with alcoholism titled *Wasted: Tales of a Gen X Drunk*. The book refers to a "Bart O'Kavanaugh," who Judge recalls vomiting in a car after a party at "Beach Week" during their high school days. Copies of the out-of-print book were listed at more than $1,800 online when Senate Democrats sought to portray Judge's memoir as reflective of Kavanaugh's history.

Kate Gibson, "Mark Judge Memoir Offered for $1,800 on eBay," CBS News, October 4, 2018, https://www.cbsnews.com/news/mark-judge-memoir-offered-for-1800-on-ebay/; Seth Kaufman, "Good Luck Finding A Copy of Mark Judge's 'Wasted: Tales of a Gen X Drunk,'" *New Yorker*, September 29, 2018, https://www.newyorker.com/culture/

culture-desk/good-luck-finding-a-copy-of-mark-judges-wasted-tales-of-a-gen-x-drunk.

"It's frustrating folks, it's maddening to watch this...."
Rush Limbaugh, "My Early Thoughts on Senate Judiciary Show," *The Rush Limbaugh Show*, September 27, 2018.

More than twenty million people watched the entirety of the Ford-Kavanaugh hearings on cable and broadcast television, according to the *Hollywood Reporter*, with viewership ebbing and flowing throughout. But 7.2 million viewers stuck with Fox News alone.
Michael O'Connell, "20 Million Watch Full Ford-Kavanaugh Hearing on Cable and Broadcast," the *Hollywood Reporter*, September 28, 2018, https://www.hollywoodreporter.com/live-feed/ford-kavanaugh-ratings-hearing-brings-20-million-viewers-cable-broadcast-1147785.

"This was extremely emotional, extremely raw, and extremely credible, and nobody could listen to her deliver those words and talk about the assault and the impact it had had on her life and not have your heart go out to her," Wallace said, without qualifying the assault as "alleged."
Chris Wallace, *Fox News: Kavanaugh Senate Hearing special coverage*, Fox News, September 27, 2018.

Chapter 6

"In her initial conversations with The New Yorker...."
Ronan Farrow and Jane Mayer, "Senate Democrats Investigate a New Allegation of Sexual Misconduct, From Brett Kavanaugh's College Years," *New Yorker*, September 23, 2018, https://www.newyorker.com/news/news-desk/senate-democrats-investigate-a-new-allegation-of-sexual-misconduct-from-the-supreme-court-nominee-brett-kavanaughs-college-years-deborah-ramirez.

"The *Times* had interviewed several dozen people over the past week in an attempt to corroborate [Ramirez's] story, and could find no one with firsthand knowledge."

Sheryl Gay Stolberg and Nicholas Fandos, "Christine Blasey Ford Reaches Deal to Testify at Kavanaugh Hearing," *New York Times*, September 23, 2018, https://www.nytimes.com/2018/09/23/us/politics/brett-kavanaugh-christine-blasey-ford-testify.html.

To limit the damage to their reputations, Farrow and Mayer appeared on CNN and CBS the next morning after the *Times* report.
CNN and CBS also served as the platforms Debra Katz turned to after the *New Yorker* published the uncorroborated allegations of her client Christine Blasey Ford.

Ramirez's recovered memory was "a fairly high level of evidence for this kind of a case," Farrow assured CNN....
John Berman and Ronan Farrow, *New Day*, CNN, September 24, 2018.

"Did he see it?" John Dickerson asked.
Aaron Blake, "Breaking down the new Brett Kavanaugh sexual misconduct allegation," *Washington Post*, September 24, 2018, https://www.washingtonpost.com/politics/2018/09/24/breaking-down-new-brett-kavanaugh-sexual-misconduct-allegation/.

...Bennet helped put Ramirez in touch with a lawyer named Stan Garnett of the Denver-based firm Brownstein Hyatt Farber Schreck....
Jesse Paul, "Colorado woman's sexual misconduct allegation against Kavanaugh made its way through Sen. Michael Bennet's office before becoming public," *Colorado Sun*, September 23, 2018, https://coloradosun.com/2018/09/23/colorado-brett-kavanaugh-accusation-michael-bennet/.

Garnett ... who considered running for the Senate seat held by Republican Cory Gardner.
Mitchell Byers, "Boulder DA Stan Garnett won't run for Congress in 2018, but won't rule out 2020 Senate run," *Boulder Daily Camera*, July 6, 2017, https://www.dailycamera.com/2017/07/06/boulder-da-stan-garnett-wont-run-for-congress-in-2018-but-wont-rule-out-2020-senate-run/.

The objectionable paragraph was replaced with an attack on Republicans: "In the #MeToo era, Republicans cannot afford to attack Judge Kavanaugh's accusers...."

Sheryl Gay Stolberg and Catie Edmondson, "Brett Kavanaugh Vows to Fight 'Smears' and Will Not Withdraw," *New York Times*, September 24, 2018, https://www.nytimes.com/2018/09/24/us/politics/brett-kavanaugh-confirmation.html.

[Kelly] did not disclose her own connection to the event as an alumna of a sister school, but reported on where Kavanaugh's classmates, their spouses, and their friends went for an after-party without Kavanaugh.

Kelly did not respond to request for comment. The *New York Times* vice president of communications, Danielle Rhoades Ha, said in an email that Kelly identified herself as a reporter for the *Times* who was covering the reunion and looking for reactions to Kavanaugh's confirmation.

"Kelly's high school affiliation was not a relevant fact in that context, given that she was not writing about herself or her alma mater, but merely covering the weekend's events as a news story," Ha said.

"[Pogrebin] caught me off guard the other day," Yarasavage texted to Berchem. "Never identified herself as NYT, but just Robin Pogrebin as [though] we knew each other." "She did the same to me," Berchem replied. "Tho u had forewarned me."

Redacted messages exchanged by Karen Yarasavage and Kerry Berchem were made public in the Senate Judiciary Committee's summary report on the investigation of misconduct allegations made before Justice Kavanaugh's confirmation vote.

Robin Pogrebin and Kate Kelly did not respond directly to a request for comment. The *New York Times* vice president of communications, Danielle Rhoades Ha, responded on Pogrebin and Kelly's behalf. She said in an email that Pogrebin identified herself as a reporter in conversation with Yarasavage. Ha added that "Yarasavage could hear her typing notes on the conversation."

"Pogrebin discussed with Yarasavage her desire not to be quoted, so it is hard to see how Yarasavage could have perceived the call as anything but a background interview," Ha said.

Ha also disputed that Pogrebin did not identify herself in conversation with Berchem. "Berchem and Pogrebin had several days of conversations as well as email and text exchanges about the possibility of Pogrebin writing about Berchem's text messages with Yarasavage and whether Berchem was ready to go public with her concerns as well as her efforts to reach the FBI," Ha said.

Neither the Senate nor the FBI seemed interested in her gossipy attempts to intimidate a friend into silence, so she turned to NBC News.
Heidi Przybyla and Leigh Ann Caldwell, "Text messages suggest Kavanaugh wanted to refute accuser's claim before it became public," NBC News, October 1, 2018, https://www.nbcnews.com/politics/supreme-court/mutual-friend-ramirez-kavanaugh-anxious-come-forward-evidence-n915566.

Avenatti's unparalleled publicity skills earned him more than 250 appearances on cable and broadcast television networks in 2018.
Bill D'Agostino, "Update: TV News Hosted Michael Avenatti 254 Times in One Year," Media Research Center, April 11, 2019, https://www.newsbusters.org/blogs/nb/bill-dagostino/2019/04/11/update-tv-news-hosted-avenatti-254-times-one-year.

***Vanity Fair* spotted Avenatti talking to an MSNBC executive, purportedly about hosting his own cable television show.**
MSNBC did not comment at the time on whether it was considering giving him a primetime slot, but Avenatti fanned the flames and told Vanity Fair, "I've been approached by a number of networks who have explored the possibility of me possibly having my own show."
Joe Pompeo, "'I've Been Approached by a Number of Networks': Did Michael Avenatti Ask Phil Griffin for an MSNBC Show?" *Vanity Fair*, May 2, 2018, http://www.vanityfair.com/news/2018/05/did-michael-avenatti-ask-phil-griffin-for-an-msnbc-show.

Avenatti, however, assured CNN there was "no coordination whatsoever" between Katz and his client's last-minute allegations against Kavanaugh.

Ariane de Vogue and Eli Watkins, "New Kavanaugh accuser has tie to firm of Christine Blasey Ford's attorney," CNN, September 26, 2018, https://www.cnn.com/2018/09/26/politics/julie-swetnick-debra-katz-settlement/index.html.

… [Avenatti] was facing up to 333 years in prison.…
Rebecca R. Ruiz, "Michael Avenatti Faces New Criminal Charges in Escalated Federal Case," *New York Times*, April 26, 2019, https://www.nytimes.com/2019/04/11/us/avenatti-indictment.html.

… Virginia Hume, writing in the *Weekly Standard*, explained how that letter was drafted and disseminated among Kavanaugh's friends.
Virginia Hume, "About That Letter from Women in Support of Brett Kavanaugh," the *Weekly Standard*, September 14, 2018, https://www.weeklystandard.com/virginia-hume/about-that-letter-from-women-in-support-of-brett-kavanaugh.

Chapter 7

[Graham] entered the U.S. Air Force after law school and served in the Judge Advocate General's Corps.
Lindsey Graham, "About Lindsey Graham," LindseyGraham.com, June 26, 2019, https://www.lindseygraham.com/about/.

[Flake] promised to block all of Trump's judicial appointments until Republican leaders brought legislation aimed at restricting the president's trade agenda to the floor for a vote.
Andrew Desiderio, "Jeff Flake: I Will Block Trump Judicial Nominees Until GOP Votes on Tariffs," the Daily Beast, June 26, 2018, https://www.thedailybeast.com/jeff-flake-i-will-block-trump-judicial-nominees-until-gop-votes-on-tariffs.

As soon as Justice Kennedy announced his retirement, however, Flake backtracked, saying he would not block a vote on the coming Supreme Court appointment.

Aris Folley, "Flake: I won't oppose Trump's Supreme Court pick over tariffs," *The Hill*, June 28, 2018, https://thehill.com/homenews/senate/394610-flake-i-wont-oppose-trumps-supreme-court-picks-over-tariffs.

[Archila] did not mention that she was co-executive director of the Center for Popular Democracy, part of the Demand Justice coalition that was committed to stopping President Trump's appointment of *anyone* to the Supreme Court.
Staff, "The Center for Popular Democracy Leadership," the Center for Popular Democracy, June 26, 2019, https://populardemocracy.org/staff-leadership-print.

"Friday, as the Senate descended into chaos, one Republican and one Democrat found a way forward with an old technique that seemed long forgotten: compromise," intoned Scott Pelley on CBS's *60 Minutes*.
Scott Pelley, "Sens. Jeff Flake and Chris Coons Explain Why They Decided to Delay Brett Kavanaugh's Confirmation," CBS News, September 30, 2018, https://www.cbsnews.com/news/jeff-flake-lindsey-graham-brett-kavanaugh-supreme-court-confirmation-inside-the-decision-to-delay-confirmation-hearing/.

Senator Chuck Grassley...and Senator Susan Collins of Maine received more than ten voicemail messages threatening assault and murder from Ronald DeRisi of Long Island, who wanted to retaliate for their failure to ruin Kavanaugh.
U.S. Capitol police special agent Lawrence O. Anyaso, "Affidavit and complaint in support of an application for an arrest warrant," *U.S. v. Ronald DeRisi in the United States District Court for the Eastern District of New York*, October 18, 2018.

"There's no value to reaching across the aisle," [Flake] complained on CBS. "There's no currency for that anymore. There's no incentive."
In his interview with his future employer on *60 Minutes*, Flake bemoaned how Kavanaugh's testimony "seemed partisan." Before Flake ruled out running for reelection, however, he created legislation that

would turn the federal judiciary into a wedge issue for Republican voters to boost his chances of reelection. A Supreme Court vacancy had been an animating issue for conservative voters in 2016 and President Trump's judicial appointments were his signature accomplishment in 2017. Flake looked to exploit this for his personal gain by authoring legislation—the Judicial Administration and Improvement Act of 2017—that took aim at the U.S. Court of Appeals for the Ninth Circuit and what Republican voters perceived as its decisions hampering Trump's agenda.

Flake proposed breaking up the 9th Circuit and creating a Twelfth Circuit, which would include primarily red states such as Arizona, Alaska, Idaho, and Montana and leave states such as California, Hawaii, and Oregon in the Ninth Circuit. Similar plans had been offered in the past, but conservative criticism of the "9th Circus" combined with one-party control of Congress and the White House made it a real possibility for the very first time. Fearful of partisan meddling in judicial affairs, two GOP-appointed federal judges— Ronald Reagan-appointed Alex Kozinski and George W. Bush-appointed Carlos Bea—came to D.C. to lobby persuadable Republicans privately against breaking up the Ninth Circuit to which they belonged. Flake's effort failed, and by the next year he was decrying the "partisan" tenor of Kavanaugh's testimony.

Ryan Lovelace, "Jeff Flake to Gorsuch Critics: Read His Rulings," *Washington Examiner*, March 20, 2017, https://www.washingtonexaminer.com/jeff-flake-to-gorsuch-critics-read-his-rulings; Ryan Lovelace, "Judges Fight Move to Break up the 9th Circuit Court of Appeals," *Washington Examiner*, March 13, 2017, https://www.washingtonexaminer.com/judges-fight-move-to-break-up-9th-circuit-court-of-appeals.

"I now keep a loaded gun by my bed," [Kelley Paul] wrote in a letter published on the date of Kavanaugh's confirmation.
Kelley Paul, "My Husband, Rand Paul, and Our Family Have Suffered Intimidation and Threats," CNN, October 6, 2018, https://www.cnn.com/2018/10/03/opinions/rand-paul-suffer-intimidation-and-threats-kelley-paul/index.html.

The night before his arrest, someone spotted him in Senator Hassan's office.

Assistant U.S. Attorney Alessio D. Evangelista, "Statement of Offense in Support of Guilty Plea," *U.S. v. Jackson Alexander Cosko No. 18-CR-303 in the United States District Court for the District of Columbia,* April 5, 2019.

The additional FBI inquiry, lasting nearly a week, produced a report of about fifty pages, including findings from interviews with approximately ten people with relevant testimony and incorporating Ford's and Kavanaugh's sworn testimony to the Judiciary Committee.

Alan Fram and Lisa Mascaro, "Kavanaugh Says He 'Might Have Been Too Emotional' at Hearing; Friday Morning Preliminary Vote Set," *Chicago Tribune,* October 5, 2018, https://www.chicagotribune.com/ nation-world/ct-kavanaugh-senate-vote-fbi-report-20181004-story.html.

Ford's responses to questions from Democrats took up ten minutes and twenty-four seconds. Her answers to the Republicans' 175 questions, by contrast, took up nearly thirty minutes.

Senate Judiciary Committee, "@senjudiciary," Twitter, October 4, 2018, https://twitter.com/senjudiciary/status/1047936553023143936.

Chapter 8

...McCaskill announced that she would vote against Brett Kavanaugh's confirmation.

Bryan Lowry, "Missouri Sen. McCaskill Plans to Vote against Embattled Kavanaugh for Supreme Court Seat," *Kansas City Star,* September 25, 2018, https://www.kansascity.com/news/politics-government/ article218694560.html.

When Trump turned the microphone over to Hawley, the candidate complimented the president on the size of the crowd, remarking that "twenty thousand people or something" were turned away.

Josh Hawley, "Trump Campaign Rally in Springfield, Missouri," NBC News, September 21, 2018, https://www.youtube.com/watch?v= vmLfwT8Dl1g.

[Hawley and Kavanaugh] were members of the same caste—graduates of Yale Law School and Supreme Court clerks. After practicing appellate litigation in Washington, D.C., Hawley returned to his home state to teach at the University of Missouri Law School and was elected state attorney general in 2016.

Josh Hawley, "Resume," University of Missouri, 2015.

Soon after Justice Anthony Kennedy retired, [Hawley] set up the website "supremeclaire.com" to spotlight the differences between the judges he wanted and those McCaskill favored.

"Hawley Microsite Highlights McCaskill's 'Wrong' Record on Supreme Court Picks," NTK Network, July 5, 2018, https://ntknetwork.com/hawley-microsite-highlights-mccaskills-wrong-record-on-supreme-court-picks/.

Campaigning in Indiana, Trump charged the incumbent Democratic senator, Joe Donnelly, of joining the "Democratic mob" against Kavanaugh.

"Trump campaign rally in Fort Wayne, Indiana," C-SPAN, November 5, 2018, https://www.c-span.org/video/?453851-1/president-trump-campaigns-republicans-indiana.

By the time Trump got to Southaven, Mississippi, a suburb of Memphis, on October 2, he knew his voters enthusiastically stood with his nomination of Brett Kavanaugh.

Donald Trump, "Trump Campaign Rally in Southaven, Mississippi," GOP, October 2, 2018, https://www.youtube.com/watch?v=WQFvO67oN0k.

Among those receiving calls from Bush were Joe Manchin, Jeff Flake, Lisa Murkowski, and Susan Collins.

Ashley Parker, Josh Dawsey, and Philip Rucker, "For Trump and White House, Kavanaugh Hearing Was a Suspenseful Drama in Two Acts," *Washington Post*, September 27, 2018, https://www.washingtonpost.com/politics/for-trump-and-white-house-kavanaugh-hearing-was-a-drama-in-two-acts/2018/09/27/6b82f8c8-c276-11e8-a1f0-a4051b6ad114_story.html.

Three days before Ford testified, scores of protesters swarmed the hallway outside [Collins] office on Capitol Hill and forty-six protesters were arrested.
Thomas McKinless, "Anti-Kavanaugh Protesters Swarm Susan Collins' Office, 46 Arrested," *Roll Call*, September 24, 2018, https://www.rollcall.com/video/anti-kavanaugh_protesters_swarm_susan_collins_office_46_arrested.

In the three months following Kavanaugh's nomination, protesters had followed [Collins] everywhere, including her houses in Maine and Washington.
NBC Staff, "Kavanaugh Protesters Gather Outside Senator Collins Home," NBC News Center Maine, September 23, 2018, https://www.newscentermaine.com/video/news/politics/kavanaugh-protestors-gather-outside-senator-collins-home/97-8260561.

One man ambushed [Collins] late at night as she made her way home, and she sprinted to her house clutching her dry cleaning and a briefcase.
Mark Leibovich, "Susan Collins Could Do Without the Death Threats," *New York Times*, November 16, 2018, https://www.nytimes.com/2018/11/16/magazine/susan-collins-could-do-without-the-death-threats.html.

The sender wrote "You" and drew an arrow to the stick figure.
Suzanne Muscara was arrested in April 2019 after the FBI found a partial fingerprint on one of the letters, and she pleaded not guilty.

Collins's speech ahead of the cloture vote was carried live across the cable news networks.
Susan Collins, "Senator Collins Remarks on Judge Brett Kavanaugh's Nomination," C-SPAN, October 5, 2018, https://www.c-span.org/video/?452493-1/senate-confirms-brett-kavanaugh-supreme-court-justice-50-48&start=20268.

"That was a difficult day," Debra Katz later told law students at the University of Wisconsin.

Debra Katz, "UWLawTalks: Debra Katz '84," University of Wisconsin, November 29, 2018, https://www.youtube.com/watch?v=XC2xSeM QkW8.

While Katz's clan mourned, Kavanaugh's supporters celebrated in the one spot in the "swamp" where it was safe to do so in public—the Trump International Hotel in the Old Post Office building.
Washington, D.C., has a height restriction that keeps the Washington Monument the dominant feature of the skyline, but Trump's hotel exceeds the height limit. The monument and the Catholic Church's Basilica of the National Shrine of the Immaculate Conception are the only two buildings in the District of Columbia taller than the Trump Hotel, which is adjacent to the Justice Department and FBI headquarters downtown.

Chapter 9

Her fans sent her nearly $650,000 through the crowdfunding platform GoFundMe.
Team Christine Blasey Ford, "Help Christine Blasey Ford," GoFundMe, https://www.gofundme.com/help-christine-blasey-ford.

"I feel like all of you who have made a contribution are on this journey with me, which is very heartening," Ford wrote in an update on October 3, 2018.
Ibid.

Ford was a finalist for *Time*'s "Person of the Year" feature....
Suyin Haynes, "Who Will be TIME's Person of the Year for 2018? See the Shortlist," *Time*, December 10, 2018, https://time.com/5475133/time-person-of-the-year-2018-shortlist/.

...Senator Kamala Harris, a future Democratic presidential candidate, noted that [Ford] "shook Washington and the country"....
Kamala Harris, "Christine Blasey Ford," *Time*, April 16, 2019, tinhttps://time.com/collection-post/5567675/chrise-blasey-ford/.

Faculty members, students, and graduates of the University of North Carolina nominated Ford for the Distinguished Alumna and Alumnus Award in recognition of the "courage it took for her to take the moral and ethical stand that she did in testifying about her sexual assault experience in front of the world."

Carolina Alumni Review staff, "Kavanaugh Accuser Put Forward for UNC Alumni Award," *Carolina Alumni Review*, October 9, 2018, https://alumni.unc.edu/news/kavanaugh-accuser-put-forward-for-unc-award/.

Raliance...named Ford its Person of the Year because of the "global impact" of her testimony against Kavanaugh.

Raliance, "RALIANCE Names Christine Blasey Ford as "Person of the Year" in New Awards Program, Raliance, March 25, 2019, https://www.globenewswire.com/news-release/2019/03/25/1760214/0/en/RALIANCE-Names-Dr-Christine-Blasey-Ford-as-Person-of-the-Year-in-New-Awards-Program.html.

The American Psychological Association established a grant in Ford's honor as the result of a GoFundMe fundraising campaign by Heidi Li Feldman, a law professor at Georgetown University.

Public Affairs, "American Psychological Foundation Establishes Grant Honoring Christine Blasey Ford," American Psychological Association, January 23, 2019, https://www.apa.org/news/press/releases/2019/01/christine-blasey-ford.

After the hearing, Katz received the *Washington Business Journal*'s C-Suite award....

Rebecca Cooper, "C-Suite Awards: Debra Katz," *Washington Business Journal*, December 6, 2018, https://www.bizjournals.com/washington/news/2018/12/06/c-suite-awards-debra-katz.html.

She told an audience at the University of Baltimore's feminist legal theory conference, Applied Feminism and #MeToo, "You bet we were angry," and, "Fighting is much better than feeling depressed."

Debra Katz, "Feminist Legal Theory Conference Lunch Keynote," University of Baltimore, April 12, 2019, https://ubalt.hosted.panopto.

com/Panopto/Pages/Viewer.aspx?id=7d87c6e6-4883-40b3-a493-aa2d01
1071a0.

...Kavanaugh said that he asks himself, "What would Justice Kennedy...think about this?"
Jess Bravin, "Kavanaugh Warns Technology Will Force Re-Examination of Rights, War Powers," *Wall Street Journal*, May 7, 2019, https://www.wsj.com/articles/kavanaugh-warns-technology-will-force-re-examination-of-rights-war-powers-11557255934.

The retired justice John Paul Stevens...told an audience of retirees in Boca Raton, Florida, that while he initially thought Kavanaugh "should be selected" as the justice to replace Kennedy, he had changed his view after watching Kavanaugh's "performance in the hearings."
Lulu Ramadan, "Retired Supreme Court Justice: Kavanaugh does not belong on the high court," the *Palm Beach Post*, October 4, 2018, https://www.palmbeachpost.com/news/20181004/retired-supreme-court-justice-kavanaugh-does-not-belong-on-high-court/2.

...Kavanaugh penned a rebuttal that was published in the *Wall Street Journal* just before the vote on his nomination:
Brett Kavanaugh, "I Am an Independent, Impartial Judge," *Wall Street Journal*, October 4, 2018, https://www.wsj.com/articles/i-am-an-independent-impartial-judge-1538695822.

"The complaints do not pertain to any conduct in which Judge Kavanaugh engaged as a judge," [Judge Henderson] wrote.
Karen LeCraft Henderson, "Statement of Judge Karen LeCraft Henderson Regarding Judicial Misconduct Complaints," United States Court of Appeals for the District of Columbia Circuit, October 6, 2018, https://www.cadc.uscourts.gov/internet/home.nsf/Content/Announcement+-+Statement+of+Judge+Karen+LeCraft+Henderson+Regarding+Judicial+Misconduct+Complaints/$FILE/PressRelease20181006.pdf.

Afterward, [Chief Justice John Roberts] referred the complaints to a judicial council formed from the U.S. Court of Appeals for the Tenth Circuit—a court with no ties to Kavanaugh.

Tim Tymkovich, "In Re: Complaints Under the Judicial Conduct and Disability Act," December 18, 2018, https://www.uscourts.gov/courts/ca10/10-18-90038-et-al.O.pdf.

While the press hyped the complaints as pertaining to "judicial misconduct," Tenth Circuit chief judge Tim Tymkovich wrote that they dealt with "some miscellaneous assertions" and with allegations that Kavanaugh "made inappropriate partisan statements that demonstrate bias and a lack of judicial temperament; and treated members of the Senate Judiciary Committee with disrespect."
Ibid.

Two men appealed Tymkovich's decision to dismiss the complaints—Jeremy Bates...and Paul Horvitz....
Jeremy C. Bates, "In re: Complaint Under the Judicial Conduct and Disability Act, No. 10-18-90050," Jeremy Bates Appeal, January 28, 2019; Paul F. Horvitz, "Misconduct Petition," Paul Horvitz Appeal, January 2, 2019.

The ads linked to a petition saying, "#CancelKavanaughGMU"....
Mason For Survivors, "Support Mason 4 Survivors #Cancel KavanaughGMU," Change.org, 2019, https://www.change.org/p/tell-president-cabrera-support-mason-4-survivors-cancelkavanaughgmu.

"This is not a crazy appointment," [Cabrera] told the faculty on video, which was captured by the College Fix.
Zachary Petrizzo, "GMU faculty want new probe of Kavanaugh: 'there has not been a full investigation'," the College Fix, April 8, 2019, https://www.thecollegefix.com/gmu-faculty-want-new-probe-of-kavanaugh-there-has-not-been-a-full-investigation/.

More than three hundred of them swarmed the law school for a sit-in, classes were canceled, and posters emblazoned with the slogans #IBelieveChristine BlaseyFord and #IStillBelieveAnitaHill littered the hallways.
Serena Cho, Isha Dalal, Lindsay Daugherty, and Asha Prihar, "200 Yale Law students gather for Kavanaugh hearing," Yale Daily News, September 28, 2018, https://yaledailynews.com/blog/2018/09/28/200-yale-law-students-gather-for-kavanaugh-hearing/; Aaron Haviland, "I

Thought I Could Be A Christian And Constitutionalist At Yale Law School. I Was Wrong," The Federalist, March 4, 2019, https:// thefederalist.com/2019/03/04/thought-christian-constitutionalist-yale-law-school-wrong/.

...Issac J. Bailey, an award-winning journalist a decade younger than Kavanaugh, attended not Yale, but Davidson College in North Carolina where he somehow acquired special insight into Kavanaugh's behavior.
Issac J. Bailey, "Issac J. Bailey," Other Press, https://www.otherpress. com/authors/isaac-j-bailey/.

...[McConnell] reportedly blamed Minority Leader Chuck Schumer, who was "scared of Brian Fallon."
Glenn Thrush, "Senate Republicans Go 'Nuclear' to Speed Up Trump Confirmations," New York Times, April 3, 2019, https://www.nytimes. com/2019/04/03/us/politics/senate-republicans-nuclear-option.html.

In partnership with the group Pack the Courts, Demand Justice announced in February 2019 that it had raised five hundred thousand dollars and would press the Democratic presidential candidates in 2020 to support its cause.
Alex Thompson, "Progressive Activists Push 2020 Dems to Pack Supreme Court," Politico, February 25-27, 2019, https://www.politico.com/ story/2019/02/25/progressive-activists-pack-supreme-court-1182792.

Senators Cory Booker, Kirsten Gillibrand, Kamala Harris, and Elizabeth Warren, as well as former congressman Robert "Beto" O'Rourke, have all indicated an openness to remaking the Supreme Court. Gillibrand also vowed that she would "only nominate judges who will uphold Roe v. Wade."
Sahil Kapur, "Democrats Shift to Seize on Supreme Court as 2020 Campaign Issue," Bloomberg, May 17, 2019, https://www.bloomberg. com/news/articles/2019-05-17/democrats-shift-to-seize-on-supreme-court-as-2020-campaign-issue.

Demand Justice's hostility was so strong that in May 2019 it paid approximately ten thousand dollars for anti-Bennet television ads in

New Hampshire, despite Bennet's failure to register any detectable support in several polls there.

John DiStaso, "Progressive judicial group targets Democrat Michael Bennet in TV, digital ads," WMUR9, May 7, 2019, https://www.wmur.com/article/progressive-judicial-group-targets-democrat-michael-bennet-in-tv-digital-ads/27380051.

The Republican State Leadership Committee spent more than one million dollars on ads in support of Brian Hagedorn's campaign for the Wisconsin Supreme Court.

Patrick Marley, "Republican Group Spending More Than $1 Million to Help Brian Hagedorn in Wisconsin Court Race," *Milwaukee Journal Sentinel*, March 26, 2019, https://www.jsonline.com/story/news/politics/2019/03/26/wisconsin-supreme-court-gop-group-spending-1-m-help-brian-hagedorn/3275973002/.

ABC News exit polls in 2018 showed that Senator Joe Donnelly's vote against Kavanaugh was an important factor for 53 percent of Indiana voters.

Gary Langer and Benjamin Siu, "Election 2018 Exit Poll Analysis: Voter Turnout Soars, Democrats Take Back the House, ABC News Projects," ABC News, November 7, 2018, https://abcnews.go.com/Politics/election-2018-exit-poll-analysis-56-percent-country/story?id=59006586.

…Thapar told the Federalist Society's law school chapters that he would accept invitations to speak about originalism that came with the promise of more than twenty undergraduates in the audience.

@BYU_FedSoc, "Judge Thapar notifies @FedSoc chapter presidents that he'd accept an invitation which included a case for originalism & promise of 20+ undergrads at his event," Twitter, July 22, 2018, https://twitter.com/BYU_FedSoc/status/1021107667736113153.

Thapar spoke at...Georgetown Law School, where attendees were promised free Chick-fil-A.

@GtownFedSoc, "On Thursday we are hosting Judge Thapar for a discussion on judicial philosophy. Come out for a great even [sic] and free Chick-fil-a!" Twitter, February 5, 2019, https://twitter.com/GtownFedSoc/status/1092969755189768192.

APPENDIX

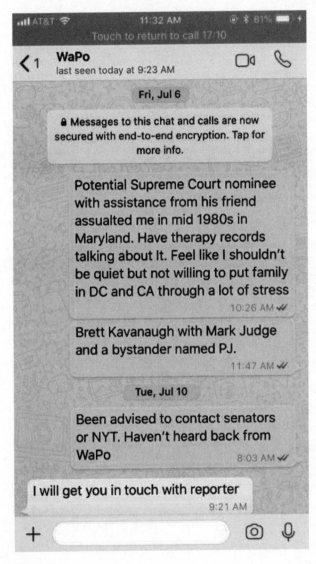

Figure 1

July 30, 2018

CONFIDENTIAL

Senator Dianne Feinstein

Dear Senator Feinstein:

I am writing with information relevant in evaluating the current nominee to the Supreme Court. As a constituent, I expect that you will maintain this as confidential until we have further opportunity to speak.

Brett Kavanaugh physically and sexually assaulted me during High School in the early 1980's. He conducted these acts with the assistance of his close friend, Mark G. Judge. Both were 1-2 years older than me and students at a local private school. The assault occurred in a suburban Maryland area home at a gathering that included me and 4 others. Kavanaugh physically pushed me into a bedroom as I was headed for a bathroom up a short stairwell from the living room. They locked the door and played loud music, precluding any successful attempts to yell for help. Kavanaugh was on top of me while laughing with Judge, who periodically jumped onto Kavanaugh. They both laughed as Kavanaugh tried to disrobe me in their highly inebriated state. With Kavanaugh's hand over my mouth, I feared he may inadvertently kill me. From across the room, a very drunken Judge said mixed words to Kavanaugh ranging from "go for it" to "stop". At one point when Judge jumped onto the bed, the weight on me was substantial. The pile toppled, and the two scrapped with each other. After a few attempts to get away, I was able to take this opportune moment to get up and run across to a hallway bathroom. I locked the bathroom door behind me. Both loudly stumbled down the stairwell, at which point other persons at the house were talking with them. I exited the bathroom, ran outside of the house and went home.

I have not knowingly seen Kavanaugh since the assault. I did see Mark Judge once at the Potomac Village Safeway, where he was extremely uncomfortable seeing me.

I have received medical treatment regarding the assault. On July 6, I notified my local government representative to ask them how to proceed with sharing this information. It is upsetting to discuss sexual assault and its repercussions, yet I felt guilty and compelled as a citizen about the idea of not saying anything.

I am available to speak further should you wish to discuss. I am currently vacationing in the mid-Atlantic until August 7th and will be in California after August 10th.

In Confidence,

Christine Blasey

Palo Alto, California

████████

Figure 2

Christine Blasey MA, PhD, MS

Palo Alto, CA

Education

Master of Science, Epidemiology, 2009
Stanford University School of Medicine
Department of Health Research and Policy
     Specialization: Biostatistics
     GPA 4.0

Doctor of Philosophy, Psychology, 1996
University of Southern California, Rossier School of Education (APA-accredited)
     Specialization: Marriage and Family Therapy, Research Design and Statistics
     Dissertation: Psychometric Development of a Measure of Children's Coping Strategies
     GPA 3.9

Predoctoral Clinical Psychology Internship, 1994
University of Hawai'i at Manoa (APA-accredited)

Master of Arts, Clinical Psychology, 1991
Pepperdine University, 1991
     Dean's Letter of Commendation
     GPA 4.0

Bachelor of Arts, Experimental Psychology, 1988
University of North Carolina at Chapel Hill

High School, 1984
Holton-Arms School
Bethesda, Maryland

Current Employment

Current   **Professor, PGSP-Stanford University Consortium for Clinical Psychology**
           Stanford University School of Medicine Department of Psychiatry and Palo Alto
           University

           Director of Student Research Competence.
           Teach Statistics, Research Methods, Psychometrics, Dissertation Preparation Seminar,
           Advanced Statistics and Scientific Writing.
           Mentor students and serve on 10-15 Dissertation Committees per year. Common student-
           led research areas include Evidence-based treatments for Depression, Anxiety, ADHD,
           Autism Spectrum and other Developmental Disorders, Trauma and other illnesses in
           Veteran populations
           Golden Apple Award, Winner 2012 and 2018

Figure 3.1

Research Psychologist and Biostatistician, Stanford University School of Medicine Department of Psychiatry

Design studies and conduct statistical analyses supporting faculty research across child and adult psychiatry. Statistical expertise in centering, interaction effects, mediation and moderation. Studies focus on child and adulthood psychiatric conditions, their etiologies and effective treatments. Provide statistical expertise to faculty in other departments within the School of Medicine (e.g., cardiology)

Prior Employment

2012-4, 2017   **Consulting Biostatistician**, Titan Pharmaceuticals, San Francisco, CA
Conduct statistical analyses regarding the efficacy of novel treatments for opioid abuse disorders.

2012-4, 2017   **Consulting Biostatistician**, Brain Resource, Sydney, Australia
Conduct statistical analyses regarding the putative psychological and biological markers of treatment response to ADD and Antidepressant medications.

2010-2012   **Director, Corcept Therapeutics**

2005-2012   **Associate Director, Statistician, Corcept Therapeutics**

Led statistical activities of Phase 3 program for development of new medicines. Designed and constructed databases, chose analytic models, wrote statistical programs, co-authored Statistical Analysis Plans, co-authored Clinical Study reports (CSR), and co-wrote manuscripts for scientific publications. Presented at professional meetings including NCDEU and APA.

1999-current   **Research Psychologist, Stanford University**

Provided data analytic and research design support for faculty and trainees in the Department of Psychiatry & Behavioral Sciences. Received formal mentoring from Helena C. Kraemer. Co-authored manuscripts, presented at professional conferences, taught statistics courses for MD and PhD postdocs and research fellows, provided training courses in SPSS. Taught statistics courses for 3 years in Child Psychiatry postdoctoral fellowship program and in the Stanford-PGSP Consortium.

1999-2001   **Biostatistician, The Children's Health Council**

Designed and conducted program evaluations. Provided project management and supervised Research Assistants in their research projects.

Figure 3.2

1995-98   **Visiting Professor, Pepperdine University**

Taught full time (10 classes per year) in the undergraduate and graduate psychology programs. Courses Taught: Psych 101 (small class and large lecture hall), Introductory Statistics, Intermediate Statistics, Computer Applications in Statistics, Psychological Testing and Assessment, Developmental Psychology, Personality Theory, Family Therapy. Nominee, Tyler Teacher of the Year Award, 1996.

Computer Skills
SPSS
QROC (signal detection)
SAS – Level 4

Statistical Reviewer
Multiple psychiatry and statistics journals

Sample of Awards and Invited Talks

2018   Invited Statistics Mentor, NIH-American Psychiatric Association Annual Meeting, New York

2017   Invited Statistics Mentor, NIH-American Psychiatric Association Annual Meeting, San Diego

2018   Golden Apple Teaching Award in Statistics, PGSP-Stanford Psy.D Consortium

2012   Golden Apple Teaching Award in Statistics, PGSP-Stanford Psy.D Consortium

2014-5   Roundtable Lead Discussant, Statistical Analysis in Industry-FDA Interactions. American Statistical Association Annual FDA meeting with Industry and Academic Statisticians. Washington, DC

1997   Ron Tyler Teaching Award Finalist, Pepperdine University

Book and Book Chapters

Kraemer HC and **Blasey C**. (2015) *How Many Subjects*? Los Angeles: Sage Publications.

Blasey C, DeBattista C, Belanoff J, Schatzberg A (2010). Psychopharmacology. In Koocher G (Editor), Psychologists Desk Reference.

Figure 3.3

Jeremiah P. Hanafin

███████████   Text   ███████████

POLYGRAPH EXAMINATION REPORT

Date of Report
08/10/2018

Date of Examination
08/07/2018

Location of Examination
Hilton Hotel, 1739 West Nursery Road, Linthicum Heights, MD 21090

Examinee's Name
Christine Blasey

Synopsis
On August 7, 2018, Christine Blasey reported to the Hilton Hotel, 1739 West Nursery Road, Linthicum Heights, MD 21090, for the purpose of undergoing a polygraph examination. The examination was to address whether Blasey was physically assaulted by Brett Kavanaugh while attending a small party in Montgomery County, MD. This assault occurred in the 1980's when Blasey was a high school student at the Holton-Arms School. Accompanying Blasey was Attorney Lisa Banks of the firm Katz, Marshall & Banks. After introductions were made, this examiner left the room so Blasey and Attorney Banks could discuss this matter. During this discussion, Blasey provided a written statement to Banks detailing the events that occurred on the evening of the assault. The statement was provided to this examiner when he returned. Blasey stated that the statement was true and correct and signed it in the presence of this examiner and Banks attesting to its accuracy. A copy of this statement is attached to this report. After a brief discussion, Banks departed.

Blasey was then interviewed in an effort to formulate the relevant questions. During this interview, Blasey described the events that occurred on the night of the assault. She stated she attended a small party at a house where the parents were not home. Those attending the party were drinking beer. Blasey stated that Kavanaugh and his friend, Mark, became extremely intoxicated. Blasey stated that she had met Kavanaugh before at previous parties and she briefly dated one of his friends. She stated that Kavanaugh attended Georgetown Preparatory School and she previously attended parties hosted by students of this school. Blasey remembers another male at this party, PJ, who she described as a very nice person. At some point in the evening, Blasey went upstairs to use the restroom. When she got upstairs, she was pushed into a bedroom by

Figure 4.1

Examinee's Name: Blasey, Christine
Date: 08/10/2018

either Kavanaugh or his friend, Mark. The bedroom was located across from the bathroom. She was pushed onto a bed and Kavanagh got on top of her and attempted to take her clothes off. She stated she expected Kavanaugh was going to rape her. Blasey tried to yell for help and Kavanaugh put his hand over her mouth. Blasey thought if PJ heard her yelling he may come and help her. Blasey stated that when Kavanaugh put his hand over her mouth that this act was the most terrifying for her. She also stated that this act caused the most consequences for her later in life. Blasey stated that Kavanaugh and Mark were laughing a lot during this assault and seemed to be having a good time. Kavanaugh was having a hard time trying to remove Blasey's clothes because she was wearing a bathing suit underneath them. She stated Mark was laughing and coaxing Kavanaugh on. Blasey recalls making eye contact with Mark and thinking he may help her. Mark continued to encourage Kavanaugh. On a couple of occasions, Mark would come over and jump on the bed. The last time he did this, all three became separated and Blasey was able to get free and run to the bathroom. She stated she locked herself in the bathroom until she heard Kavanaugh and Mark go downstairs.

Following this interview, Blasey was given a polygraph examination consisting of the following relevant questions:

Series I

    A. Is any part of your statement false? Answer: No
    B. Did you make up any part of your statement? Answer: No

Four polygraph charts (which included an acquaintance or "stim" chart) were collected using a Dell Inspiron 15 notebook computer and Lafayette LX4000 software. This software obtained tracings representing thoracic and abdominal respiration, galvanic skin response, and cardiac activity. All of these physiological tracings were stored in the computer along with the time that the questions were asked as well as text of each question.

The format of the test was the two question Federal You Phase Zone Comparison Test (ZCT). As part of a 2011 meta-analysis study done by the American Polygraph Association (APA), the ZCT is one of the polygraph examinations considered valid based upon defined research protocol. As part of the validation process, the APA chose techniques that were reported in the Meta 22 Analytic Survey of Validated Techniques (2011) as having two, independent studies that describe the criterion validity and reliability. The ZCT includes relevant questions addressing the issues to be resolved by the examination, comparison questions to be used in analysis, symptomatic questions, and neutral or irrelevant questions. All questions were reviewed with Blasey prior to the test. The charts collected were subjected to a numerical evaluation that scored the relative strength of physiological reactions to relevant questions with those of the comparison questions. An analysis was conducted using a three (3) point scale (-1, 0, +1). If reactions were deemed to be greater at the relevant questions, then a negative score was assigned. If responses were deemed to be greater at the comparison questions, then a positive score was assigned. A decision of deceptive is rendered if any individual question score is -3 or less or the grand total of both questions is -4 or less. A decision of non-deceptive is rendered if the grand total of both questions is +4 or more with a +1 or more at each question.

Figure 4.2

Examinee's Name: Blasey, Christine
Date: 08/10/2018

Blasey's scores utilizing the three (3) point scale are +4 at Question A and +5 at Question B with a total score of +9. Based upon this analysis, it is the professional opinion of this examiner that Blasey's responses to the above relevant questions are **Not Indicative of Deception.**

A second analysis was conducted utilizing a scoring algorithm developed by Raymond Nelson, Mark Handler and Donald Krapohl (Objective Scoring System Version 3) which concluded " **No Significant Reactions- Probability these results were produced by a deceptive person is .002.**" Truthful results, reported as "No Significant Reactions," occur when the observed p-value indicates a statistically significant difference between the observed numerical score and that expected from deceptive test subjects, using normative data obtained through bootstrap training with the confirmed single issue examinations from the development sample. **Truthful results can only occur when the probability of deception is less than .050.**

Deceptive results, in which an observed p-value indicates a statistically significant difference between the observed numerical score and that expected from truthful persons, and are reported as "Significant Reactions."

When the observed p-value fails to meet decision alpha thresholds for truthful or deceptive classification the test result will be reported as "Inconclusive." No opinion can be rendered regarding those results.

A third analysis was conducted utilizing a scoring algorithm developed by the Johns Hopkins University Applied Physics Laboratory (PolyScore Version 7.0) which concluded **"No Deception Indicated—Probability of Deception is Less Than .02."**

3

Figure 4.3

One summer
~~While in~~ high school in ~~early~~ 80's,
I went to a small party in the
Montgomery County area. There were
4 ~~people~~ boys and a couple of girls.
At one point, I went up a small
stairwell to use the restroom. At
that time, I was pushed ~~by this~~
~~person~~ into a bedroom and was
locked in the room ~~and pushed onto a~~
bed. ~~Brett~~ ~~My boys were in the room.~~ laid ontop of me
and tried to remove my clothes
while groping me. He held me
down and ~~he~~ put his hand on
my mouth ~~so~~ to stop me ~~from~~
~~from the~~ screaming for help. His
friend Mark was also in the room
and both were laughing. Mark
jumped on top of us 2 or 3
times. I tried to get out from
under unsuccessfully. Then Mark
jumped ~~again~~ and he toppled
over. I managed to run out of
the room across to the bathroom
and lock the door. Once ~~they~~
I heard them go downstairs,
I ran out of the house and
went home.

Christie Blasey August 7, 2018

Figure 5

KATZ, MARSHALL & BANKS, LLP

By Electronic Mail
September 18, 2018

The Honorable Charles E. Grassley
Chairman, Committee on the Judiciary
United States Senate
135 Hart Senate Office Building
Washington, D.C. 20510

Dear Senator Grassley:

Thank you for reaching out yesterday afternoon. Dr. Christine Blasey Ford looks forward to working with you and the Committee.

As you know, earlier this summer, Dr. Ford sought to tell her story, in confidence, so that lawmakers would have a fuller understanding of Brett Kavanaugh's character and history. Only after the details of her experience were leaked did Dr. Ford make the reluctant decision to come forward publicly.

In the 36 hours since her name became public, Dr. Ford has received a stunning amount of support from her community and from fellow citizens across our country. At the same time, however, her worst fears have materialized. She has been the target of vicious harassment and even death threats. As a result of these kind of threats, her family was forced to relocate out of their home. Her email has been hacked, and she has been impersonated online.

While Dr. Ford's life was being turned upside down, you and your staff scheduled a public hearing for her to testify at the same table as Judge Kavanaugh in front of two dozen U.S. Senators on national television to relive this traumatic and harrowing incident. The hearing was scheduled for six short days from today and would include interrogation by Senators who appear to have made up their minds that she is "mistaken" and "mixed up." While no sexual assault survivor should be subjected to such an ordeal, Dr. Ford wants to cooperate with the Committee and with law enforcement officials.

As the Judiciary Committee has recognized and done before, an FBI investigation of the incident should be the first step in addressing her allegations. A full investigation by law enforcement officials will ensure that the crucial facts and witnesses in this matter are assessed in a non-partisan manner, and that the Committee is fully informed before conducting any hearing or making any decisions.

Figure 6.1

◢ Katz, Marshall & Banks, LLP

The Honorable Charles E. Grassley
Chairman, Committee on the Judiciary
September 18, 2018
Page 2

We would welcome the opportunity to talk with you and Ranking Member Feinstein to discuss reasonable steps as to how Dr. Ford can cooperate while also taking care of her own health and security.

Sincerely,

Debra S. Katz

Lisa J. Banks
Attorneys for Dr. Christine Blasey Ford

cc: The Honorable Dianne Feinstein
       Ranking Member, Committee on the Judiciary

Figure 6.2

INDEX

A

ABC, 60
ABC News, 159, 160, 161
abortion drug, 56
Akin Gump, 159
Akin Gump Strauss Hauer &
  Feld, 92
Alex, Cristóbal, 19
Alito, Sam, 25, 131
Alliance Defending Freedom
  (ADF), 25
Alliance for Justice, 17
American Bar Association, 115
American Psychological Associa-
  tion, 140
America Rising, 5
Antonin Scalia Law School, 147,
  148
"Applied Feminism and #MeToo"
  conference, 71, 142, 143
Arabella Advisors, 19
Archila, Ana Maria, 111
Arnold & Porter Kaye Scholer, 46
Article III Project (A3P), 158
Associated Press, 9
Atwood, Margaret, 32
Avenatti, Michael, 94–97, 100,
  122, 128, 137
Ayotte, Kelly, 24

B

Bailey, Issac J., 149, 150, 151
Baker, Peter, 14
Baldwin, Henry, 12
Banks, Lisa, 63, 141
Bannon, Steve, 36
Barkoff, Kendra, 80
Barrett, Amy Coney, 4, 8, 9, 13,
  17, 126, 162, 163, 164, 165
Barry, Maryanne Trump, 10
Bash, John, 25
Bash, Zina Gelman, 25, 26, 50
Bates, Jeremy, 146
Beck, Glenn, 8
#BelieveTheWoman, 91, 110
Bennet, Michael, 89, 158
Berchem, Kerry, 92, 93, 94
Berman, Marc, 140
Biden, Joe, 2, 21, 69, 80
Blackburn, Marsha, 161
Blatt, Lisa, 46, 47, 50, 132
Blevins, James Dean, 113
Blue Orca Capital, 58
Blumenthal, Richard, 93, 128
Booker, Cory, 20, 40, 41, 42, 43,
  44, 50, 108, 128, 157, 158
Bopp, Jim, 8, 9
Bork, Robert, 21, 22, 23, 24, 28,
  49
Braun, Mike, 159
Brigham Young University, 165

Bromwich, Michael, 79, 80, 81, 141

Brown, Emma, 55, 71

Brown, Eric Renner, 2

Brownstein Hyatt Farber Schreck, 89

Bruce, Eric, 84

Burck, Bill, 36, 38, 39, 43, 44

Burnett, Erin, 13

Bush, George H. W., 24

Bush, George W., 7, 8, 10, 24, 35, 36, 37, 38, 39, 44, 56, 129, 131, 146

Buttigieg, Pete, 157, 159

BuzzFeed, 70

Byrd, Haley, 17

C

Cabrera, Ángel, 148

Camerota, Alisyn, 72

#CancelKavanaugh, 68, 90

Carmona, Rachel O'Leary, 32–33

Catalan, Jeffrey, 100

CBS, 74, 101, 112, 129

CBS Evening News, 61

CBS News, 112

CBS This Morning, 70

Center for American Progress, 17, 18

Center for Popular Democracy (CPD), 32, 112

Citizens United, 9

Clifford, Stephanie. *See* Daniels, Stormy

Clinton, Bill, 10, 19, 20, 47, 61, 66, 80, 103, 130, 155, 156

Clinton, Chelsea, 28, 29

Clinton, Hillary, 18, 19, 20, 46, 47, 61, 66, 103, 156, 165

Clinton Global Initiative, 19

Clune, John, 89

CNN, 13, 44, 55, 61, 67, 70, 72, 74, 88, 97, 101, 129, 161

College Fix (GMU), 148

Collins, Susan, 12, 19, 33, 113, 129, 130, 131, 132, 133, 135, 136, 137, 143

Colorado Sun, 89

Congressional Research Service, 131

Contemplation of Justice (statue), 137

Coons, Chris, 112

Cooper, Anderson, 44

Corcept Therapeutics, 56, 57, 58

Cornyn, John, 42, 43, 44

Cosko, Jackson, 114

Coyle, Patrick, 153, 154

Cozen O'Connor, 84

Cramer, Kevin, 159

Cruz, Ted, 8, 113, 161

C-SPAN, 81

C-Suite award, 141

Culvahouse, A. B., 22, 23

D

Daily Mail, 26

Daines, Steve, 136

Daniels, Stormy, 94, 97

dark-money group, 19, 20
Davidson College, 149
Davis, Kolan, 77
Davis, Mike, 35, 81, 158
"DC's Leading #MeToo Lawyer,"
    62
Demand Justice, 18, 19, 20, 27,
    28, 31, 32, 47, 112, 147, 148,
    156, 157, 158, 164
Denhollander, Rachael, 140
Denver Post, 89
DeRisi, Ronald, 113
Deutsche Bank, 11
Dickerson, John, 88
Distinguished Alumna and Alum-
    nus Award, 140
Dixon, Monica, 19
Donnelly, Joe, 12, 19, 127, 159
"Don't Ask Don't Tell" policy
    (military), 130
Dorgan, Byron, 146
Douglas, William O., 21
Drudge Report, 68
Duca, Lauren, 28
Duck, Jennifer, 73
Duncan, Arne, 55
Dundas, Chris, 32
Durbin, Dick, 47, 48, 49, 107,
    108

E

eBay, 66
Eid, Allison, 126
Entertainment Weekly, 2

Equal Employment Opportunity
    Commission, 69
Ernst, Joni, 161–62
Eshoo, Anna, 54, 59, 67

F

Facebook, 137, 147
fake news, 65, 67, 128, 129
Fallon, Brian, 18, 20, 27, 47, 156,
    157, 158
Farrow, Ronan, 61, 68, 69, 70,
    71, 87, 88, 89, 90
FBI, 78, 80, 82, 83, 88, 93, 94,
    97, 100, 107, 108, 112, 115–
    19, 121, 122, 147, 149
Federal Election Commission, 19
Federalist 76, 130
Federalist Society, 3, 4, 6, 7, 49,
    51, 144, 158, 165
Feinstein, Dianne, 4, 35–38, 41,
    43, 45, 46, 47, 49, 52, 54, 59,
    60, 66–73, 108, 118, 119, 127,
    128, 153
Feldman, Heidi Li, 140–41
Ferriero, David, 37, 38, 39
Flake, Jeff, 110–13, 129, 136, 162
Flores, Sarah Isgur, 34
Ford, Christine Blasey, 52–60,
    62, 63, 68, 70–86, 87, 97, 98,
    100, 101, 104, 105, 108, 109,
    111, 114, 116, 118–21, 125,
    128, 129, 132, 134, 135, 139–
    43, 149–51
Ford, Gerald, 144

"Forrest Gump of Republican politics," 47
Fox News, 12, 86, 99
Franklin, Benjamin, 137
Freed, Dara, 19

G

Gallagher, Maria, 111
Gardner, Cory, 89
Garland, Merrick, 2, 131
George Mason University (GMU), 147, 148
Georgetown Law School, 165
Georgetown University, 141
George W. Bush Presidential Library, 37
Gerken, Heather, 27, 28, 148, 149
Gillibrand, Kirsten, 20, 157, 158
Ginsburg, Douglas, 23
Ginsburg, Ruth Bader, 46
GoFundMe, 139, 140
"Golden God," 114
Good Morning America, 60
Gorsuch, Neil, 1, 2, 5, 9, 10, 12, 17, 18, 24, 35, 89, 101, 123, 126, 131, 143, 144, 147, 158, 165
"Gorsuch 2.0," 10
Gotti, John, 118
Graham, Lindsey, 108, 109, 110, 114, 137, 162
Grassley, Chuck, 11, 13, 31, 35, 36, 37, 38, 39, 40, 42, 44, 45, 57, 73, 74, 77, 78, 79, 81, 94, 95, 97, 109, 113, 122, 137, 142, 158, 162
grassroots donors, 20
Greenwald, Glenn, 66
Grier, Robert C., 12
Grim, Ryan, 66, 67
Griswold v. Connecticut, 21, 22
Gu, Eugene, 26
Guantanamo Bay, 48

H

Haaland, Deb, 33, 34
Hagedorn, Brian, 158
Hamilton, Alexander, 130
Hanafin, Jeremiah P., 63
Handmaid's Tale, The, 31, 32
Hardiman, Thomas, 10, 18
Harris, Kamala, 20, 31, 39, 40, 43, 48, 119, 140, 157, 158
Harvard, 150
Harvard Law School, 27
Hassan, Maggie, 24, 114
Hatch, Orrin, 22, 114, 162
Hattaway, Doug, 19
Hawley, Josh, 125, 127, 159, 162
Hayes, Chris, 43, 44
Haynes, William "Jim," IV, 48
Hearron, Marc, 35, 36
Heitkamp, Heidi, 12, 19, 127, 136, 159, 161
Heritage Foundation, 3, 14
Hewitt, Hugh, 10
Hill, The, 26
Hill, Anita, 49, 69, 101, 102, 120, 161

Hillsdale College's Kirby Center, 163
Hill-Snowdon Foundation, 20
Hillyer, Quin, 10, 156
Hoffman, Susan, 141
Holder, Eric, 18
Holiday, Ryan, 65, 66, 67, 68, 70
Hollywood Reporter, 86, 94
Hoover Institution, 5
Horvitz, Paul, 146
Huffington Post, 67
Human Resource Executive, 62
Hume, Virginia, 98

I

"I am Spartacus" moment, 43
Instagram, 137
Intercept, 66, 67, 68, 70
Internet Age, 65
Iran-Contra affair, 80

J

Jackson, Robert, 163
"Jane Doe," 119–21, 122
Japanese Americans, internment of, 41, 163
John F. Kennedy Profile in Courage Award, 140
Jones, Paula, 61
Jones, Van, 32
Jones Day, 163
Judge, Mark, 54, 59, 63, 76, 77, 78, 84, 94, 95, 96, 134, 151
"Judge Dogma," 4, 164

Judicial Conduct and Disability Act, 146
Judicial Crisis Network, 27
"judicial misconduct," 145

K

Kagan, Elena, 27, 108, 131
Kanter v. Barr, 164
Kantor, Jodi, 61
Kasowitz Benson Torres, 48
Katz, Debra, 60–63, 65–74, 77, 79–81, 91, 97, 101, 136, 137, 141–43
Katz, Marshall & Banks, 61
Kavanaugh, Ashley, 104
Kavanaugh, Ed, 105
Kavanaugh, Liza, 104
Kavanaugh, Martha, 105
Kelly, Kate, 91
Kennedy, Anthony, 2, 5, 10, 11, 12, 18, 21, 23, 34, 36, 53, 55, 110, 111, 126, 132, 144, 147
Kennedy, Edward, 21, 22, 49, 80
Kennedy, John, 110
Kessler, Eric, 19
Kethledge, Raymond, 10, 18
Keyser, Leland, 82, 83, 84, 134, 135
King, Jeff, 33
Kirby Center (Hillsdale College), 163
Kirkland & Ellis, 25
Klion, David, 1
Klobuchar, Amy, 40, 41, 43, 107, 108, 158

Korematsu v. United States, 41, 163

Korlym, 56, 58

Kozinski, Alex, 27

Kubrick, Stanley, 43

Kupec, Kerri, 25

Kyl, Jon, 24, 25, 161

L

Larsen, Joan, 126

Law360, 141

Leadership Conference on Civil and Human Rights, 17

Leahy, Patrick, 41, 107, 128

LeCraft, Karen, 145

Lee, Mike, 41, 42, 114

Lee, Thomas, 165

legacy media, 66, 68

Lenkner, Travis, 11, 98

Leo, Leonard, 7, 12

Lescaze, Alexandra, 151, 152

Limbaugh, Rush, 8, 29, 49, 85

Lodes, Lori, 32

Loudon, Gina, 137

Louisville Courier-Journal, 9

Luther, Robert, 6

M

MacCallum, Martha, 99

"Making Black Lives Matter Initiative," 20

Malcolm, John, 3, 4, 14

Manchin, Joe, 12, 19, 129, 136, 160

Marcum, Anthony, 50

Marcus, Ruth, 53

Mayer, Jane, 68–71, 87, 88, 89, 90

McCabe, Andrew, 80

McCain, John, 161

McCaskill, Claire, 125, 126, 159, 160, 161

McConnell, Mitch, 2, 3, 9, 11, 12, 101, 114, 121, 122, 157

McGahn, Don, 3, 4, 6, 7, 14, 23, 24, 25, 36, 101

McLean, Monica, 83

McSally, Martha, 161

media manipulation, 66

Meese, Ed, 14

Meese Center for Legal and Judicial Studies, 3

Megaphone Strategies, 32, 33

Merkley, Jeff, 2

#MeToo movement, 27, 55, 60, 62, 65–86, 91, 104, 161

Michigan State University, 140

Milano, Alyssa, 104

Mitchell, Rachel, 81, 82, 85, 101, 106

Mordente, Patrick X., 38

Morrisey, Patrick, 160, 161

Morrison & Foerster, 35

Ms., 141

MSNBC, 43, 53, 94

Mueller, Robert, 36, 48

Munro-Leighton, Judy, 119, 122

Murkowski, Lisa, 12, 19, 33, 129, 136

Murray, Claire McCusker, 25

N

NARAL Pro-Choice America, 28
Nation, 1
National Football League, 140
National Law Journal, 35
Native Americans, 33–34
NBC, 93, 94, 96
Nelson, Bill, 160
New Venture Fund, 19
New York City Bar professional
    ethics committee, 146
New Yorker, 55, 61, 68, 70, 87,
    88, 89, 97, 100
New York Times, 1, 5, 14, 18, 54,
    61, 66, 88, 90, 91, 100, 129,
    152, 155
New York University, 154
*New York University Journal of
    Law & Liberty*, 6
Nieman Fellowship (Harvard),
    150
Nixon, Richard, 21, 50
North, Oliver, 80
Notre Dame, 10, 163, 165
Notre Dame Law School, 4

O

Obama, Barack, 2, 9, 37, 46, 55,
    57, 108, 126, 131, 159
Obamacare, 3, 8, 131
Obergefell v. Hodges, 131
Ocasio-Cortez, Alexandria, 112
O'Connor, Sandra Day, 45, 46,
    132
Omidyar, Pierre, 66

One Nation, 3
Open Society Foundations, 19
O'Rourke, Robert "Beto," 157,
    161

P

Pacific Legal Foundation, 51
Palo Alto University, 72
Paoletta, Mark, 101
Paul, Rand, 113, 114
Pelley, Scott, 112
Pence, Mike, 4, 32, 101, 136, 159
People, 2
People for the American Way, 17,
    22, 32
Pepperdine University, 59
Perabo, Piper, 33
Peretz, Evgenia, 154, 155
Pew Research Center, 12
Planned Parenthood, 28, 32
Planned Parenthood v. Casey, 45,
    46, 55, 132, 144
Pogrebin, Letty, 91
Pogrebin, Robin, 90, 91, 92, 155
Politico, 67, 94
polygraph, 62, 63, 71, 73, 80
Portman, Rob, 33
postal inspector, 130
Powell, Lewis, 21, 50
Presidential Records Act, 36, 38
Priebus, Reince, 36
Project on Government Over-
    sight, 57
protesters, 17, 18, 33, 60, 111,
    113, 129, 130, 136, 137, 148

Pulitzer Prize, 61
Purvis, Burton, 32

R

Ramirez, Deborah, 87–94, 97, 98
Reagan, Ronald, 10, 21, 22, 23, 24, 28, 46
RealClearPolitics, 68
Rehnquist, William, 50
#Resistance, 26, 60, 90, 119
Roberts, John, 3, 7, 8, 11, 131, 137, 145, 146
Robinson, Peter, 5
Roe v. Wade, 21, 22, 28, 32, 45, 46, 48, 55, 59, 132, 143, 144, 157
Rolling Stone, 1
Ronald Reagan Presidential Library, 23
Roosevelt, Franklin, 163
Rosenstein, Rod, 34
R Street Institute, 49, 50

S

Samuel, Ian, 6
Sanders, Sarah Huckabee, 7, 12
Santorum, Rick, 10
Sarsour, Linda, 33
#SaveSCOTUS rally, 18
Scalia, Antonin, 2, 4, 6, 14, 17, 110, 118, 131, 163
Scalia, Maureen, 14
Schatzberg, Alan, 57

Schneiderman, Eric, 61
Schumer, Chuck, 11, 18, 31, 38, 118, 127, 157
Scott, Rick, 160
Seidman, Ricki, 80
September 11 attacks (2001), 41
Sessions, Jeff, 24, 60
Seven-Sky case, 3, 4, 131
sexual misconduct accusations, 61, 69, 79, 87, 96, 146
Shah, Raj, 24
Singh, Anisha, 18
Siskind, Amy, 26
Sixteen Thirty Fund, 19
60 Minutes, 112
SKDKnickerbocker, 80
Slate, 151
Smyth, Patrick J., 84, 134
Snow, Kate, 96
Snowden, Edward, 55
social media, 1, 2, 47, 49, 51, 68, 70, 92, 137, 147, 162
Society of Professional Journalists' Code of Ethics, 91
Soros, George, 19, 20
Sotomayor, Sonia, 80, 108, 131
Souter, David, 23, 132
Southern Investigative Reporting Foundation, 58
Southern Poverty Law Center (SPLC), 25
"Spartacus" moment, 43
Specter, Arlen, 10
Sports Illustrated, 140
Stanford University, 55, 67

Stanford University School of Medicine, 56, 59
Starr, Kenneth, 10, 29, 47, 156
Stevens, John Paul, 144, 145
Strong Arm Press, 67
Super Lawyers, 141
Swetnick, Julie, 94–98, 101, 122, 153
Sykes, Diane, 165

T
"Taxicab Tom," 10
Tester, Jon, 160
Thapar, Amul, 9, 126, 165
Thomas, Clarence, 4, 23, 49, 51, 68, 69, 80, 101, 102, 161
Thurm, Eric, 1
Tillis, Thom, 41
"Titan of the Plaintiffs Bar," 141
To Kill a Mockingbird, 22
Toobin, Jeffrey, 55, 56
"torture memos," 5
Trump, Donald, 1–9, 11–15, 17–21, 24, 28, 33, 34, 48, 49, 53, 60, 66, 69, 80, 89, 90, 92, 94, 101, 103, 110–12, 116, 123, 125–29, 131, 137, 142, 143, 146, 147, 157–65
Trump International Hotel, 136
Trump National Golf Club, 13
Trust Me, I'm Lying: Confessions of a Media Manipulator, 65
Twitter, 1, 2, 8, 26, 42, 43, 44, 68, 94, 114, 162
Twohey, Megan, 61

Tymkovich, Tim, 145, 146

U
University of Baltimore, 71, 142
University of California, Berkeley, 5
University of Missouri Law School, 126
University of North Carolina, 140
University of the Pacific, 147
University of Pittsburgh Law Review, 6
University of Southern California, 59
University of Virginia, 22, 163
University of Wisconsin, 62, 136
USA Today, 18, 20
U.S. Food and Drug Administration (FDA), 56, 57
U.S. National Institutes of Health, 57
U.S. National Library of Medicine, 57
U.S. News–Best Lawyers, 141
U.S. Postal Service, 130

V
Van Gelder, Barbara "Biz," 84
Vanity Fair, 94, 154
"vast right-wing conspiracy," 66
vetting, 5, 13, 70, 84, 89, 110
Villanova University, 163
Vinneccy, Richard, 96

W

Wallace, Chris, 86
Wall Street Journal, 144, 156
Walsh, Alex, 101
Walsh, Howard, 83
Walton, Reggie, 114
Warren, Elizabeth, 20, 40, 157, 158
Washington Business Journal, 141
Washington Examiner, 10, 156
Washingtonian, 62
Washington Post, 10, 53, 54, 59, 63, 65, 66, 68, 69, 70, 71, 72, 74, 82, 84, 97, 100, 116, 129, 152, 153
Weekly Standard, 17, 98
Weinstein, Harvey, 61
"Weinstein effect," 65, 66
Weissmann, Shoshana, 49, 50
whistleblower, 61, 72
Whitehouse, Sheldon, 51, 82, 100, 106, 107
Whitewater investigation, 47, 56
WikiLeaks, 61
Wikipedia, 114, 116
Wilkinson Walsh + Eskovitz, 99
Willett, Don, 126, 162
Willey, Katharine, 73, 74, 77, 79
Williams, Nat Chioke, 20
Wired, 1
Witt, John Fabian, 149
Women's Bar Association, 141
Women's March on Washington, 32, 60
Wonder Woman award (*Ms.*), 141
Wong, Candice, 34

Y

Yale College, 10, 107
Yale Law School, 10, 27, 107, 126, 149
Yarasavage, Karen, 90–94
"Year of the Woman," 161
Yoo, John, 5, 6